The South Side of Queen

The
South Side of
Queen

A BURLESQUE THEATRE FAMILY SAGA

BARRY J. LITTLE

Published in 2022 by
Kinetics Design, KDbooks.ca

ISBN 978-1-988360-78-2 (paperback)
ISBN 978-1-988360-79-9 (ebook)

Edited by Michael Carroll

Cover and interior design, typesetting,
online publishing, and printing by Daniel Crack,
Kinetics Design, KDbooks.ca
www.linkedin.com/in/kdbooks/

Some of the names of people in this book have been changed
from actual to fictitious ones.

Contact the author at
bjlittlemd@hotmail.com

To my father, Murray Little,
whom I dearly wish could have lived to see this book's publication.

Contents

Cast of Characters

APPELBAUM/APPLEBY FAMILY

Abraham (Avner or Abe) Appelbaum/Appleby

Esther Brucha Appelbaum/Appleby, wife of Avner

Louis (Lou) Appelbaum/Appleby, first son of Avner and Esther

Frieda Appelbaum, mother of Avner

Lemel Appelbaum, father of Avner

Aaron Appelbaum, brother of Avner

Moishe Appelbaum, brother of Avner

Rivka Appelbaum, wife of Moishe

Beryl Appelbaum, brother of Avner

Harry Appelbaum, brother of Avner

Chanala Appelbaum, wife of Harry

Maxie Appelbaum, son of Harry and Chanala

Morris Appelbaum, son of Harry and Chanala

Joseph Ber Appelbaum, father of Esther

Rachel Appelbaum, mother of Esther

Becky Appelbaum Persiko, sister of Esther

Sam Persiko, husband of Becky

Shandlia, sister of Esther and Becky

Malka, sister of Esther and Becky

Aaron Appelbaum, brother of Esther and Becky

Bertha, daughter of Becky and Sam Persiko

Chemia Appelbaum, brother of Esther and Becky

Beryl Appelbaum, brother of Esther and Becky

Faga, daughter of Beryl

Sam Appelbaum, cousin of Lou Appelbaum/Appleby and son of
    Aaron Appelbaum

Eva Appelbaum, wife of Sam Appelbaum

LETOVSKY/LITTLE FAMILY

Morris (Murray) Letovsky/Little

Shandlia (Lily or Lil) Appelbaum Letovsky/Little, daughter of
    Avner and Esther Appelbaum/Appleby and wife of Murray
    Letovsky/Little

Samuel Letovsky/Little, father of Murray Letovsky/Little

Anna Letovsky/Little, mother of Murray Letovsky/Little

David (Dave) Letovsky/Little, brother of Murray

Mary Letovsky, sister of Murray

Gert Letovsky/Little, sister of Murray

Gerald (Gerry) Little, first son of Lil and Murray

Barry Little, second son of Lil and Murray

Alan Little, third son of Lil and Murray

CASINO THEATRE EMPLOYEES

Robert (Bob) Alda, house singer and master of ceremonies

Walter (Wally) Crosby, janitor and caretaker

Rex Doyle, house singer and master of ceremonies

Bobby Goodman, house singer and master of ceremonies

Chuck Gregory, choreographer and stage manager

Percy Grisewood, scenery painter

Mrs. Haley, costumer

Charlie Mackie, jack-of-all-trades employee

Lester Montgomery, choreographer and stage manager

Eon O'Sullivan, Percy Grisewood's assistant

Ida Rose, choreographer replacement for Chuck Gregory

Dave Sherman, assistant manager

Carl Steiner, chief stagehand

Archie Stone, orchestra leader

DOCTORS, LAWYERS, POLICE OFFICERS, AND POLITICIANS

Willie Anderson, Toronto solicitor

Sergeant Brown, Toronto police officer bribed by Fred Piton

Jacob Cohen, Toronto magistrate, father of Arthur Cohen

M.M. Crawford, chief Toronto coroner

Dr. Dyck, an abortionist

Sergeant Evans, Toronto No. 2 Station

Detective Hutchinson, Toronto Police Headquarters

Dr. Moses Jacobson, Esther Appelbaum/Appleby's doctor

Edward Johnson, Toronto alderman

Detective Sergeant Jones, Toronto No. 2 Station

R.J. Kelly, Fred Piton's lawyer

Detective Keyes, Toronto No. 2 Station

Jim McNeally, Toronto Police detective

Peter Miles, Toronto Police detective

Frank Mitchell, Toronto solicitor

Moses Mulholland, Toronto Police assistant inspector

Walter Robb, judge and chairman of the Liquor Control Board
    of Ontario

Sidney Rosenthal, lawyer for the Allen brothers

Joe Sedgwick, lawyer for the Roxy Theatre Management Company

Rick Smith, Toronto Police detective

William Teasdale, Toronto Police detective

Edmund Tong, Toronto sergeant of detectives

Harold Waterhouse, Toronto Police sergeant of detectives

Detective Sergeant Whitelaw, Toronto Police

Sergeant Wilder, Toronto police officer bribed by Fred Piton

Detective Sergeant Winters, Toronto Police

OTHER PEOPLE

Gersten Allen, financial manager for Allen brothers, Toronto movie
    and stage theatre impresarios

Jay Allen, Toronto movie and stage theatre impresario, partner of
    Murray Letovsky/Little and Lou Appelbaum/Appleby

Jules Allen, Toronto movie and stage theatre impresario, partner of
    Murray Letovsky/Little and Lou Appelbaum/Appleby

Herb Allen, Toronto movie and stage theatre impresario, partner of
    Murray Letovsky/Little and Lou Appelbaum/Appleby
Murray Anderson, Brant Inn owner
Ollie Baskin, shady partner of Lou Appelbaum/Appleby
Walter Blenkenship, Murray Letovsky/Little's banker
Edwin Alonzo Boyd, Toronto bank robber
Arthur Cohen, Justice Jacob Cohen's son, theatre partner of Murray
    Little and Lou Appleby
Roy Cooper, Montreal theatrical booker
Antony Ferry, Toronto playwright and arts journalist
Adolph Frankel, friend of Appelbaum/Appleby family
Sadie Ginsberg, a midwife
Rabbi Jacob Gordon, senior rabbi at the McCaul Street Synagogue
Harvey Hart, Canadian movie and television director and producer
Max Hoffman ("Uncle Max"), friend of the Appelbaum family
Dennis Hyland, movie theatre owner
Walter Murdoch, president of the Toronto Musicians' Association
Reverend James Mutchmor, relentless Toronto moral crusader
Nathan Louis Nathanson, Toronto movie theatre impresario
Jane Peterson, Barry Little's third-grade teacher
Fred Piton, owner of the Globe Theatre and partner of Avner
    Appelbaum/Appleby
Jimmy Rizzo, a boxer
Doris Robinson, cashier for Dennis Hyland
Milt Shuster, Chicago booker for Casino Theatre talent
Jim Sullivan, a clerk at Toronto's City Hall
Teddy Swain, a boxer
Ray Wong, Chinese community member leasing the Roxy Theatre

Prologue

The interview with Adolph Frankel, the elderly, well-mannered gentleman in my medical clinic, had gone as usual with the typical questions about his past health. I had asked him to go into the examining room and change. A few minutes later I entered the room to find him seated on the examining table. "I know who murdered your grandfather, Dr. Little," he said.

I heard myself gasp as the blood drained from my face. "What did you say?"

"You *are* an Appelbaum, aren't you?"

I was stunned, and for a moment, unable to respond. *Who was this man? How come he knows the family name and that my grandfather was murdered? And how could he know who murdered him? The murder was never solved.*

My patient looked puzzled and asked again, "You're an Appelbaum, aren't you?"

"Yes," I answered warily. "My mother's name was Appelbaum."

"Well, I knew your grandfather very well."

"I see," I said, groping for something else to say.

My thoughts raced. I had never heard Adolph Frankel mentioned by anyone in our family, but he certainly seemed like a responsible fellow to me.

"It's nearly fifty-five years since my grandfather was killed," I said. "Why are you talking to me about this now?"

"I don't want to take this knowledge to the grave without somebody like you knowing, and let's hope, doing something about it. I told two of your family members years ago, but one didn't believe me and the other didn't want to do anything with the information."

By now, I had recovered my composure. "With respect, Mr. Frankel," I cautioned, "this is neither the time nor the place to talk about matters concerning my personal life and family. Perhaps another time outside the clinic? Now let's get on with your examination."

The old man agreed, and the examination went smoothly. There were no abnormal findings, and I reassured him about his health. As I left him to get dressed, he repeated, "Believe me, I know who killed your grandfather. Here's my telephone number. Please call me. I need to talk to you."

Alone in the office, I was overcome by the multitude of images that streamed through my head: my grandparents, our old house on Grace Street, faded pictures of relatives looking rigid and antiquated in nineteenth-century costumes, family members left behind in the mad escape to the New World. I remembered my grandmother's black beaver coat, favoured on blustery winter days, and her beautiful hand-woven white silk shawl, worn as if she were a hooded monk in prayer. I recalled the smell of mothballs that permeated her bedroom and pictured her dresser topped with a crystal bottle half filled with what I thought were precious stones but which turned out to be cheap imitations from Woolworth's. And beside this jewellery container lay a pearl-and-ivory hairbrush, a wedding gift to a child bride in Poland. After my grandfather's death, I often saw her sitting in that room, seemingly for days, in quiet bereavement.

Now, as I sat in my upholstered green leather chair, I imagined a young woman packing her clothing as she prepared to make her way to the New World in 1900, excited yet stoical. What, I wondered, would have gone through her mind with the hairpin turn in her life that she was about to make?

Grandmother Esther Brucha Appelbaum was the village beauty in the small town of Lagow, Poland, her soft, pale skin and tiny, delicate facial features making her appear quite fragile. She was betrothed to her first cousin, Abraham "Avner" Appelbaum, the marriage having been arranged by her father, Joseph Ber Appelbaum, and his brother, Lemel. The wedding would take place in Toronto, Canada, away from the growing dangers and restrictions for Jews in the Old World. And so it was that Esther, accompanied by her plucky younger sister, Becky, boarded a large steamer at Hamburg, Germany, to cross the icy black North Atlantic to America. Avner would follow about six months later.

The sisters travelled in steerage, seasick and lonely. They got off the steamer at Halifax where they were shunted through a large wooden immigration building by stern officials who had little patience with their speaking in Polish or Yiddish. When they boarded a train to Toronto via Montreal, it was possibly the first such ride they had ever had in their lives. Finally, they arrived at Union Station in Toronto, and after a long, bumpy ride, they were met by Max Hoffman, "Uncle Max" to the Appelbaums, who took them by carriage to their new home on Nassau Street in the southern part of the city, the centre of the Jewish ghetto.

Uncle Max wasn't a blood relative but a friend of the two brothers in the Old Country. He had come to North America two years before to seek his fortune and promised to look after any of the children the brothers sent forth. Uncle Max could speak a little English, and unlike the newly arrived Esther, wasn't handcuffed by any religious baggage.

Once they had settled into their small flat, the sisters chatted endlessly about Avner, speculating what he might be like. They knew he was short and somewhat enigmatic in demeanour, always well dressed, or at least as well as he could be in a small, muddy shtetl. He had a good job in that town, but he, too, was anxious to leave the perils and uncertainty of life in the Pale of Settlement for a good life elsewhere. No army for him! He was bright, though quiet, introspective, and not well educated. He had street smarts and was considered affable in a dignified kind of way. In any event, Esther had no choice: she would have to marry him.

"You're getting a good man, Esther," Becky stated decidedly one evening.

"Maybe … maybe."

"No, you'll have a good life here in Canada. Avner will look after you and you'll have lots of children."

"But I don't know him," Esther demurred.

"Don't worry," the ever-optimistic Becky replied. "These marriages always work out. You'll be okay."

Esther had a difficult time adjusting to her new and different surroundings. She was, after all, living with the goyim, strangers who practised another faith. She began to spend much of her day cooped up in her private quarters, incessantly praying, pleading to a being she feared and trusted, and with some emotional gymnastics, loved. Esther seldom stepped outside her front door, even though she knew she must make some attempts to acclimatize herself. She thought it was sinful to acquire a facility in English, and in all her days, spoke only Yiddish or Polish, with Hebrew, being holy, used solely for prayer. Becky, in contrast, would taunt her, anxious to learn English and become part of the community about her.

Gradually, Esther familiarized herself with some of the streets in the neighbourhood, the merchants, and of course, the local synagogue. But everything was on hold until Avner arrived.

1

AVNER'S ARRIVAL

The big day at last arrived when Avner was to appear, almost six months to the day since Becky and Esther had landed in this strange, foreign country called Canada. Uncle Max had dutifully checked in each day to monitor the two immigrant girls, now settled in the flat he'd rented for them on Kensington Avenue in the Toronto Jewish ghetto. There were no telephones in 1901, at least not for poor people, so news for them came by word of mouth and by mail, usually the former.

Each morning, Uncle Max ascended the rickety wooden stairs to the second floor above the grocery store and overlooking the street. Max was solicitous. His daily ritual was to ask them whether they'd had enough to eat, whether the rooms were warm enough, and had the nosy downstairs proprietor been bothering them, knowing the crippled and grotesque little man had a roving eye and might even be an out-and-out child molester. Max had heard the local market gossip.

Becky opened the windows to let in the morning air, excited that her future brother-in-law would be arriving at Toronto's Union Station in three hours, at twelve noon to be precise. She drew the blinds, and with the window partially open could hear the tumult in the street below: peddlers announcing their wares as their horses and carts passed by, greengrocers hawking freshly arrived vegetables, squawking chickens being led to slaughter by the ritual animal killer, the yelps and laughter of children playing in the street. All of this melded with the odours of rotting vegetables, putrefying ice-packed fish, and freshly deposited horse dung. Still, Kensington and the flat above the grocery store were her new home, at least for the time being.

"Esther, have you washed yet?" Becky called out.

"There's plenty of time."

"I picked one of your nicer dresses to meet Avner. Aren't you excited at all?"

"Of course, I am, but what's the hurry?" Esther sounded only half-convincing. The "doubting Thomas" response was so typical. This quality of an instant state of suspicion and mistrust, Becky knew, would likely persevere for the remainder of her sister's life! In any event, Esther wasn't going to be hustled by her younger sister no matter what, and she obviously hadn't finished her morning ablutions and prayer, either — a combination of history recital of the Old Testament and pleading, a prayer ritual that was repeated at least twice a day, morning and sunset. Special prayers and exaltations, too, were uttered throughout the day for a constellation of daily events: bathing, washing of hands before meals, lighting of ceremonial candles. There was probably even a prayer before defecation. In fact, it seemed to Becky that the entire waking experience was one of fearful devotion, even though the prayers weren't nearly as formidable and time-consuming as they were for the male members in her Judaic Orthodox faith.

"Esther, you're such a slowpoke! Maybe you don't want to meet him. Maybe you don't want to marry him."

"Well … of course, I do …" she responded with her usual lack of enthusiasm.

"Esther, what's Avner planning for your life together over here?" Becky asked. "You hardly share anything with me. Why don't you? Or are you hiding something from me?"

"I don't keep secrets." Esther was hurt and a little put off by her sister's brusque comments and innuendo. "Don't be ridiculous. I've got nothing to hide, and as you very well know, I've only had two letters from the Old Country, and Avner didn't say very much other than to tell me about his travel plans and when he was arriving. And you know, anyway, Becky, that he doesn't say very much even at the very best of times. Remember his brother Joseph's wedding a year ago? Avner could hardly even say hello and sat quietly in a corner of the schul's banquet hall. He only danced once, and it wasn't with me, either. Just as well. I don't go in for that dancing and drinking stuff, as you know. That's for the goyim." Esther was a little more discursive than usual. "Fortunately, I know he's a good man and comes from a good family. We are, after all, a part of it! He's our first cousin. I'm sure once I get to know him better, things will work out for the best and we'll have a good marriage. And besides, what will be will be. It's in God's hands, isn't it?"

Esther believed that all events were preordained by some supernatural being. In her case, it was Yehuda. Becky thought similarly, though she was more worldly-wise than her older sister.

Finally, the two girls were dressed in their Sabbath best. Esther had chosen her frosty white frilly blouse, long black skirt, and black high-button shoes. A firm-fitting bonnet, creating a picture not unlike a *Police Gazette* cover girl, topped her black hair. Becky was similarly bedecked with a hand-knitted wool cap framing her cherubic face with its two amber, always scanning eyes.

The doorbell rang, cutting short their chatter. It was Uncle Max, about to escort them to the train station. As the two girls descended the wooden circular stairs from their flat, they saw Uncle Max in front of the grocery store, seated on his wagon, looking elegant in his dark pinstriped suit, white shirt, black bow tie, and freshly polished black boots. He looked like the king of Poland seated on his chariot, the victorious conqueror about to lead a ceremonial procession with his two female charges. What a paradoxical scenario Max portrayed: sartorial elegance juxtaposed against a background of squalor, dignity personified on a rag peddler's wagon.

It was March 3, 1901, and a typically overcast, chilly Toronto day. But there was warmth and sunshine in Max's face as he proudly watched his two entrusted "nieces" mount his regal carriage. Never mind that his horse had just defecated on the cobbled street.

Becky turned to Esther. "What's wrong with you? You don't seem to be happy or excited."

"You know, Becky, I don't have to jump around like a puppet or act like a clown in a circus ring. I'm happy … really, I am. Don't worry so much."

"I'm not worried," Becky retorted. The horse began to clippety-clop down the cobblestones toward Spadina Avenue, a street not without its own charm of sorts, at least for the girls. There was certainly nothing like it in their hometown of Lagow. Spadina was a cavernous boulevard with tall Norway maples, old oaks, and elms lining the roadway and peppering the sidewalks. A ribbon of trees and bushes seemed to carve the street in half, with each side of the boulevard an endless row of small factories, retail shops, butcher shops, delicatessens, and outdoor markets. Many of the store windows advertised their wares in Yiddish, making the girls feel a little more at home, even though they were far from acclimatized to their new living conditions. But at least they could continue to speak in Yiddish and pray in Hebrew, provided they limited their geographic boundaries to the several blocks within the Kensington Street ghetto.

Max, seated majestically in the driver's seat, cajoled and exhorted his tired grey mare to get a move on. "You stupid horse!" he shouted. "You lazy slowpoke. Get a move on!"

The carriage moved a little more quickly, heightening the anticipation for all three, and finally they arrived at Front Street. Two blocks to the west was Union Station and Avner.

Max stopped the carriage at one of the horse stalls across from the train station where gigantic steam-powered "horses" from as far away as New York disgorged passengers. What a marvel! The girls remembered very little of what they saw on the night of their own arrival at the station, but they couldn't help but be impressed by the enormous Victorian structure. The overly elaborate four-storey building, its facade of Corinthian pillars seemingly supporting its enormity, was festooned with plaster figures and flowers, making it an impressive and fitting testimonial to the grandiose British Empire. They admired the marbled floor, so highly polished, and the huge, cavernous space where footsteps and voices reverberated with curious ghost-like whispering echoes, making conversation, even at close range, sound otherworldly.

"Max, what's the number of the platform where we're to meet Avner?" asked Becky.

"It's gate 4 and the arrival time is twelve noon. I hope you won't expect too much, girls. I don't think he's travelling in first class, though knowing Avner, he'd like to. It's been an overnight ride for him, anyway."

The three sat expectantly on a bench across from gate 4, Esther's heart pounding, perhaps in synchrony with her sister's.

Will I even recognize him? Esther asked herself, losing her inner composure for the moment at least.

"There he is!" shouted Becky, appearing more excited than the bride-to-be.

"Yes, I see him," said Esther as Max nodded approvingly.

There was no mistaking Avner, even in this crowd of tired, babbling passengers. One could hardly say that Avner cut an imposing figure; if anything, it was quite the opposite. Still, there was a striking uniqueness about his physical presence. He stood no more than five foot four, showing signs of early balding even at the age of twenty-one. Thick rimless glasses punctuated a moon face, while a slight squint — the result of a turned-in left eye — and slightly swarthy skin betrayed his ancestral Semitic heritage, giving him a rather mysterious, almost exotic, appearance. His dark blue suit, now wrinkled from travel, with its matching vest, tie, and stick pin, reflected a person of sartorial discernment — a feature that had distinguished him throughout his life from his other brothers. He quickly spotted Max, Becky, and his bride-to-be amid the maelstrom of humanity at the station, and clutching his two leather suitcases, containing all his worldly possessions, walked smartly toward them. Dropping his bags on the floor, he embraced Uncle Max in a bear hug.

"Welcome to Canada!" Max exclaimed.

"Oi ... I'm finally here." Avner's voice was soft, wispy. "It was such a long journey from Lagow to Hamburg. And the boat ride, Max, you wouldn't believe! There was hardly room to breathe on that ship, and on the first day I got really seasick. I was so embarrassed! But it seemed as though every second person had the same trouble. We were so jammed together, Max, that I felt like a herring in a barrel, and I was so happy when the ship docked at Montreal. Yes, yes," he added quickly, "I knew there would be a long train trip to Toronto. Max, you know I don't smoke, but so many of the men on the train did, and it was so uncomfortable! So if I look like a mess, I am."

As he stopped, breathless from his explanation, Esther slowly moved forward to greet her future husband, reluctantly uttering that she was so glad he had arrived. It was said in such a half-hearted way that even romantic Becky could envision a catastrophic marriage. Becky attempted to welcome him warmly.

"Let me help you with your bags," Max said, suddenly in a hurry to get going.

"I'm all right," Avner answered, displaying his usual independence.

The quartet made its way through the masses of people and across Front Street to the carriage where the tired old horse waited, obviously not looking forward to yet another journey. The two suitcases were placed on the carriage, and the four passengers somehow squeezed in, the two men in front, the women in back — the typical male/female seating arrangement.

"Gee-up!" shouted Max, and the mare did her best to lug the migrants home to the ghetto. A blanket had been placed over the two girls for warmth, but the day was still too damp and miserable for what should have been a joyous occasion.

"Avner, I got rooms for you on Nassau Street," Uncle Max said. "It's not much — just a small space on the third floor where the Frankels live. You don't know them, but they're very nice people and won't charge you very much rent. You need to get settled. You'll want to make arrangements for the wedding, and of course, spend some time with Esther." Max displayed a peculiar order of priorities.

Esther could hear only snatches of the conversation, what with the racket on the street and the two men being up front, but Becky listened more intently and muttered to her sister, "You're going to be living on Nassau Street, just around the corner from us. You'll also have lots of time now to get to know Avner."

Becky wondered again why husband-to-be had so readily agreed to this union, arranged by his father and uncle when he scarcely knew his cousin at all. She presumed that Avner must have been truly smitten by her sister, the village beauty — Esther, the pale-complexioned maid with the sculptured face and sharp, steely-blue eyes. It must have been love at first sight for him. There could be little else to explain it.

From Spadina, the horse made a westerly turn onto Nassau Street, stopping in front of the Frankel home — a relatively new house with a small garden and big chestnut tree masking the ordinariness of Avner's new dwelling.

"You'll like the Frankels, Avner," offered Max. "Mr. Frankel has a little bakery and confectionery store on Kensington Avenue. He works hard. His wife sometimes works with him. They have a couple of daughters living with them, and their young son, Adolph, should be coming over within the year, as soon as he can get the papers and money together. He's been talking of trying to avoid conscription into the Polish army by mutilating himself, and the family there has done everything to prevent him from doing this desperate act. The boy's really scared about serving on the Russian front. You know, the border seems to change from day to day — Tsar Nicholas is quite crazy, need I tell you." It seemed Uncle Max would talk forever.

"Anyway, let's meet the Frankels and then we'll leave you to settle in. I'll make arrangements for an evening meal over at my house on Baldwin Street tomorrow, and we can talk then about finding you a job. I hear they're looking for cutters, tailors, and pressers at Eaton's — a big goyishe company that sells everything you can think of. Funny, though, they don't sell tobacco. The old man — Timothy Eaton — is a very strict Methodist and has a lot of influence in this city. Anyway, you have a great deal of time to settle in and learn for yourself."

2

NEWS FROM THE OLD COUNTRY

It rained the day after Avner arrived, making Kensington, Baldwin, and Nassau Streets even smellier and greyer, the rain and mist giving the ghetto a surrealistic ambience.

"I'll be happy to go with you, Esther," Becky enthused.

"No, no, it's not for you to go with me this time." Becky appeared saddened by her older sister's response, but still Esther added, "Don't worry. I'll manage on my own. After all, I'm the one who's getting married." In her heart of hearts, Esther knew that her bubbly little sister was the one who had sufficient courage to speak up and be forthright. This meeting with Avner wasn't going to be easy for her.

Esther put on her new clothing, kissed her sister goodbye, and reluctantly made her way to Nassau Street and the Frankel residence. With each step, a new uncertainty entered her mind. When finally she reached her destination, after checking the number three times, Esther opened the squeaky iron gate and walked up the path and onto the verandah. With tremulous reluctance and sweaty palms, she pressed the doorbell.

Within moments, the door opened and Mrs. Frankel, wearing a bright yellow speckled apron, greeted her warmly. "Oh, it's Avner's new bride! Welcome. He's been expecting you."

Stunned by the unexpected appellation, Esther forced a smile. "Yes, he asked me to come over today." The forthcoming marriage almost an afterthought, she added apologetically, "He's going to give me news of the family from the Old Country."

"Esther, don't stand on the verandah," Mrs. Frankel said. "Come on in. Avner's waiting for you upstairs."

"Oh, yes," answered Esther. She kissed the mezuzah on the doorway arch, removed her galoshes and heavy coat, which Mrs. Frankel neatly placed aside in the dark hallway, and proceeded up the stairs to join her future husband.

What will I say to him? she wondered. *This is so embarrassing, even humiliating. I have nothing to say to him. Maybe he'll take the initiative. But he's so shy. I hope we don't sit and stare at each other. If he doesn't talk, I won't know where to begin.*

These thoughts and concerns swirling in her mind, Esther began losing her composure. Just as she reached the top of the stairs, the door opened and there stood Avner, a slight Cheshire cat smile on his face.

"Oh, please come in," he said in a quiet, mannerly way.

Esther mentally sighed in relief, sensing he would lead the conversation.

"Let me pour you a cup of tea and we can sit and talk and I can tell you about the family back in Poland. I'm sure you'd like to know the latest news of them, and perhaps some of the local gossip. Come into the kitchen, sit, and make yourself comfortable and we'll have a glass of tea."

The kettle boiled, tea was poured, and they sat at the table in the tiny cupboard-sized room that passed for a kitchen.

"Esther, you've never looked better! In fact, I think you might have put on a little weight since I last saw you. Seems like years ago." Avner seemed to be fumbling with his opening pleasantries. "Mostly, I've got good news from the Old Country, but I have to tell you that your father, Joseph, and your mother, Rachel, are very mixed about your coming to this Gentile country. They asked me to make sure you remain a good Jew and pray every day."

There will be no question about that, thought Esther, but she didn't interrupt.

"Your mother and father are both well, and their clothing business is doing fine, though the break-ins and stealing, especially by drunken soldiers, makes business very difficult. Your sisters and brothers there are, thank God, well, too, but they're all talking about leaving Poland and coming to Canada, which is causing a little trouble. Aaron and Chemia are so fearful of conscription that they've already booked their passages."

Esther, now breathing a little easier, interjected, "Thank you for this news. I hardly ever get a letter from my sisters and none at all from Aaron. I just know he's always too busy to write. And as for Chemia, I don't think he can read or write that well — maybe he can a little — but he never writes to me." She hesitated for a moment, then changed the subject. "You know it's not easy here for me. I know I have to learn English, but I really don't want to because I think somehow I'm betraying my mother and father and my God-given traditions. Becky seems to have much less trouble in this matter. She's so smart and worldly-wise, and she's only eighteen. I'm so happy she came to Canada with me."

The words had come tumbling out. Esther paused to collect her thoughts, ruminating briefly, thinking that maybe Becky could help her with some personal and more intimate problems, concerns that could never be discussed with her mother, and certainly not with father.

Avner, ever so perceptive and obviously anticipating her apprehension, gently said, "There are so many problems in Lagow, Esther, you can't imagine. You can't open a business without getting a special licence, which takes months and months, and you can so easily be rejected by some arrogant civil servant, often on a whim. Stealing is everywhere a problem, and I never want to see a soldier — drunk or otherwise — again!"

Esther and Avner sat across from each other in the kitchen, sipping tea, exchanging whatever news they could muster, each carefully avoiding the subject of their impending marriage. Avner had also resisted getting onto the subject of his brothers — Josef, Beryl, Harry, Lazar, and Moishe.

"So how are your brothers?" asked Esther finally.

"Harry's a big mystery to me. I don't know him really. I don't think anyone does. He seems to go his own way, doing what he wants when he wants to. I think he's spoiled by Mother and Father. Moishe and Lazar are growing up nicely. All three of them want to come to Canada, but I think Josef and Beryl are really stuck on Poland even with all its problems. Josef thinks he would lose his *Yiddishkite* if he came to North America. He and his wife are very religious and fearful of Gentiles. And as for Beryl, he's doing extremely well in business in Warsaw and feels he has too much to lose by leaving."

When will he ever get around to talking about our impending marriage? Esther wondered. She worried that Avner, slightly fidgety across the table, might read her mind. *Is he going to back out of the arrangement? If he does, what will I do? And do I really want to go through all this business with this man, anyway?* Questions without answers continued cascading through her mind. Finally, in a rare moment of uncharacteristic utterance, Esther blurted, "Avner, what about our marriage?"

3

A NEW JOB

"So how did you get along with Avner?" asked Becky. She had sat shivering on the verandah, waiting for her sister's return. "Was he nice?" Becky could hardly contain herself. "When are you going to see him again?" She watched as Esther opened the door. "I must hear all about it. Have you decided on a date?"

"I've hardly got my galoshes off, Becky. Give me a chance. I'll tell you all about it soon enough. There's lots of time."

Becky began to fantasize, as she often did when mentally blocked. Esther was hiding a secret. She hoped to learn some intimate details, if only her sister would co-operate. "It sounds as if you've had a good afternoon, Esther."

"Becky, please, there will be lots of time. Help me off with these galoshes first, and later tonight I can tell you a little bit more … please!"

Becky, unable to help herself, blurted out, "Are you going to have a honeymoon? How will you know what to do?"

"Please, Becky, all in good time. I'll let you know what you have to know."

This explanation didn't satisfy her. "You must be hiding something. I know you, Esther."

"I'm not, Becky. For heaven's sake, stop all the questions. You'll know what you have to know, and should know, soon enough."

The interrogation continued as they ascended the stairs to their apartment, the questions ongoing until Esther, with no option, entered the little room with her sister trailing and slammed the door in her face. "That's it!"

"I only wanted to know."

"I told you Becky … in time!"

Not placated, but acknowledging her sister's wishes, Becky retired to the tiny kitchen, with its gas burner, and put on a kettle for tea. Esther was always such a great irritation, what with her silence, inaccessibility, and seeming indifference! Becky sat at the flimsy kitchen table, still mentally in hot pursuit of what had transpired between her sister and her soon-to-be brother-in-law.

Their little apartment was hot and stuffy. In keeping with curious Victorian practice and Toronto's inclement weather, windows were kept tightly shut, creating a pervasive atmosphere of stale air, which when inhaled, made sleep come quickly and thoughts arise slowly.

Becky fell asleep at the kitchen table, having consumed her cup of tea and a biscuit. She awoke to find Esther exhorting her to get ready.

"Wake up, Becky. It'll soon be sundown and we must get to the butcher shop and grocery store before the Sabbath."

"Promise to tell me at least a bit?"

"Didn't I say I would … in time? Let's go to the marketplace. Please put on your warm sweater and coat — now!"

Just at that moment, the doorbell rang downstairs. It was Uncle Max.

Becky quickly put on her winter apparel and ran down the stairs. "What is it, Max? Did something happen? You usually come around in the mornings, not the evenings."

"It's actually good news for you and your sister. I just got a letter from your father who says Aaron and Chemia will be in Toronto the second week of May. That's even sooner than we all expected. Now isn't that good news for you both?"

"Oh, yes, of course, it is. We miss them. But we miss the rest of the family, too, Max."

Becky's first thought had been: *Well, this is going to delay the wedding until at least June.* But quickly rethinking the issue, she decided, *Well, maybe I didn't expect them to get married until the summer, anyway. Wait until Esther hears this!*

"Esther, Esther!" she called. "Aaron and Chemia will be here in the middle of May. Isn't that exciting?"

"Yes, it'll be nice to see them, and it'll be good to have them at the wedding."

So she knew! Becky thought. It was the first hint of the conversation that had so gouged her curiosity. "Esther, will you let me help you pick out the wedding dress?"

"Let's do the pre-Sabbath shopping first, Becky. How many times do I have to tell you that I'll let you know?"

This last comment, at least by its tone, momentarily squelched the usually smiling Becky.

Max, ever the perpetual peacemaker, interjected, "Girls, I've brought you only good news. Let's not fight! I promise you, Becky. You won't be left out of anything." Having delivered his message, he would leave the girls on their own to do their shopping. "I'll see you in the synagogue on Sabbath morning, and we can speak to the rabbi after the service. Esther, you and Avner can arrange the marriage ceremony, reception, and so forth."

This last comment only rekindled Becky's enthusiasm for particulars about the upcoming marriage. Max having left them on the dirty grey sidewalk in front of the house, the two girls turned the other way and walked toward Kensington Market. Undaunted by Esther's silence, Becky continued to pepper her silent sister with a barrage of embarrassing questions.

"Have you talked to Avner about the honeymoon? Tell me, Esther, do you know what people do on their honeymoon? I do. One of my girlfriends in the Old Country told me all about it. Her mother had told her. Maybe you're too shy or ashamed to tell me anything, Esther."

"Please, Becky, leave me alone. I know a lot more than you think I do, and shame on you for asking me."

A slight drizzle had added to the gloom and discomfort of the street — and the conversation. Now the onset of rain marked an end to the inquisition, at least for the time being.

The following Monday, another overcast, wet day in Kensington, the doorbell rang just after breakfast.

"I'll get it!" Becky said, scrambling down the stairs to greet Avner.

"Good morning, Becky. I've come to speak to Esther. I want to tell her about my job interview this afternoon and some other details. Can I come in?"

"Yes, yes, please come in!" Unable to restrain her unbridled curiosity any longer, Becky blurted out, "So when's the wedding?"

"Soon, soon," Avner said in a soft, hesitant voice. "You'll know about it soon enough, Becky."

He was no better than Esther! Becky thought. "So what's the big secret, Avner?"

"All in good time," he mustered as they ascended the stairs.

"Esther, are you there?" Becky called.

Hurriedly putting on her household smock, Esther joined them in the front room where in mellifluous, retiring tones Avner told them that very afternoon he had a job interview at the T. Eaton Company.

"Oh, I know about that place," Becky said. "They have a big store on Queen Street with all kinds of wonderful clothes and other things for sale."

Avner seemed a little displeased by this interruption. "As you know, I used to work in the family tailoring business back in Lagow. I never really liked the work, but I felt I had to help out. Anyway, at least I gained some good experience there."

"Oh, I remember that," piped up Becky.

"Okay, okay!" Avner snapped, uncharacteristically peeved by yet another disruption. He was a man used to taking his time and seldom lost his composure. "Anyway, it'll be a start for us, Esther. I'm sure I can get something there. Max told me he'd heard they're looking for help because the store's expanding. They're already the biggest store in the city. And Toronto's growing steadily. Max says there are already two hundred thousand people here. Can you believe it?"

The conversation ended and Avner left abruptly. Like Esther, he was proving to be a person of few words; unlike Esther, however, he was a man of many ideas. Somewhat placated, Becky decided to do some housecleaning. Unable to restrain herself, when Esther wasn't looking, she peeked out at the street below through the faded front-room window blinds looking for Avner to return from his job interview. Esther sat quietly on the sofa reading her prayer book, as always, oblivious to the world surrounding her.

"Oh, there he is. I see him coming." Becky had aimed the words excitedly in the direction of her sister.

"Thank you, Becky. Go downstairs and let him in."

Even Becky understood how very important it was for Avner to obtain work if all of them were to survive in Canada. They were well aware that their father and uncle were only able to send modest sums of money from Poland for their support. Uncle Max received the money, and each month delivered it to the girls.

"I'll be able to tell right away whether he has the job by the look on his face, Esther."

"Well, it won't be the end of the world if he doesn't get this first job now, will it? Don't be so excited. Something will work out. It always does, and for the best, God willing."

Becky raced down the stairs, opened the door, and greeted Avner with a hug and kiss, taking the poor fellow by surprise, he being unaccustomed to overt displays of inner feelings. "I'll bet you got the job. I can tell by the look on your face, Avner!" She squeezed the little man, causing him to choke and catch his breath.

"Well, I start next Monday. I had a long interview with a Mr. Bradshaw who asked me a lot of questions, but I got the job!"

Having never gone for a job interview herself, or for that matter even contemplating going for one, Becky continued the inquisition once they reached the sitting room. "What did he ask you, Avner, what did he ask you?"

"Stop with the questions!" Esther's voice sounded even more maternal than usual.

"All right, ladies!" Avner seated himself on the overstuffed sofa. "Mr. Bradshaw seemed very stern but polite. He was wearing a black suit with a wing collar, and to be honest, was every bit a gentleman. He did ask a lot of questions. First of all, he asked me how old I was, and I told him I was twenty-one.

"He wanted to know where I came from and asked me what my religion was. When I told him I was Jewish, he gave me something of a funny look that I find hard to describe — maybe, because of his sigh, a little displeased. He then asked how I spelled my name and I told him 'Appelbaum.' He again gave me a funny look and told me that the more usual spelling was 'Applebaum.' I told him English wasn't my first language, that I was having some trouble with it and that my spelling might have been incorrect.

"Then he asked me about my past work experience, and I told

him that in the Old Country I'd done some work as a tailor for my father and was a good cutter and that I'm also able to press clothing. He wanted to know about my education, and I told him I had to leave school when I was fourteen to help in the family business.

"He wanted to know other things about my background — whether I was single or married. And if I was married, or going to be married, who the wife was or was to be. The questions went on for about half an hour! Then he finally stood up behind his big oak desk and told me to report to the third-floor tailoring department next Monday morning." Avner stopped, suddenly out of breath.

Becky could hardly contain herself: Avner had a job!

Esther, with a half-smile, nodded approvingly.

4

AN UNEXPECTED TURNAROUND

March melted into April, and the Polish immigrants found themselves still trying to establish roots in the not-so-welcoming Canadian soil. Avner had a dull and tedious albeit steady job, while Becky had found herself a part-time position behind the counter of a delicatessen on Spadina Avenue, the de facto main street for the ghetto dwellers. Esther remained a less certain transplant in Canada. After all, she had left the bosom of a warm, loving family, having been the adored village beauty to boot. Arrangements for her marriage had been finalized for the third week in June: a small post-service reception would take place at the tiny synagogue on Baldwin Street.

A few streaks of yellow sunlight, the first in weeks, entered Becky's tiny bedroom, waking her earlier than usual. Scarcely awake, she went to the window to fully close the blinds left half drawn the evening before, and out of the corner of her eye, spotted a little russet-coloured bird on a branch of the large Norwegian maple tree at the rear of the house. *What a perfectly pretty little bird*, she mused. A customer in the delicatessen had told her to look for a bird like this. It was the first sign of spring. She must tell Esther. Still in her nightdress, she tiptoed down the hallway to her sister's bedroom door. But as she approached the door, the second surprise of the morning startled her — a barely audible sobbing coming from Esther's bedroom.

"What's the trouble, Esther? Are you crying? Please let me in!" When the sobbing continued without a reply, Becky persevered. "What's the matter, Esther? Please tell me." She began to bang furiously on the door.

The sobbing stopped, there were a few shuffling footsteps, and the door slowly opened, revealing a red-eyed Esther.

"Something bad has happened, hasn't it? What is it? Everything seemed all right last night at supper. I noticed you were a little quieter than usual, and Avner seemed a little different, too."

Esther's words came faintly. "It's nothing … nothing."

"It's not nothing! I know you, Esther, you almost never cry — always keeping things to yourself. You must have heard some bad news. Was it from Uncle Max? Has something bad happened back in Lagow? You must tell me!"

Trying to compose herself, Esther, in a rare moment of outward emotion, clutched her sister by the hand and blurted out, "I want to go home."

"What?" Becky was stunned.

"I do, Becky. I'm so unhappy here in Canada. I miss our family, and everything is so strange and different. Even the people look different, and I never understand what they're saying."

"But, Esther, you're surrounded by so many people from the Old Country here in Kensington. Doesn't that make you feel even a little bit at home?"

"A bit," conceded Esther. "But that isn't enough."

"It isn't Avner, is it?"

Esther let go of her sister's hand, turned abruptly, and sat on the edge of the bed.

"I knew it. It is Avner, isn't it?"

"No … not exactly."

"But I thought you really liked him, maybe even loved him." Becky had never before used the word *love* with her sister, and certainly not in relation to Avner. "Esther, how could you let things go this far? You told Papa you were happy to marry Avner, and for goodness' sake, you've already spoken to the rabbi about the wedding arrangements. Does Avner know anything about this?"

"As I said, it's not just Avner. It's a lot of things." Attempting to sound convincing, Esther continued. "The people here in Canada, the winter so cold and wet, and I feel like such an outsider."

"But what about Avner? Does he know?" Becky was losing her patience.

"Before you came home from your job last night, Avner showed up. I told him I didn't want to go through with the marriage, at least not right now, that I needed time to think it over. I told him about my mixed feelings, about everything. And I told him I have to go back to the Old Country." Esther was sobbing again. "I was so ashamed to tell him."

"Well, what did he say?" Becky stood solemnly, trying to withhold her tears as the confession continued.

"I don't know how to describe it to you, Becky, but in a funny sort of way, Avner was more disappointed than shocked or angry. He told me he was very upset but that he'd respect my decision. He then when on to tell me how he'd always adored me, ever since he first met me when we were both very young children. I guess, for him, it was love at first sight. I was so surprised. And to think that I hardly noticed him during all the years we were growing up. It wasn't until I was seventeen and Mother and Papa told me we were to be married that I paid any attention to him at all! And as for love, well, no, I've never had that kind of feeling for him. I did feel respect for him, though, and I thought that would be enough."

At this point, Becky interjected, "Why didn't you object to the marriage, Esther, tell them how you felt?"

"I didn't think I had a choice … no say. Papa and Uncle Lemel had already obtained the rabbi's blessing. Besides, almost everybody in Lagow has their marriages arranged. Even though I didn't feel love for Avner, I thought that would come with time. I thought I could live with the situation. And all the rest you know."

Becky was saddened by what Esther had to say and surprised by her sister's atypical frankness.

I'm sorry, Becky, but I'm going back to Poland!"

5

RETURN TO POLAND

Avner accepted the inevitable, but Becky was heart-broken. Max expressed surprise, but it was the rabbi who found Esther's decision particularly upsetting. It was unthinkable for a child to disobey her parents' wishes. Marriage was a sacred institution, indeed a holy covenant between a man and a woman with God as an omnipresent intermediary. Esther, of all people, was flouting God's intention in the eyes of Rabbi Chaim Jordan, the de facto senior rabbi in the ghetto.

Two days after learning of her decision, the rabbi angrily paid Esther a visit to remind her in no uncertain terms of her Judaic and filial obligations. As though on a pulpit, he delivered a sermon explaining to Esther that the institution of marriage was fundamental to healthy living as well as serving as an antidote to loneliness. In his finest tone, he reminded her that the Bible clearly stated it wasn't good for man to be alone. It was for that reason God had made for him a companion — a woman.

Although shaken by the cleric's outburst, Esther remained firm in her resolve to return home. The rabbi, infuriated with the morning's visit and Esther's apparent intransigence, couldn't help but attempt one last verbal assault as he hastily put on his overcoat to leave. His bearded face red with fury, his grey eyes staring upward, heavenward, he spluttered a departing, "One who does not have a wife lives without joy, without bliss, without happiness." It occurred to him, only then, that he might have neglected to learn why she wanted to return to Poland. When he slammed the door at the bottom of the steps, the forced closure seemed to rock the house. Esther began a subdued wail.

Despite the sudden turnaround of events, Avner, Max, and Becky all volunteered to help Esther return. Avner would see to it that the marital arrangements were cancelled and pledged to do his best to contribute half the cost of Esther's ticket. Max, agreeing to similarly contribute toward the cost of passage, promised Avner and Esther his support and volunteered to inform their families in the Old Country. Becky would help with the packing and was to stay behind and continue to work. Aaron and Chemia, when they arrived in May, would move into Becky's apartment.

Avner was caught. He couldn't return to Poland for reasons of personal safety and the risk of being conscripted into the army. He also realized the futility of chasing unrequited love. With no choice but to continue in his new job at the T. Eaton Company, he remained convinced that he had a future with the giant retail store. He'd been so lucky to get that job, in the first instance, with such a company. Despite his menial participation as a tailor and presser, he had become part of a new world — aligned with a growing enterprise far removed from the age-old haggling and bartering practices that were such an integral part of business in Eastern Europe. It was his resolve to stay in Canada and work. He must somehow overcome the bitter disappointment of losing Esther, even though the departure of his beloved immersed him in a quagmire of depression approaching bereavement.

Esther, remaining steadfast in her resolve to return home, more than ever withdrew herself from contact with the few family members and friends she had in the ghetto; spending endless hours alone in her bedroom in a self-imposed imprisonment, keeping her bedroom door locked. Occasional faint mutterings, incantations, and prayer could be heard, but the only contact Becky now had with her sullen sister occurred at the evening meal where Esther sat silent in a mock catatonic, fugue-like state. Whatever spontaneity she'd once exhibited had now evaporated, conversations being reduced to "yes," "no," or "I guess so."

Avner having been discouraged from visiting, only Uncle Max was granted permission to enter the sanctuary of the girls' apartment.

On the day Esther left for her long journey home, the mood in front of Union Station was one of cold sobriety, in vivid contrast to the joyful excitement several months earlier. As the bags were being unloaded from the carriage Max had arranged, Becky, in one last-moment plea to her ashen elder sister, stammered, "Do … do you really want to go, Esther? Look how unhappy you are and look how unhappy you're making everyone else."

Esther, clearly unmoved and stubborn as always, replied, "You know my feelings, Becky. I have nothing more to add." She said the words tersely as she descended the horse-carriage steps.

Avner had pleaded with his foreman for time off work to be at the farewell, but Esther, having severed all contact with him, was unaware that he stood some twenty feet away, swamped in the throng of milling passengers and passersby, hoping to get one last glimpse of her. Avner called out "Shalom," but no heads turned as the crowds swallowed Esther, Max, and Becky.

The next day, when Max visited him, Avner confided, "Max, you know I'm sandwiched between two worlds. I can't go back to the old one. It's simply too dangerous. But how am I to endure the new one without Esther?"

Max nodded sagaciously. "I understand, Avner. How could you possibly be happy with such a dilemma? I really didn't think she was so unhappy here in Canada. As you know, I visited the girls quite often, but it was always Becky who spoke up. Esther said very little. I knew her, but I didn't know her. Was she really that unhappy?"

"Well, maybe it was me," Avner mustered. "I thought she liked me." He'd stumbled over the word *liked*. "I thought she was starting to get fond of me. You know what I mean."

Max placed a reassuring hand on his arm. "Now don't go blaming yourself, Avner. You're a fine young man. You're not the first person to be disappointed this way. Just be patient. Time will heal you, my good friend." Anxious to change the focus of what had become a somewhat emotional topic, Max rose from the sofa, cleared his throat, and in his most diplomatic manner, asked, "So how's work?"

Relieved at the change of direction in the conversation, Avner replied, "They treat me well. The pay isn't bad, but the hours are long. I think the biggest problem is the boredom. And I never get to see the finished suits. And from the factory floor we never get to speak to the customers. Not like the Old Country. But we get a nice lunch break and the foreman on the floor is polite to us. Maybe, with luck, I can get some kind of promotion from the factory floor to the sales department."

Avner knew he was babbling but didn't want Max to go. "You know, Max, he has a good thing going, this Timothy Eaton. He closes his store at eight o'clock in the evening, which is two hours earlier than any of the others, and would you believe, he actually closes on Saturday afternoons in July. And August, too. I have a great deal of respect for this man, even though I hear he's very stern. He doesn't approve of smoking or drinking or dancing or card playing; I'm told he's basically a mensch. But he does well, even without the tobacco and schnapps as does his competition, Mr. Robert Simpson, who's just across the street from us! You know, Max, I hope that one day I, too, might have my own business — perhaps a department store."

Max left the apartment, leaving Avner alone to contemplate what he'd been trying to avoid: What would he say to his parents and brothers about Esther's departure?

6

A TELEGRAM AND A LETTER FROM HOME

The doorbell rang. It was six o'clock in the morning, and though his mind was scrambled with half-forgotten dreams, Avner knew that something was wrong. Hurriedly, he put on a coat, ran down the stairs, and opened the door, to be handed a telegram, something that always meant trouble. It was from Poland — Lagow — and was from his mother, Frieda. It read quite simply: "Sadly, your father, Lemel, has died."

It had been only a week since Esther had left, and a profusion of thoughts and emotions tumbled through Avner's mind as he quickly signed for the telegram, returning the slip to the impatient delivery boy. He was beyond the point of weeping but was tormented by mental images of his mother trying to manage without his father. A sense of duty suddenly overwhelmed him, and he resolved to become more actively involved in helping his younger brothers in their quest to come to Toronto. Before reporting for work at eight o'clock, he'd send a telegram to his brother, Beryl, whom he trusted implicitly and viewed as the best candidate to assist him. It would be a matter of logistics and finance, of course. Beryl had no intentions of leaving Poland himself but was supportive of the younger boys' plans to do so. And, most important of all, he could be depended upon to attend to family matters and look after their mother over the long term.

Avner set these ideas forth in his telegram home. And then, unable to attend his father's burial and shiva, he was left to observe a period of mourning on his own.

While at work during the day, Avner had recurring images of his father and the family growing up in Lagow. When his foreman approached him just after the lunch break, it was to ask, "What's wrong with you, Appelbaum? You usually manage to cut a dozen patterns. But you've cut only two this morning."

"I can't seem to concentrate," Avner replied timidly, holding back tears. "You see, I received a telegram this morning that my father died."

"Oh, you're some strange kind of Jew. Don't you people usually stop everything and bury your dead within twenty-four hours?"

Avner was stunned to hear that his supervisor knew about the custom, more so by his crudeness and insensitivity. "No, my father lives in Poland and has likely been buried by now, Mr. McGregor."

McGregor was surprised by the response, cleared his throat, and said, "Well, in that case, Appelbaum, just do what you can today and you can make up the work tomorrow."

Fearful of yet another calamity, like losing his job, Avner smartly answered, "Yes, sir."

In mid-May, as planned, Esther's brothers, Chemia and Aaron, arrived and moved in with Becky, who continued to work in the delicatessen on Spadina Avenue. Aaron soon moved out to a small basement room on Nassau Street, having found full-time work in a local grocery store. Chemia took the only job he knew: he became a peddler of small dry goods.

Three months had elapsed since Esther's return to Lagow and the tender embraces of her family. Becky continued to write weekly, pleading with Esther to return. Becky felt deserted, having heard nothing from Poland, and in particular, nothing from Esther with whom she'd felt a strange yet unassailable kinship.

Finally, on a hot, late-August morning, a letter from Lagow arrived. Excited, Becky opened it with a burst of enthusiasm, tearing the envelope in anticipation, and read it aloud, hoping to simulate her beloved sister's voice.

My dearest Becky,

Sorry for not writing sooner. Everything is fine with me. Mother and Father and our sisters are well. I guess Aaron and Chemia are well settled by now. All of us here are thinking of joining you and the boys — even Mother and Father.

God bless you,
Esther

Becky's first instinct was to show this letter to Avner. Maybe Esther will change her mind and marry him, after all!

Avner was happy to see Becky the next Sunday when she came over for tea and cookies and to gossip, as she often did. When he read the letter she handed him, Avner's face beamed. "I'm so glad for your family, Becky. I do hope Esther comes with them. My family is leaving, too. Well, all except Mother and Beryl and his family."

"Has Esther written to you lately?" Becky knew full well her sister hadn't.

"Not at all. And I don't have to tell you my feelings about her and about her not writing." He paused, then added wistfully, "Becky, maybe Esther will reconsider marrying me when she returns."

Becky nodded without answering and directed her attention instead to queries about Avner's brothers.

"My brothers are all in good health," Avner continued. "My oldest brother, Joseph, is going to the United States. He was very reluctant to consider leaving Poland at first, even with all the problems there, but luckily a very good friend who went to Detroit a few years ago has persuaded him to start a business there. I'm helping Lazar, Harry, and Moishe to come to Toronto. It looks as though the Apple Tree, as I like to call our family, is transplanting its roots. Before long, we may all be in North America."

Avner's buoyancy dropped suddenly to a hushed tone. As though someone were listening or spying, he whispered, "Becky, I'm thinking of leaving the Eaton Company. I'll give it a little while longer, but from what I can now see, there probably isn't much room for getting ahead, and besides, I like being my own boss. McGregor, the foreman, isn't the nicest person, and I'd rather be on my own. But I'll give it a little more time." Shifting gears, he asked, "And you, Becky? You seem to be doing nicely. You're always so happy. Have you met a nice young man yet?"

Becky, momentarily losing her composure, blushed. "Well ... yes."

Avner laughed at her embarrassment.

"Oh, well, I must meet him. What's his name?"

With uncharacteristic terseness, she replied, "Sam Persiko."

"A nice name. A good Jewish boy no doubt."

Becky found his use of the word *Jewish* surprising. Avner rarely, if ever, referred to Jewishness as an attribute. Whenever the issue of religious affiliation came up, Jewishness was regarded as a liability rather than an asset. It never made sense, in Becky's mind, that her older sister should be so diametrically opposite to Avner when it came to matters of religious faith and practice.

7

NO MORE EATON'S

One Thursday after work, Avner dropped into Shapiro's delicatessen on Spadina to have a word with Becky, knowing she'd be there for a short while. Thursday usually not being a busy evening, he felt he wouldn't unduly interrupt her.

"Becky, I've got wonderful news. Harry, Lazar, and Moishe will be arriving here next week! I'm so happy. By the way, what news of your family?"

"Well, I know they're preparing to move here, but I haven't heard anything from them in many weeks. I'm hoping they'll surprise us and arrive unannounced."

"And Esther? Is she going to join them?"

Becky looked up from behind the smoked meat counter and said reassuringly, "Oh, I'm sure she'll join them, Avner."

Avner resisted making further mention of Esther. He was anxious to share some special news. "Becky, I've made up my mind." The words tumbled out in a rush. "Today, McGregor came over to the cutting desk, and in front of all the other workers and in a loud voice, yelled, 'Appelbaum! What the hell's wrong with you? You spend half the time daydreaming. I heard through the grapevine that you've got a girl in Poland who walked out on you. Is that your problem? Get on with your work, meet your quota, or you're out of here.' Becky, it was so embarrassing! So that was it. I'm leaving."

"But what will you do? Jobs aren't easy to get, Avner."

"You remember I told you that I'd start my own business? Well, I've decided! I'm going into the furrier and dry goods business. Max is going to help me get some money, and Moishe has agreed to come in with me. It's a perfect job for Moishe — he's a leather worker by trade. There's a small retail space available down on King Street. It's a good business area. I've looked and asked many times and I don't see anybody, even Eaton's, selling beaver pelts and other accessories like special buttons, things I might sell to independent tailors and furriers. Maybe I could add more items the department stores don't sell — imported schnapps perhaps, or whisky." Avner was running out of breath.

"Aren't you a little nervous? I mean, going into your own business?"

"A little." He hesitated for a moment. "But anything would be better than listening to that McGregor barking like a wild dog. Funny, he reminds me of my old Jewish schoolteacher — that same loud, irritating voice."

"Avner, I wish you only luck. Maybe if you become a big success, Esther will change her mind about marrying you!"

What a sweet, naive little girl, Avner thought. He left the delicatessen with a supper of pastrami on rye under his arm.

The following morning, he rose earlier than usual, took a hot bath, then shaved and clothed himself in his dark blue pinstriped suit, topping it all off with his favourite hat, a black bowler. Like some fashionably tailored gentleman in the *Police Gazette*, he took the horse-drawn streetcar to the T. Eaton Company, arriving ten minutes earlier than usual. Stomping up the three flights to the cutting room, he headed straight for Mr. McGregor's dusty little closet of an office at the back of the shop floor.

McGregor seemed to anticipate a confrontation, but before he could rearrange himself and utter a word, Avner had maximized his five feet four inches, arched his back, clicked his heels, and straightened his collar. Mustering his strongest stentorian voice, he thundered, "Mr. McGregor, I'm leaving!"

Not to be outdone, McGregor managed to stand up. "Appelbaum," he bawled, "you beat me to the punch. You're fired! Get the hell out of here. You can pick up whatever's owed to you at the cashier on the first floor." Now standing firmly, face florid, his temporal veins pounding, McGregor couldn't help asking, "And what's with the fancy garb, Appelbaum?"

"I'm seeing my banker this afternoon."

"You must be joking — you seeing a banker?"

A half-smile suddenly painted itself on Avner's round, pudgy face as realization dawned: *I can now tell him anything I want.*

But Avner said nothing further. Instead, he turned and marched past his fellow workers on the cutting floor — the eavesdroppers couldn't believe what they'd just seen and heard — and descended the stairs. Picking up the $10 pay owing to him, he smartly left the building and strode to the corner of Bay and Queen Streets to meet Max at Bowles Lunch, a popular eating and meeting place across from City Hall.

"I've made all the arrangements, Avner," Max told him. "Once we've had some lunch, we'll go to the Imperial Bank and I'll introduce you to my bank manager. He's assured me I can sign for you for up to $500. I've got good credit there now — finally."

Avner was over the moon and scarcely listening as Max continued. "You can then make arrangements to sign that lease for the King Street store. I trust you, and know both you and Moishe will work hard. You'll make a go of it! It's a great idea, starting a furrier and dry goods business!"

Max, as always, was nothing if not supportive, even though to Avner and everyone else, he had always seemed enigmatic. Why the unquestioning loyalty? For reasons that remained unclear to most of the family, it seemed that Max, too, had been forced to leave Poland. Each Appelbaum had a different version as to why he was so loyal to the family members and their friends.

One story was that he nearly drowned in the Baltic Sea during a Sunday picnic, that Avner's father rescued him moments before a giant wave nearly swept him away. Yet another had it that he'd been a former lover of Frieda, Avner's mother, and vowed to remain loyal to her even though she'd married Lemel.

Whatever, the connection remained unclear and didn't matter. Max was simply there for his family and friends — and this time for Avner.

Within days, the bank loan was obtained, the space was rented, and Avner busied himself preparing the store for business. Meanwhile, Avner's three brothers had arrived in Toronto, and once settled in, Moishe and Avner officially opened the store for business. The buying and selling of fur pelts, once begun, immediately became profitable. For the two brothers, it was hard work — eight to eight daily, Monday to Friday, with half days on Saturdays, just like Eaton's.

But not a day went by without Avner thinking of Esther. He continued his contact with Becky, and occasionally with her brother, Chemia: a Sunday afternoon tea, an over-the-counter encounter, a chance meeting in his own store, Chemia looking for an extra piece of cloth or an unused fur pelt to peddle. Occasionally, Avner heard rumours of Esther's possible return — usually from Becky — but the months evaporated and the seasons passed.

By 1903, Avner had been in Canada for nearly two years, but his passion for Esther hadn't diminished. Since his letters were always unanswered, he couldn't be sure whether they actually reached Esther, either as a result of inept postal systems or possible interception by Esther's mother, Rachel. Avner had heard she disapproved of his religious indifference.

One Saturday in late April, having just closed the shop, Avner chanced to spot Max at the corner of King and Yonge Streets. Even at a distance of several hundred feet, Avner could sense that Max was depressed. Walking slowly, his head bent forward, Max looked unusually grey and sullen as he clung tenaciously to a newspaper.

Avner called to him, "Max, Max, wait, it's me, Avner!"

Max lifted his head and smiled, attempting to put on his usual good front, but he couldn't fool Avner, now somewhat breathless from running to catch him. "Max, tell me what is it? Is it bad news? You're upset. You look terrible."

"Let's go have a cup of coffee and I'll show you what's in today's *The Forward*."

The two men sat at a small table by the window, the bleak wetness of an April Toronto a perfect backdrop for the unhappy story Max had read in the daily Jewish newspaper. "In the Pale of Settlement," Max told Avner, "there's been much more trouble. Look, right here, dozens of Jews in Kishinev in Russia were murdered in a pogrom on Easter morning. The Cossacks went wild, raping and murdering everybody in sight. According to the paper, government officials themselves might have started the pogrom. Who knows? This massacre is the biggest in a quarter century. Tsar Nicholas thinks that Jews have been responsible for some five hundred strikes in factories this year, that they've been organizing all kinds of revolutionary groups to overthrow him. Of course, Kishinev isn't near your family, but it's still in the Pale of Settlement. This kind of trouble could spread throughout the entire region."

Max paused to take a breath and then continued. "Christian peasants have been angry for some months in Poland, too. A little Christian boy was killed, and a lot of these peasants believe the Jews killed him and used his blood to prepare for the Passover. To make matters worse, a little Christian girl on the eve of Easter died for reasons that aren't clear. But, apparently, on Easter Sunday morning, there were handbills throughout Kishinev announcing that the tsar was giving permission to local Christians to avenge the deaths and wreak 'bloody punishment' upon Jews. According to the story, half the Jewish section of the city was wrecked. I'm fearful that my own family, and your beloved mother and brother — your Esther and her family — could be caught up in this tidal wave, which I fear will drown the Jews like rats."

Avner buried his face in his hands. "This is terrible, Max."

"Listen, Avner, I'm going to make a phone call to my brother." This was the first time Max had made any mention of his family. "He lives in Lublin, a few hundred miles from Lagow, and he's well connected. Maybe he can arrange for your mother and Beryl and his family to come over. I'll also ask him to try to contact Becky and Esther's family. There's also our local Jewish agency, though I'm sure it will be flooded with hundreds of calls — everybody wanting to get out. Don't worry. Somehow we'll get all of them out."

MARRIAGE AT LAST!

The summer of 1903 was dry, hot, and seemingly endless, causing some men to brave wearing tropical shorts, unheard of in a decent city like Toronto. But for the Appelbaum family, the atmosphere wasn't simply an issue of physical discomfort; theirs was the pervasive and continuing anxiety known only to those with relatives left in the Pale of Settlement. Even U.S. President Teddy Roosevelt had sent a petition to Tsar Nicholas II, protesting the Russian treatment of Jews, only to have it rejected out of hand by an imperialistic madman.

On August 19, 1903, the local press reported that Theodor Herzl, founder of the Zionist movement, had declared that Palestine would be the best place for a Jewish state, given the continued religious harassment. The British offered up Uganda as a haven for those fleeing pogroms. But to many Jews, Palestine, the site of ancient Israel and given by their God, seemed the more logical sanctuary. To Max and Avner, the sensible refuge was Canada. Somehow, in the eyes of Avner, by a mixture of alchemy and perhaps chicanery, Max had been able to raise enough funds and make contacts in Lublin. Within months, papers were arranged to allow the remainder of the family of Joseph Ber Appelbaum to come to Canada. Which, of course, included Esther, the reluctant bride-to-be. To Avner's dismay, his mother and brother, Beryl, declined to leave Poland.

Just three weeks before their scheduled departure for North America, there was disturbing news. A young cousin of Esther's had died. Within a day of complaining of pain in his stomach, following an evening meal, he suffered a perforated appendix, suddenly, dramatically, in an ill-equipped, small-town clinic that passed for a hospital. One day after the shiva, Esther's mother, Rachel, was shot in the thigh in the village square by a drunken farmer wielding a shotgun and screaming, "Death to the Jews." Transferred to a hospital in the bigger city of Lublin, Rachel — and naturally her husband — would be obliged to remain behind. The children, however, would leave as planned. If there had been any doubts before, there was absolutely no question now. They were to depart to a safer land, the parents following once Rachel's wounds had healed.

Max received a telegram to that effect and hurried to tell Avner, who couldn't conceal mixed emotions of dismay and delight.

"You know, Max, tragedy is bringing Esther back to Toronto," he declared. "I'm sure she's going to think a lot differently about life here in Canada and she won't run away from me this time. The family's very close, and I just know Esther will be my bride, if only to please her father. Max, you're a real mensch! Our family owes so much to you."

It was December 31, 1903, when Max and Avner received Esther and her sisters, Shandlia and Malka, at the railway station. A special horse-drawn carriage had been arranged, and they huddled under mounds of sheepskin as they made their way to the safety of the Toronto ghetto that would be their home.

Esther moved in with Becky and Chemia, while the two remaining sisters settled into an apartment atop a creamery store on Baldwin Street. The ever-restless Aaron, tiring of his grocery shop job, moved to Lindsay, Ontario, having heard about an opportunity in the small town from a mutual friend already living there — a job in a junk shop.

After giving further thought to a life with Avner, Esther married him in a small synagogue on Baldwin Street within six months of her return, with Max and all the family members from both sides in attendance. The ceremony under the canopy was brief: the vows were made, the glass broken, and a brief honeymoon in Niagara Falls followed. Rabbi Jordan officiated, the same man who had so castigated Esther for what had seemed to him a flagrant disregard for her religious and filial obligations.

Curiously, as they would later acknowledge, the wedding took place on the very day of the death of Theodor Herzl — that founder of the Zionist movement to establish the Jewish state in Palestine — on Sunday, July 3, 1904. Although few in this sequestered and isolated Toronto community had any idea who he was — years later Avner would insist he did know — none could have imagined the effect Herzl's notions would have on future generations. In any event, his ideas were reported in *The Forward* on that hot July day; the Appelbaum-Appelbaum union wasn't.

Becky couldn't wait to see her sister on her return from the honeymoon in Niagara Falls. "Esther, it was such a lovely wedding," she said. "And you looked so beautiful! Mother's wedding dress and pearls fitted you perfectly, and everybody was so happy for you."

Esther had to admit it was very nice having family there from both sides, but lamented, "I'm only sorry that Mother and Papa weren't there. Fortunately, everybody seemed to have a good time."

"I'm glad to hear you say that, Esther," Becky responded. "When I looked at you standing under the canopy, while the rabbi was telling us about the importance of the marriage and family, you had no expression on your face. I could see it even through your veil. Were you unhappy, Esther? I didn't see any tears."

Esther hesitated for a moment, cleared her throat, and mustering as much enthusiasm as she could in that moment, whispered to Becky, "Of course, I was happy. After all, I was being married."

"Avner looked so nice in his tails and had such a warm glow on his face." Becky was trying hard to believe her sister, returning the whisper as though there was some need to carry on this intimate conversation. "You never would have known it was the same rabbi who was so angry with you."

"Never mind all that, Becky. It's in the past now. You may not have noticed, but after the ceremony he did come up to me and apologize."

Becky pressed for more. "The reception was wonderful, too. Such nice music and food, and the toast given by Uncle Max — it was all just perfect." Lowering her voice to an almost inaudible whisper, she asked, "Was it a nice honeymoon, those three days? And were you able to eat? You always keep kosher."

Esther, now a little more than irritated at her young sister's perpetual inquisitiveness, stood motionless and stared at Becky. "If I tell you, do you promise you won't tell anyone?"

"What do you mean?"

"I actually packed some of my own food. Now, is there anything else? It was a proper honeymoon, and that's all you need to know!" Sensing that one admonition probably wouldn't be sufficient, Esther added, "Avner has bought a house on Denison Avenue, and since it seems you must know everything, we're planning on having a big family."

Becky, surprised by this sudden explosion of unrequested revelations, quickly excused herself from Esther's presence with "Oh, my God, I'm late for work."

Within weeks, Avner and Esther had moved into their small two-storey house on Denison, just south of what was now informally known as the Kensington Market. Setting up house was no easy task for Esther, a woman already recognized as having no interest in, or ability with, culinary skills. But with Avner, in effect, managing the household — everything from paying the bills to cutting the lawn — the house on Denison became something of a meeting place and second home for members of the family. Sunday afternoons featured a parade of rotating relatives, with tea in glass cups and honey cake served continuously in the parlour.

On Sunday afternoons, the Denison house parlour also functioned as a courtroom for debate and resolution of every imaginable issue. Typical of the architecture of the day, the small room with its sparse furnishings had a heavy sliding oak door separating it from the kitchen at one end. A set of framed glass windowed doors divided it from the so-called "front room" at the other — the room that faced onto Denison Avenue. A highly polished circular oak table sat in the centre of the parlour, covered always with a large white crocheted tablecloth and surrounded by six imitation Chippendale chairs. An overly large crystal chandelier with small ornate oil lamps hung from the centre of the ceiling where a blue fret-patterned mosaic trim provided, paradoxically, the overall appearance of a small mosque. A large rosewood cabinet, replete with several rows of matching dishes and assorted china teacups, stood against the pink-flowered wallpaper.

Sunday afternoons in the parlour could be, and often were, heated, lively events, with Avner usually acting as peacemaker and mediator. Issues considered to be gossip were discussed softly, discreetly; political and religious matters usually degenerated into shouting matches.

Lazar was the first to arrive early one Sunday afternoon, followed soon after by Moishe. Avner was in the kitchen helping Esther prepare tea.

"So hows by you, the business, Moishe?"

This was a pretty standard opening with the Appelbaum brothers, but on this particular Sunday, Moishe, usually quick to respond with "Very good, we're making a living," hesitated. He then whispered, "I haven't told Avner yet, Lazar. I'm thinking of leaving the furrier business. I think I can do much better in the picture business."

"Picture business? You mean photography, Moishe?"

"No, I mean moving pictures. Already people are paying good money to see these moving pictures. Lazar, it's like looking at real people — alive! They've been around for a few years already in New York. Someone came up with this special machine that makes pictures move, and now moving pictures are a big business.

"I'm not very happy arguing over the price of fur pelts with tailors, cutters, furriers, and jobbers. So I'm thinking of telling Avner today about my intentions. I'll need a small loan to buy the machine and lease a room. All I'll need then are chairs and a plain wall with a sheet — they call it a screen — where you can see the moving pictures. Lazar, did you know there's already a place on Yonge Street, just north of King, called Robinson's Musee Theatre, where they charge ten cents to see these moving pictures? And there's another place across the street doing the same thing. I think we should get in on it now, Lazar. Or at least I should."

"Does this mean Avner will be left with the business by himself? Running the store alone with all that responsibility?"

"I'm hoping maybe he'll be interested in getting out of the furrier business, too. When he's had his cup of tea, we'll talk about it."

Avner's face lit up when he heard about the new venture. "How different, how inventive, Moishe. It sounds profitable! I'll investigate it first thing in the morning. There might be several places in downtown Toronto we could try to show these pictures. First, though, we must keep the store open until we're sure. We don't want burned bridges. If I hire help, I could keep the store open during the day and be in the moving picture business at night when people will have the time to come. But most of all, we'll have to find out how easy it is to obtain this new machine. It sounds good to me, and it's certainly very different. I think people will pay for something that's different and entertaining. Moishe, I like it!"

Three days later, a HELP WANTED sign went up in the store window on King Street, and the brothers Appelbaum were on their way into moving pictures and show business.

"Avner, how could Moishe give up such a good business for a toy?" admonished Esther. "He's making such a good living in the store. I think you and Moishe are making a big mistake. Do we really need this — and in the evening?"

"My dearest Esther, you have to trust me."

"You and Moishe are gambling." Esther paused, and embarrassed, turned her back to Avner. "I thought we were going to raise a family."

Her opposition coming as no surprise, Avner put his arms around her. "Esther, stop being such a pessimist." He laughed softly. "It'll work out. I think I can make more money this way, and so much more easily. Besides, it won't be every evening. We'll have a family. Believe me, I'm not doing anything foolish. I knew Moishe didn't like the garment business. I, too, would like something that's new and exciting — and profitable. I don't blame Moishe. We'll see." Avner appeared to be half pleading.

She pulled away from him. "Have it your way, Avner. You will, anyway. Let's stop this conversation. I must go now and say my evening prayers."

LIGHTS, CAMERA, ACTION!

Avner's enthusiasm for moving pictures prevailed. Although a quiet, introspective man, he was enjoying his involvement in the potentially profitable, perhaps even glamorous business. Besides, anything was better than the needle trade with Eaton's, and owning and operating a store in the garment business wasn't exactly fun, either. For Avner, it was, at times, actual drudgery. Still, his family's security was uppermost, with placating Esther a close second.

"I told you not to worry, Esther," he reminded her patiently. "We'll keep the store open during the day with the new help. His name's Joe. You'll like him. He's young and reliable and a friend of the Frankels. Esther, don't worry. My brother and I aren't crazy."

"Have it your way," Esther answered testily.

"Esther, show a little imagination."

"Who's going to pay good money to see a photograph that moves?"

"Esther, I know you aren't interested in things like this, but you should at least know something about what we're talking about. There's a picture called *The Great Train Robbery* that's made a lot of money for everybody involved. The people who come to see it really enjoy it. The audience actually shrieks out loud when the robber points a gun in their direction."

Her response was predictable: "People pay to see that?" Esther wasn't looking for greatness — peace with God and a flock of children would do.

While convincing Esther was an obstacle, it still wasn't as formidable as obtaining the actual machine, the means that would allow them to get into the picture business in the first place. The projection machines and films weren't only scarce; they were also very expensive. So after further inquiries, it was soon apparent that, just as Avner had anticipated, others in the local community had caught on to the idea. Avner and Moishe would never have an exclusive, not in Toronto, or even within the Jewish community.

Moishe tried to make an initial arrangement with one of the owners of Robinson's Musee. The man wasn't exactly helpful. In fact, he was downright rude. "Look, Mr. Apple-bum," he said, "I'm not going to tell you how, when, or where I got the machine. Get it from your own people. Besides, the subtitles are in English."

Moishe had turned out to be a bad choice as ambassador to the world of show business. Easily flustered and ill-equipped for the refined duplicity of diplomacy, he left the encounter with the Musee spokesman humiliated.

Ashamed to tell his older brother of his failure to get even a toehold or make a positive impression, he began to think that Esther might have been right. Maybe they were just "gambling with a toy."

But Moishe's rejection only heightened Avner's resolve. "Moishe, don't worry. You find the hall and I'll find the machine. In the past couple of days, I've made some more inquiries, and I know for certain I can get one in New York. I'm told by a reliable source that there's a supplier of projection machines on Hester Street. He has a deal with Vitagraph, a relatively new film company! Would you believe, he's a mechanic from the Old Country who actually was a friend of our father back in Lagow. So it's a good connection. Don't worry. I'll get a machine and some films and guarantee we'll be in business in a few months. So Esther thinks we're dealing with toys? I think we're dealing with a gold mine!"

Avner's zest and enthusiasm, however, proved to be a bit premature, and for the time being at least, Esther seemed vindicated. "See, I told you" became an all too frequent utterance in the Denison Avenue kitchen, parlour, and bedroom. The brothers would have to wait and continue to operate their King Street store for a while.

The delays weren't always Toronto-generated. Avner's connection in New York also appeared to be hedging his bets — working as a mechanic while acting as a motion picture machine retailer part-time. Some six months after his initial contact, Avner finally received a telegram from New York: "Abe can't help yet. Joseph Karnofsky."

Max Hoffman explained it to the family one Sunday afternoon over a cup of tea. "So far, nobody can get their hands on equipment and film. There are copyright battles between Mr. Thomas Edison's company and others who are making projection equipment and films. There are lots of people in on the act." Always reassuring, he added, "Boys, you're on the right track."

Max was right. Motion pictures were gaining ascendancy, currency, and acceptability in the United States. By 1906, independent companies were renting films, others were leasing projectors, and some were even training projectionists — many of them electricians in already established vaudeville houses. Some companies purchased films from the manufacturers and rented them to theatres; those companies were called exchanges.

The months following their initial enthusiasm turned out to be a painful period for Avner and Moishe. As time passed, the green leaves on the maples of Denison Avenue began to fade much like the hopes of the two Appelbaum brothers, until one day in early fall.

"Are you Mr. Avner Appelbaum?" inquired a delivery boy at the front gate. Avner nervously ripped open the telegram from New York. It read: "Abe have machine. Film available. Joseph Karnofsky." Avner returned to the house and yelled upstairs, "Esther, I'm taking the overnight train to New York to meet Karnofsky! Moishe and Joe can look after the store today. I'm going to meet Max and ask him for some money and get my ticket."

For once, Esther had no response.

The overnight train trip to New York was exhausting. Avner hardly slept at all in his coach seat, mainly due to anticipation. But Karnofsky turned out to be obliging, even helpful in making arrangements for the transportation of the new motion picture projection machine. He even promised to put Avner on to a film exchange firm and advised him that, regrettably, there were no Yiddish films, nor were there any Yiddish subtitles, at least not yet.

January 1907 might have been a cold and bitter month for others in Toronto, but for Moishe and Avner it might just as well have been the tropics. The equipment and films arrived at the train station, ready to be received. Tipped off by one of his customers, Moishe had managed to locate a large grocery store that was going out of business. It was situated on the south side of Queen Street, just west of Spadina Avenue and midway between the main centres of Jewish habitation — Kensington Market and a region called The Ward, bounded on the west by University Avenue and on the east by Yonge Street. The location was right in the commercial centre of Toronto!

"It's perfect," announced Moishe. "It faces the main street! It's a large box-like structure with a flat floor, and it's so cheap. It's literally a fire sale. The owner has to sell."

And so, delayed but not dismayed, the Appelbaums opened a small cinema, which they named the Crystal Theatre. Avner had heard of the Crystal Palace in Hyde Park, London, built for the Great Exhibition in 1851, and fancying himself to be a knowledgeable man of the world, was proud to use such a prestigious name.

Although the original Crystal Palace had been constructed of iron, glass, and laminated wood, a perfect example of nineteenth-century modern architecture, Avner's boxy theatre was a far cry from all that the word *crystal* might convey. But it mattered little. He also remained blissfully unaware that in 1891, long before he'd thought up the name, 91 Yonge Street, midway between King and Adelaide Streets, had been the site of the Wonderland Museum, which for a time had been known as the Crystal Theatre before its name was changed. In December 1905 that building was destroyed by fire, apparently caused by defective wiring in a projection machine. It was an event that left Avner shaken when he learned of it.

After many months of waiting, and much to Esther's annoyance, Avner next made a momentous decision. The brothers sold the King Street clothing store and entered show business full-time.

Their Crystal was no palace. The one-time grocery store continued to emanate odours from the many bits of vegetables that had fallen into the cracks of the wooden floor and rotted there; traces of well-used sawdust remained in the corners of the dark, airless room. The one large window, facing the street, was covered with cardboard advertisements proudly announcing "The Crystal Theatre, Real Living Pictures, Admission 10 cents."

The local Imperial Bank at Queen and McCaul Streets, in a display of uncharacteristic adventurism, and with Max's co-signature, gave the brothers a loan of $1,000. Two dozen wooden chairs were acquired in a church sale, and it was a simple matter to obtain a clean white bed sheet, the harbinger of the silver screen. Moishe was quick to learn how to operate the motion picture projector, while a separate slide projector provided announcements and dialogue that occasionally was out of sync with what the characters were mouthing on the screen.

"Maybe we should have some music in the background," Avner suggested. "In New York and Chicago, they're using a piano player to accompany the activity on the screen to add to the entertainment experience, I gather. Anyway, if people enjoy it, it's good enough for me, and besides, I like music. If we can find one of the young girls in the neighbourhood who can play, maybe we could rent a piano from Heintzman on Yonge Street."

Moishe, ever cautious and not particularly musical, seemed less enthusiastic about this proposal. "Don't you think this is getting too complicated and expensive, Avner? After all, we've waited a long time for this, a couple of years already."

"Yes, and that means we're going to have even more competition now, so we'd better do it right. Fortunately, we're going to be able to rent films right here in Toronto from the new exchange that's opening." Avner's eyes grew wide with excitement. "We can get hold of *Cinderella*, *A Trip to the Moon*, *The Great Train Robbery*. They're popular movies. And that's just the beginning. There are lots of companies now making pictures! But, Moishe, the competition here in Toronto worries me. Already Manny Gebertig and Jacob Smith are in the business, and I hear there are several others, so we'll just have to offer something better!"

Moishe seemed placated by his brother's enthusiastic explanation, but almost by way of apology, as a final face-saver, Avner looked him squarely in the eye. "We can always go back into the clothing business." After a long pause, and in his best resonant voice, he added, "But we won't have to."

Moishe smiled. "At least my Rivka is a little more supportive than your Esther. Why is she so uncomfortable?"

"She's very conventional, just like Shandlia, Malka, and Chemia. I told them I was finally and absolutely committed to the new business. Moishe, they're just old-fashioned … Old Country. I put it down to lack of imagination." Clearing his throat and clutching his pinstriped jacket lapel with some hesitancy, Avner added, "I like Esther's family just the same." In uttering this necessary familial obligation, Avner sensed he was becoming Esther's greatest apologist.

Moishe decided to change the subject. "Avner, the words on the projector screen that you call 'subtitles' are in English, no?"

"Yes, they are."

"Are there no Yiddish films with Yiddish subtitles?"

"There are, and I think we can get hold of them for our audiences, who I expect will be mainly Yiddish." Avner glanced at his vest watch; he was growing weary of this discussion. "Moishe, I'd better get going. I'll be late for supper and Esther will start to worry." Putting on his pant clips, Avner hopped on his bicycle. How he yearned for one of those new automobiles. But for the time being, cycle riding would have to do, being more efficient and less expensive than taking the horse-drawn carriages of Toronto's public transportation system. Moishe, under less duress, decided to walk home to his new bride.

#

A FIRE

Esther was never pleased that Avner worked on Saturdays. So when he said, "Esther, I'm leaving for the theatre and I might be a little late in coming home," she let him know of her displeasure. Saturday was, after all, the Sabbath, and the thought of her husband working on that holy day was both embarrassing and revolting. Other members of the family might not feel as strongly about Avner and Moishe working on the Sabbath, but Esther's depth of passion had been noted as being akin to Joan of Arc's. Constantly reminding Avner of his sinfulness, she insisted there would be penalties both he and his family would pay for his indiscretions.

"It's the law of necessity," Avner would say in his defence when confronted by Esther, and on this particular Saturday morning, she was pleased that Avner seemed somewhat agitated. But it wasn't sinning that worried him this day. "I have to meet Harry a little earlier, Esther, so please, no lectures about the Sabbath. I'll be back home as soon as I can."

There was no reason for Avner to feel apprehensive that morning. If anything, life was turning sweet. The little Crystal Theatre, though not a runaway financial bonanza, had been generating enough income to support Avner and Esther and the now newly married Moishe and Rivka. To the brothers' surprise, they had found that their audience wasn't restricted to the local Jewish community as they had thought it would be, its appeal having transcended cultural, class, and economic barriers. Here was a new art form that was entertaining and understood by all — to enjoy motion pictures one simply had to be human. Words were seldom necessary to explain them.

Needless to say, Avner and Moishe were pleased. They ran four shows a day, including Saturdays, and were happy to have in their audiences an eclectic representation of the local Toronto community. Just down the street at Bay and Terauley (now Bay) Streets stood the imposing sandstone structure of City Hall, its massive scale and stylistic exuberance reflecting the region's self-confidence in the late nineteenth century. Avner loved the building's boldness, perhaps because in some way it mirrored and magnified his own sense of self. The clerks and lawyers of City Hall were his customers. Of course, they were intrigued and entertained by the movies, but Avner felt he was mixing with equals in his little movie house. He was part of the local scene, a bona fide member of the community at large.

Just a few blocks to the west stood venerable Osgoode Hall, the site of Ontario's courts and law school. Avner felt proud to welcome the occasional member of the bench to his little theatre; some he'd even come to know on a first-name basis. The imposing Osgoode Hall itself gave Avner yet a deeper sense of local pride, because like City Hall, it, too, represented strength, stability, and fairness. It was an impressive structure, with massive columns and arched windows, as well as an ornate iron fence and peculiar cow gates encompassing the enormous property. *In some way, I'm part of all this*, Avner often reflected.

As Avner cycled his way to the theatre to meet Harry, his rambunctious younger brother, he felt again that sense of apprehension, wondering what was so important that Harry had called him on the telephone. Avner and Esther now had a party line, but of course Esther wouldn't use the modern instrument on a Saturday. So he warned her he'd be a little late returning home, not wanting to let on that he planned to buy a little gift for her. *I'll get her a nice piece of china that she can put in the parlour, or something she can wear*, he decided happily as he cycled up Spadina Avenue, his accustomed route to the theatre. His beloved Esther deserved lovely gifts. Willing to ignore their serious moralistic-religious-idealistic differences, he simply thought she was the most beautiful and intelligent creature in the world. He was so lucky to have had such a marriage arrangement.

I wonder what Harry wants, he considered again as he came within a block of Queen. *He's such a strange man, always with harebrained schemes, flitting from job to job. What can it be this time?*

But he knew in his heart that whatever the problem he'd always do whatever was needed for Harry, whom he cared for deeply: placate him, give him advice, perhaps arrange for him to meet someone who would give him a job, even if his brother never seemed to hold on to one very long. Harry simply didn't have the discipline or the ambition of Avner or Moishe. Unlike them, in his spare time, Harry was more likely to be dreaming up deals, often concocted through endless idle conversations with like-minded buddies, passing their time sipping tea and eating pastrami sandwiches in the delicatessens along Spadina. Harry's idea of taking chances was gambling — poker being a favourite — and betting on horses with the local bookies on the street.

The remarkable thing about Harry, however, was that though five years younger than Avner, he resembled him enough to be his twin. Harry, too, was of short stature, had an eye squint and a moon face, and was always dressed like a businessman with, of course, a bright stickpin. There had often been times in the past when people had shown difficulty distinguishing between Harry and Avner. But as much as they looked alike, the similarity ended there, their ideas, thoughts, and priorities being certainly very different.

Avner arrived some twenty minutes before the first movie presentation at one o'clock, and there, standing outside the theatre, was the fashionably tailored Harry. Beside him stood a tiny young woman with jet-black hair and remarkable emerald eyes. She was wearing a tight red-and-white floral dress with a large white knitted shawl over her shoulders, matching white gloves, purse, and shoes. A small bib necklace hung around her slender throat.

"Avner, I want you to meet my dear friend, Chanala."

Had Harry called him just to meet his latest girlfriend at the theatre? He could see why his brother might not bring her home — Esther would undoubtedly be upset by her presence. After all, this woman didn't exactly fit the bill of a desirable mate and potential sister-in-law. "Pleased to meet you, Chanala."

She had a fiery intensity about her, and without hesitation, shot back, "So you're the big brother. Is this where Harry gets all his ideas?"

His choice not mine, thought Avner. *A mind of her own — and a mouth.*

"Avner, I need a little money," Harry said suddenly. "I lost my job in the hardware store yesterday."

Probably fired, thought Avner.

"I met this guy, Jim Jones, a couple of weeks ago when he came into the store. He's a do-it-yourself engineer kind of guy. Anyway, he'd been down in the States visiting a cousin in Dearborn, Michigan, and he'd met this guy down there named Henry Ford who's set up a car factory. So this Jim fellow is thinking of setting up his own company here in Toronto and is looking for some start-up money. It sounds like a good investment to me. This guy Ford seems to be making a success out of his cars, Avner, so I'm thinking I should get in on this deal."

Yet another of Harry's money-losing schemes, thought Avner, who was usually impressed with new ideas. Still, not wanting to hurt his younger brother and unable to say no to him, he took $50 out of the cash register in the little office at the front of the theatre and handed it to him.

Harry was surprised. "You keep that much cash on hand, Avner? You must trust people an awful lot. Don't you think it's dangerous to do that sort of thing? Thank you, anyway. I just know this Jones thing is going to pay off."

"Go already! It was nice to meet you, Chanala. I hope we see each other again."

Avner watched as Harry cheerfully bounced out of the theatre office onto Queen Street, holding the $50 in his left hand, his right arm around Chanala. Avner then inspected the ground-floor theatre, seeing to it that the chairs were correctly positioned, that the projector was properly loaded with the day's film. Moishe and Avner rotated responsibilities, so Moishe, today, would look after the tickets and the front-office work when not selling confectionery at the door.

The week's take could easily be as high as $150, especially when one added in Avner's innovative idea of selling candy bars, cigars, and cigarettes at the door. Sometimes the cigar smoke was so thick that the people in the seats had difficulty seeing the screen, but most of the time the customers didn't seem to mind, fascinated as they were by the action playing out before them.

When Moishe arrived, Avner advised him that he'd have to leave a little early. "So you can close up today on your own if you don't mind. Most of the stores are closed on Saturday afternoon, but I know a small jewellery store owned by a Mr. Levy that stays open. I have to get a gift for Esther — it's her birthday tomorrow. I was going to go to Eaton's, but now I'm too late. They closed at noon. You know, Moishe, I sometimes get the feeling that I enjoy giving her little gifts more than she enjoys receiving them. Never mind, though. She's still my wonderful wife."

Avner left the theatre early as planned and excitedly pedalled to Levy's Jewellery where on a previous visit he'd spotted a delicate gold wristlet with a small heart-shaped locket in which one could place a tiny picture. Surely, Esther wouldn't object to wearing a little bit of jewellery, especially if it held his photograph. The jeweller carefully wrapped the birthday present, Avner paid the $12 he'd saved, then headed home.

Esther was waiting at the front door as he rode up Denison. Having spotted her as he turned the corner, he knew something must be up. *She doesn't usually wait out on the porch, especially on a Saturday.*

"Avner, the phone rang three times in the past twenty minutes. I can't answer it because the sun hasn't gone down, but this makes me nervous."

Avner had no sooner opened the front door than the phone rang a fourth time. A series of staccato questions followed. "There's a what? A fire? When did it start? But that was before the second show and everything seemed okay when I left. You mean the film caught on fire?"

Avner could hardly believe what Moishe was saying. Esther stood by listening pale-faced and emotionless. He thought he could read her mind as she glared at him unsympathetically, almost taste her thoughts: *Now do you see what you get for working on the Sabbath!*

"The fire engine and police are still there?" Avner continued with his questions to Moishe. "I'm coming right down!" He bolted out the door, in his alarm and dread, leaving his precious little gift on the small hallway table beneath the telephone. He'd had no time to mention it to Esther.

As he rushed along Queen Street, his heart pounding with the intensity of a steam locomotive, he could see in the distance the horse-drawn fire engine in front of his precious Crystal Palace. Black smoke in recurring waves billowed out of the upper and lower windows. Water was everywhere.

Bystanders had formed an enormous horseshoe around the fire engines, but curiously the scene had an ethereal silence. Avner yelled, "Moishe, Moishe!"

Although his brother had called him at home, Avner was concerned that he might have gone back into the inferno, perhaps to help customers or retrieve property.

"I'm over here by the barber pole!" screamed Moishe, and Avner breathed a sigh of relief.

The two brothers stood in front of the barbershop some two hundred feet away and knew their lives had suddenly changed, at least for the time being.

"Are you all right?" Avner asked. "Was anybody hurt?"

"No, as far as we can tell, nobody was hurt."

"That's good. I can only see smoke. Are you sure it was the projector? Could it have been something else — like somebody smoking?"

"No, the film got hot and caught on fire. I ran for the extinguisher but couldn't find it, Avner. Suddenly, there was fire and smoke everywhere and then the customers started yelling and running toward the door and out onto the street. Fortunately, the Solzbergs, who live upstairs, were able to run down the back stairs, even with her sore hip, kvetch that she is."

"Were you able to save anything?"

"To tell you the truth, Avner, I think it's a total loss."

Avner, by now feeling very weary, sighed. "Well, at least we have the insurance." He had no sooner said the words than he saw his brother slap his own prematurely balding forehead. "What's wrong?"

"Avner, the insurance — I didn't pay the last two premiums. I don't think we'll be covered."

"Moishe, how could you? Our lives are going to be ruined!"

"I thought we could save some money, then I changed my mind and was going to make the premium payment last week, but I forgot. Who could have dreamed that —"

"Your who-could-have-dreamed has turned into a nightmare. How could you, Moishe?"

As they later learned, indeed, the insurance policy had lapsed and the insurer was off the hook, leaving the brothers with property damage totalling some $5,000. The building being gutted, nothing was salvaged. The brothers promised to pay back the building owner, reaching an amicable repayment agreement. Somehow they would also reimburse Max, he being stuck with the bank loan he'd so generously co-signed.

The Solzbergs from upstairs moved to Leonard Avenue, and

Moishe got a job as a manager in a grocery shop. Avner and Esther sold their beautiful home on Denison Avenue and relocated to rented rooms at 76 Elizabeth Street, above a very noisy Chinese restaurant.

11

TWO NEWBORNS

"Avner, the doctor told me I'm pregnant."

"You went to see the doctor today, Esther, and didn't tell me?" A mixture of excitement and pride overcame him. "When, when ... I mean, when did the doctor say you were going to have the baby?"

"Sometime in the middle of May."

"Are you all right? I'm so excited I don't know what to say."

"Everything's fine, Avner. Stop worrying. It's still five and a half months away." Esther uttered the words with her customary lack of enthusiasm. "And God willing he'll be a boy."

"Esther, I'm so happy for both of us. I know you must be, too. It'll be the first Appelbaum born in the new country. And you didn't even tell me you were going to the doctor. How could you keep this a secret? You should be proud!"

"I knew there was nothing to worry about. Dr. Jacobson has assured me that a midwife will be available for the delivery, which we'll have here at home. I shouldn't have to go into one of the goyishe hospitals."

Avner couldn't wait to tell his friends at Dworkin's News Agency, just down the street, where there was always talk and free conversation to go along with the coffee, cold drinks, and cake, and even the Yiddish newspapers from New York City. For most of the regulars, Dworkin's was a second home; for some, perhaps an only home.

News of the impending birth spread quickly within the family, and all were pleased and excited, especially young Becky who was the first to volunteer as mother's helper.

Avner was now working hard in a makeshift tailoring shop he'd created at the back of the home kitchen. On Fridays and Saturdays, he helped Dennis Hyland in his successful downtown movie theatre as an assistant manager.

On May 13, 1908, Shandlia Appelbaum was born at 76 Elizabeth Street, with the assistance of a midwife sent by Dr. Moses Jacobson, who was unable to attend the birth. Esther's labour being neither prolonged nor complicated, her only birthing problem was that she'd given birth to a girl and had hoped for a boy. Not so Avner, who could scarcely contain himself with the joy of having a girl. He insisted, though, on referring to her as Lily rather than Shandlia, a choice he thought old-fashioned.

Esther and Avner soon found Elizabeth Street to be increasingly difficult as a place to bring up a child, being so very busy and noisy a neighbourhood, with hordes of milling people, pushcarts, open produce stands, hawking merchants, retail stores, Chinese restaurants, and late-night gambling offered in backrooms.

"We'll move to the country, Esther," Avner suggested.

Shocked, Esther couldn't believe her ears that Sunday morning. She was breast-feeding Lily at the time and nearly dropped the infant. "What? You mean you'd have us leave Elizabeth Street? Avner, you know we can't afford anything more just now. The debt, the rent, the food, Lily's needs — do I have to tell you?"

"There's a chance to run a dry goods store in St. Christopher, a small town near Lake Scugog. It's not too far from Aaron in Lindsay."

"But what about the synagogue? At least here I can walk to the one on McCaul. There'll be nothing for me, up in this — what did you call it — St. Christopher? Why would you do this to me, and to a place that even has Christ's name in it?"

"I want to get out of debt as quickly as possible. You know this, Esther. And here isn't the place to bring up a family. It's true there are only a few Jewish families living there, but we'll come back to Toronto as soon as we have enough money. A small town is a good place to bring up a child. There's fresh air in the country, and there will be children for her to play with. Esther, don't worry! She won't turn out to be a shiksa. Trust me. The movie business is still doing well, and if it means putting up with inconvenience for a time so we can clear our debt and reopen the theatre, so be it. We'll come back to Toronto eventually, but in a better financial situation."

Esther didn't speak to Avner for the next week, so frightened was she of losing whatever identity she had. Moving to a small Christian village conjured up memories of the old life in Poland — all that she knew and feared as a child. And she didn't relish the return of a theatre in the family, either. But it seemed such was to be her sorrowful lot.

Avner was determined to open the dry goods store that had become available upon the sudden death of a proprietor with no heirs. And so, in the cold spring of 1909, Esther, Avner, and young Lily moved northeast to the small village of St. Christopher, much to Esther's disgust. The very name "St. Christopher" was so repugnant that she told her family only that she was moving to a small town not far from brother Aaron, and she wasn't sure of its name.

Life for Esther became increasingly cold and lonely in this small Ontario settlement. How she longed for the day when she could return to what she termed her "own people." Helping Avner behind the counter, selling various foodstuffs and clothing were, for Esther, an imposition; looking after Lily was a duty. Aware that some of the customers considered her as something of a witch, with her obviously shaven head, wig, and black shawl, Esther, in turn, regarded the local customers with equal disdain.

Communication with these strangers was often in pantomime, much like the silent movies she also scorned. And to make life more miserable, she increasingly saw Avner as an apostate, perhaps devoid of any religious feeling whatsoever. For Esther, time was becoming as frozen as the grey waters of Lake Scugog, and even Avner's cheerful buoyancy and warmth would never melt away its icy grip.

But Avner persevered, faithfully sending whatever savings he could to brother Moishe back in Toronto. As correspondence with the other brothers and their wives gradually diminished, the only joy remaining for the isolated Esther was the occasional buggy ride to visit her brother, Aaron, who remained happily ensconced in Lindsay. Her one friend — Charlie, the old horse Avner kept in the barn at the rear of the store — also seemed rejuvenated by these trips. Perhaps he alone somehow understood her sense of isolation and confinement.

Lily was nearly three when Esther became pregnant once again, and Avner decided it was time to move back to Toronto. Moishe and Avner hadn't quite met their financial obligations, but no matter; Avner knew Esther wouldn't tolerate another winter in St. Christopher. The little dry goods store on Main Street, affectionately known as "Apples" by the locals, sold quickly. And much to Lily's chagrin, along with it went her ever-faithful Charlie.

But the move back to Toronto was, in most respects, a triumph for Esther, who could hardly wait to return to her familiar Jewish community. For Avner, too, the move was a victory of sorts. Mr. Hyland had written him a letter offering him a full-time job as manager of the Photodrome Theatre that, now more prosperous than ever, had begun showing first-run movies.

The new house on Nassau Street was affordable and satisfied Esther, being just four short blocks from the Henry Street Synagogue. Avner had even promised he'd join and attend, effectively establishing a domestic ceasefire. The move would also bring him closer to his brothers, men who were, in varying degrees, empathetic with Avner and his ambitions.

But it wasn't only the movies that spurred Avner's imagination; he also found the prospect of involvement in some form of live theatre intriguing. He had once enjoyed being with important people, and already the local Lyric Theatre had caught his fancy. *Imagine watching Hamlet in Yiddish, performed in a renovated Methodist church on Terauley Street.*

"Some day, Esther, I'm going to own my own theatre," he promised her, hoping she might care. "One with live entertainment."

Esther wasn't thrilled at the prospect. "Avner, I understand that at the Lyric they have performances on Saturday evenings after the Sabbath. I've even heard that some of the women in our neighbourhood go to the synagogue on Saturday mornings and then they go to what they call a matinee in this theatre in the afternoon. This isn't acceptable behaviour! I don't want you being part of anything like that. Haven't you got a good enough job with Mr. Hyland? And doesn't he treat you nicely? It's bad enough that you must work most Saturdays. You should be thankful for what God has given us, and—He will bless us with another child …"

Would this woman never be happy? "Esther, for goodness' sake, show a little interest and enthusiasm. Can't you see all we have around us — and just around the corner? Famous people come to Toronto. There are theatre stars from New York — actors like Jacob Adler and David Kessler and musicians like Boris Thomashefsky and many others. Please, already! Maybe you don't like them, or have never even heard of them, but many people have. And they'll pay good money to see them! Stop the worrying and let me look after the finances. You just look after the children."

It was an admonishment he hated delivering to his dear Esther but one that was long overdue. In the early morning hours of March 7, 1911, Esther went into labour. "Avner, quick, call the doctor," she said as she shook him awake. "I'm starting to have very strong contractions."

Startled out of a sound sleep, Avner leaped from the bed, and still in his long underwear, grabbed Esther's hand in an attempt to calm her. "Relax," he said breathlessly, trying not to panic. "I'll go downstairs and call the doctor." As with Lily, home delivery had been insisted on — categorically.

In his bare feet, Avner ran, scarcely breathing, along the tiny corridor and down the stairs to the telephone. But there was no answer at the doctor's home each time he called. With every yelp from the upstairs bedroom, Avner grew more agitated and nervous.

"Esther, I'll be right back!" he hollered. "I just remembered there's a midwife about ten houses away. I'll see if I can get her." He didn't want to tell her the doctor wasn't available.

Avner quickly jumped into his galoshes, put on his long, heavy overcoat, and hoping nobody would see him, dashed outside into a street now thick with a topping of wet snow. Half awake and confused, heart thumping, fingers freezing, he remembered only that Sadie Ginsberg, one of several midwives in the area, lived in a big brown house, the one with the oversized verandah at the corner of Nassau Street and Augusta Avenue.

He knocked frantically on the solid oak door for what seemed an eternity, calling, "Sadie, the midwife, come quick! My wife's about to deliver!"

Eventually, the second-floor window opened and a squeaky voice answered, "I'll be right down."

"This way, this way!" Avner shouted when she finally reached the street. "For all I know, she might have delivered the baby already."

Sadie seemed remarkably serene. "Try to calm down," she told him.

Snow had begun to fall quietly in the early-morning darkness, diffusing the glow of the gas street lamps and giving the surrounding area a misty, ethereal quality. The two figures appeared like ghosts in a white swamp. As they approached the Appelbaum house, the first wails of a newborn could be heard. Avner, with Sadie right behind him, galloped up the stairs to the bedroom where the tiny infant, Louis, lay at his mother's side, the umbilical cord still intact.

Sadie was unruffled, Avner frantic. "Go get me some hot water and I'll look after things," she ordered. "She's going to be all right. The baby appears to be a healthy boy, and your wife looks just fine. And what a handsome son he is, Mr. Appelbaum. You couldn't ask for anything better. He's going to be quite something when he grows up," she added sagaciously.

As the snow continued to fall, Esther fell asleep. Louis cried softly in his new blanket while Avner paced the floor, not without a sense of pride and relief.

12

THE GREAT WAR

As Lily and Louis grew older, Avner and Esther increasingly orchestrated their children's lives, each employing a different baton.

"Lily's going to take piano lessons, and Louis will play the violin," Avner declared.

"Avner, what foolishness! You want our Louie to be a fiddler and beg? And Lily? What's she going to do with her music? Besides, lessons cost money. We should be very careful of every penny."

Avner laughed. "My dear Esther! I guess I forgot to tell you. I've been carefully saving my money and have actually notified Mr. Hyland that I'll be leaving. I'm going to open a new theatre as soon as I can find one."

Esther could barely conceal her disgust. "Avner, I really don't know what you want out of life. You seem to have to let everybody know just how important you are, forever buying new clothes for yourself. Yes, I know you buy me, Lily, and Louis nice things, too, but you aren't careful enough."

Avner, however, wouldn't be put off. "Esther, you're such a worry-wart. I'm doing just fine, and when the opportunity presents itself, I'm going to leave the Photodrome and be a somebody. Please understand. I like meeting important people who have done things. I like new ideas. I'm determined to own my own theatre again, maybe more than one. There are business opportunities happening all the time! If you want to get stuck in a prayer book, that's your business."

It was one of the few times Avner had launched a direct assault on Esther's preoccupation with her faith. She decided to remain silent.

While Esther continued in her intellectual and emotional prison, the movies and the newspapers somehow emancipated Avner. At the outbreak of war in 1914, Hollywood, California, was becoming the new film capital of the world. Motion pictures were now reflecting something of the real lives of people, and techniques and ideas were being both traded and stolen within the filmmaking community. Avner smugly fancied himself as part of this exciting new commercial art form.

But the Great War might just as well have occurred on some distant planet as far as Avner and Esther were concerned. Their respective parents being far removed from actual combat, only one event did seem to strike home. Avner, always in touch with world events, to some degree at least, knew of the Serbian nationalist assassination of Archduke Franz Ferdinand, heir to the throne of Austria-Hungary, and his wife, Sophie, the Duchess of Hohenberg. That seminal event had led to the horrific conflict in Europe and the senseless slaughter of millions of people. Avner had received a telegram from an old acquaintance of his from Lagow who was travelling to the United States but tragically lost his life on the *Lusitania* in May 1915 when the ship was torpedoed ten miles off the Old Head of Kinsale, Ireland. Avner never forgave the Germans. But then he had no love for the British or French, either. Esther, in her cocoon, paid no attention whatsoever to these events, further adding to Avner's irritation with her indifference to world affairs.

"Esther, how can you not remember my friend, Michael Zalman, from Lagow? I must have told you about him a thousand times. And now he's drowned in this stupid, senseless war being fought by these crazy royal families. Such a waste!" He paused for effect. "Well, Lily and Louis aren't going to grow up and be out of touch — you can be sure of that! They're going to go to school and get a good education."

"I'm sorry to hear about Michael." Her answer came belatedly and reluctantly. "But it's somebody else's war, not ours."

As time evaporated and the Great War ended in 1918, Lily and Louis remained in public school, using English as their primary language. Avner's accent and poor English remained a source of embarrassment for him as he sought to integrate and be like everyone else. Of course, he still wanted to be better than all the rest.

13

ACCUSATIONS

"Avner, it's been how many years since you've been the manager at the Photodrome?" Esther was at him again. "It's 1923, and the war's been over for five years. Why are you giving Lily piano lessons and Louis violin lessons? What do they need them for? You still expect them to be musicians?" The barrage of questions seemed endless.

"You're always buying me gifts. What are you trying to prove? You give the children gifts. You give your brothers gifts. You told me you were saving money to buy a theatre, but you never tell me how much money there is in the bank and you only give me enough money for food. You never tell me what's going on and you know there are lots of problems in the family, especially with Harry. I've got my own troubles with my sisters and Aaron, who reminds me a lot of Harry. I've told you he likes cars and ladies — lots of both. It's all very sinful."

Avner pushed himself back from the kitchen table, folded his arms, and stared at his wife. "Esther, morning and night it's like the Spanish Inquisition. I'm saving money and I'm very soon going to have my own theatre. I'm helping Harry and Chanala, but I don't think I can save their marriage. At the very least I'm trying to save ours!"

Esther, momentarily stunned, looked across the table at Avner, then asked in her most direct way "What is there to save? You've got your ideas about how to live and I've got mine. Let's face it, Avner. We've never been suited for each other. That's been pretty clear from the start. I think our fathers, by playing matchmakers with us, made a very, very big mistake."

They had visited this territory a million times.

"Esther, the kids are growing up nicely. They're going to school and meeting people. I give you nice clothes. There's food on the table ..." Avner's voice trailed off into an exhausted whisper of exasperation.

Obviously, something had triggered this post-breakfast ideological indigestion. Esther's beautifully sculpted face turned death-white as her clear, steely eyes took on a misty soulless quality. "You've been seeing other women, Avner!" Her voice was cold and steady.

Avner was paralyzed with surprise. He'd just received a death sentence for a crime he hadn't committed. He gazed out the kitchen window, trying to avoid eye contact with Esther, catching a glimpse of a branch of an elm tree from which he could imagine suspended, a hangman's noose.

"Esther, you must be crazy. Where ... where did you ever hear such craziness?" He watched as she stood, anger rising with her voice.

"People talk. I won't mention any names. I was told you were seen with that red-headed cashier from the Photodrome out on Queen Street a couple of times. And you've been seen having lunch with Dr. Dyck. That man performs illegal operations, Avner. What are you doing with people like that? Is this your idea of being a somebody? You're a disgrace to me. And in the eyes of God … who knows what!"

Avner had never seen Esther livid with rage. She appeared transformed, her usual quiet, icy demeanour utterly changed into some kind of grotesque and insensitive creature.

"Esther, sit down and I'll quietly explain. No, don't walk out. Just pull up a chair by the table. I'll make a cup of tea and you'll understand the whole situation."

Esther stood speechless and motionless for what seemed an eternity before finally taking a seat at the table. Here he was confronted by the inspector, the judge, and the jury, with the trial, the conviction, and the sentence all in one great indigestible lump. She sat at the end of the kitchen table, white knuckles clasping a glass of tea, stony eyes transfixed on Avner, imprisoning him by her very presence.

"Look, Esther, this is the way it is, so please listen carefully. The redhead you're upset about is Doris Robinson, Mr. Hyland's cashier. As it happens, my meeting with her was a favour for Mr. Hyland. He told me that Doris needed some special help and that because I knew Dr. Dyck maybe I could resolve a delicate situation. Doris was apparently pregnant — no, Esther, not by me! I didn't ask who the father was."

Avner continued. "One day, a few weeks ago, I arrived about a half-hour before the first picture show, and she was there, obviously very upset and nervous. So I asked her to have a coffee and a bagel with me. She told me she needed to have the pregnancy fixed, and I said I'd do what I could to arrange a meeting with Dr. Dyck. I called him, and all I know is that within two days the matter was resolved and I presume everything went all right. Doris was back to work within a week, and when she returned, both she and Mr. Hyland took me out for a quick lunch. I wasn't involved in any way except making the contact between her and Dr. Dyck. Again, Esther, I don't know who the father was. For all I know, it could have been Mr. Hyland, but I doubt it. So, my dear Esther, that's the first point. Secondly, as you know, Mr. Hyland has been very good to me and I've been able to save money. And because of what I did for Doris, Mr. Hyland said he'd help me obtain a loan at the Imperial Bank, which would mean I wouldn't have to ask Max any more for help, or go to other members of the family. And as it turns out, my darling Esther, with the loan and the money saved and Mr. Hyland's signature, I can purchase my own theatre — finally."

Esther pushed back her chair slowly and stood, cheeks flushed, lips quivering. "So these are the kind of important people you're dealing with, Avner."

"I was doing what I thought was right and I was helping a friend. I didn't have to ask any questions and ultimately the decision was between the doctor and Doris. What do you want? At least it wasn't me ... fooling around."

Esther wasn't about to be put off. "Jewish law doesn't allow for frivolous abortions. Avner, you'll be punished for such behaviour. I just know it." The kitchen trial was to continue.

"Esther, you've never even met Mr. Hyland. He's a mensch — a good man. And what happened to Doris can happen to a good woman. I don't care about your rabbinical law. She needed help, and I helped her obtain what she needed. Am I guilty as an accessory? How am I to plead?"

Esther regarded him fiercely. "Only God has the final answer. I've nothing more to say."

Head high, back arched, Esther regally exited the kitchen courtroom. Avner sat quietly and finished his cup of tea.

14

FIRST MOVIE THEATRE

"Esther, I've got great news!" Avner could hardly contain himself. "The deal's done, and I've bought a theatre at the corner of Queen and McCaul. Isn't that exciting?" He knew full well all he'd get would be blasé neutrality. "Mr. Hyland told me he has somebody to replace me as the full-time manager in about two months, which is about how long it'll take for the new theatre to become available."

"Well, at least it's not bad news," Esther responded.

"The children can continue with their music lessons, and Louis can keep on after school with his Bible studies at the Henry Street Talmud Torah. After all, we want Louis to be a mensch, too, don't we, Esther?" He said that sardonically.

Esther saw her opportunity. "Avner, I want you to be a contributor to the Henry Street Synagogue. Don't worry. You don't have to go on a regular basis, just as long as people know you care to be a member of the congregation."

"Fine, Esther, fine," he agreed. "As soon as I have enough money, I'll make a contribution and maybe even buy a seat so my name gets listed as a donor. But in the meantime, I've got a lot of work to do. I've made contact at the film exchange on Adelaide Street and am promised rental privileges. We won't have first-run films, of course, like Jay and Jules Allen or Nathan Nathanson, who own a lot of theatres, but we can get some good second runs, maybe even a Chaplin or a Mary Pickford that's made the rounds at the expensive big-shot theatres like the Tivoli. I've thought of special evenings where we can give away door prizes to bring in the customers. You know, dishes I can buy very cheaply from a wholesaler Max introduced me to. Children love to go to the theatre on Saturday afternoons. The Tom Mix serials and *Our Gang* comedies are very popular. Lily can play the piano for some of the matinees, and Harry's Chanala is willing to help. She's already agreed to be our cashier until she starts to raise a family."

Avner's joy knew no bounds. In September 1925, the former Orange Hall at Queen and McCaul became the Reo Theatre, offering silent pictures twice a day, matinees on Saturdays, free ladies' prizes on Tuesdays. Avner enjoyed playing the impresario, even if was in a five-hundred-seat film emporium. He was becoming a familiar figure at the film exchange, too — a sharp dresser with equally sharp ideas. Before long he was a senior member of the Henry Street Synagogue, placating Esther and a goodly number of the faithful in the family.

At his theatre, he enjoyed greeting customers at the door, including the occasional alderman or civil servant from City Hall who would straggle over to the little Reo. Rudolph Valentino in *The Sheik* or Mary Pickford in a rerun of *The Hunchback of Notre Dame* were well worth the twenty-five-cent admission. And who couldn't enjoy the comedic capers of Mack Sennett's Keystone Kops with Fatty Arbuckle and Mabel Normand?

One day, unexpectedly, Jim Sullivan, a senior clerk at City Hall who liked Avner and was a frequent visitor to the little cinema, suggested he become a Mason. "Avner, this would be a good opportunity for you to extend yourself. You know what I mean — get to know people; make business contacts, maybe give some of the local big boys in the movie business a run for their money. You know about the Masons, don't you? It's a fraternal organization. I think you could benefit from that kind of thing, and we'd enjoy having you around."

The invitation caught Avner by surprise. "I'm flattered, Jim, but aside from the business connections, what's it really all about?"

"Well, it's not really a religious organization. You only have to believe in a Supreme Being and not necessarily a Christian one. Masonry uses the Isaac Newton idea that God is the great architect of the universe. Really that's all there is to it."

Avner had heard of Isaac Newton but knew little about his ideas. However, Jim's explanation being clear enough, his response was, "By all means." He smiled, knowing Esther would never approve of such blasphemy. *What do you need it for?* she'd say. *If you want to help people, Avner, you can do it through the synagogue. Why would you join a goyishe organization?*

No sense telling her he wanted to meet new people, make new acquaintances and friends, maybe help somebody while helping himself — and feel good about it. Anyway, it wasn't such a big issue. He told Sullivan he'd think it over.

Another day brought a chance meeting. Avner had always enjoyed the lunch specials at Bowles. The food was good and cheap, and there was lots of it. But for Avner, most of all it worked as an opportunity to rub shoulders with some of the more significant men at City Hall, and local businessmen, as well. The place hummed, especially at noon, with men's voices reverberating off the tiled walls and floors and marble tabletops.

Avner was about to make his way back to the Reo to open for the matinee when he was joined at the table by a trim, nattily dressed young man with a strong Polish accent. "You're Avner Appelbaum, aren't you?" the man asked politely. "I've heard about you from my parents — the Frankels. They used to own a bakery and confectionery store on Kensington Avenue. You rented a room from them many years ago. I'm Adolph."

Avner recalled them instantly. "Oh, yes, very nice people! I haven't seen them in years."

"Sadly, my parents died just last year. My mother had heart problems, and I think my father, who died just after the shiva for her, must have suffered a different kind of heart problem. Call it a broken heart. Maybe it was better that way. They often spoke of you fondly."

Avner was distressed by this news. "Oh, I'm so sorry to hear about your mother and father. They were such nice people. But what about you? What are you doing?"

"I'm working on Spadina Avenue in the clothing business. My partner and I have a little factory and make men's shirts. We sell them to the larger stores, like Eaton's and Simpson's. My partner's a very good designer from the Old Country. I mainly do the promotional work, and we've got ten women working for us. And we're doing just fine. But did I hear you've opened the Reo Theatre?"

Avner was impressed with the young man's eagerness but suddenly realized it was 12:30. Trying not to be rude, he excused himself quickly. "Look, I'm running a little late. I must open the theatre. But please come around anytime. Just tell Chanala, my cashier, I sent you. We're playing *The Hunchback of Notre Dame*." Avner hustled off, little suspecting that this chance meeting might be the beginning of a long-standing friendship with Adolph Frankel.

15

FUTURE SON-IN-LAW

For Avner and many others in the entertainment industry, 1927 was an important year. When *The Jazz Singer* opened at the Warners'

Theatre in New York City on October 6, it was billed as the world's first talking picture. Curiously, its plot reflected Al Jolson's life, and to some degree, that of Avner's, as well. Jolson came from a Jewish family that frowned on his show business career, leading to disenchantment and estrangement from his parents and mirroring the antipathy Esther had always shown toward Avner's "show business" involvement. But Wall Street and Avner's business were booming. And in November of that year, when General Motors declared the largest dividend in U.S. history, Avner, having surreptitiously purchased a few shares — unknown to Esther, who shared no knowledge of his business affairs — cashed in, making a neat $2,500 profit.

It was time to tell Esther about his plans. "I'm going to buy a theatre for live performances. Yiddish, in fact. As much as I like the movies — and they're getting better all the time — I really enjoy seeing people up on the stage. It doesn't matter whether they're singing or dancing, or if it's a play, for me, it's exciting. And if it's exciting to me, it's going to excite other people, too. A while back Isador Axler sold me a few shares in the new Standard Theatre on Spadina, a full-time Yiddish playhouse. Imagine, Esther, we now own a movie house, we have shares in a live theatre on Spadina, and soon I'm going to own a new one on Richmond Street. I'll call it the Comedy Theatre. You should see this place. It's small, just a four-hundred-and-fifty-seat auditorium with a small balcony, but it has beautiful sight lines. And I can pick it up for a bargain. The owner suddenly died, so it's another fire sale. I put in a bid this morning. My idea is that we can have special live Yiddish theatre. Esther, we should celebrate."

Exhibiting a rare moment of business acumen, Esther quietly asked: "Avner, do you think there are that many Jews in Toronto who would want to waste their money with singing and dancing? You're already involved with one live theatre. Do you need a second? I want you to spend more time at home with the family. Do you need such a headache?"

How pitifully right Esther was to be in her caustic observation. The Comedy Theatre was purchased, Yiddish vaudeville acts were booked, but the theatre folded within six months for lack of attendance. Even the Standard itself, which had prospered for several years, began to struggle as audiences came to prefer Hollywood movies. And when it came to stage performances, it was American English-speaking stars they wanted to see, not Yiddish performers, no matter how talented they might be. Who wanted to be reminded of a Yiddish background when it was difficult enough being singled out as a Yid, a foreigner, especially in Toronto, the city of churches, Toronto the Good?

Avner was beginning to realize that he himself wanted to be a North American somebody; it had been a mistake to get involved in strictly Yiddish entertainment.

In addition to Avner's reversal regarding the Comedy Theatre came other disappointments. Esther seemed to become more rigid and inflexible in her ways. Young Louis, now known as Lou, had dropped out of high school in his second year and was now selling newspapers on street corners and meeting up with all kinds of nefarious toughs. No more violin lessons for him when there was money to be made.

Lily, now widely known as Lil, had become the bright spot in Avner's home life. She was pert and pretty like her mother but certainly far more popular with both sides of the family. Lil now played the piano and was acknowledged to be a good dancer. So Avner was very proud of his accomplished young daughter.

He was also pleased that Lil had met an intelligent and ambitious young man about to graduate from Central Technical School. Morris Letovsky, known as Murray, was one of five siblings in a typical Eastern European Jewish family who, like the Appelbaums, had found refuge and sanctuary in Canada. Lil and Murray were, as the local parlance had it, "keeping company." His parents, Samuel and Anna, were hard-working and God-fearing. Deprived of a formal education in their native Russia, they had married very young and hoped their future family in Canada would acquire knowledge, skills, and maybe even wisdom.

Lil invited Murray to tea and cake on a Sunday afternoon — an opportunity to meet Avner and Esther.

"Father, this is Murray Letovsky," she said. "You've heard about him from Aunty Becky and Mother, I'm sure." Lil's manner was ebullient, self-assured. "Murray's going to be an electrical engineer and hopes to join the Bell Telephone Company when he finishes Central Tech at the end of this year."

Stocky and shy, Murray, in a faint whisper, affirmed Lil's comments. "Yes, Mr. Appelbaum, I hope to get a job with Bell in Toronto. My father's in the fuel business. We deliver wood, coal, and ice, and my brother, David, and I help out when we can. I also deliver telegrams for Western Union." Murray seemed suddenly cast in the role of self-promotion, a part he'd obviously never played too well.

Avner immediately liked the lad. "Well, that's very impressive, Murray. I like people who are ambitious and work hard. Have you been to our movie theatre?"

"Oh, yes, Lil and I have gone a number of times. You know, the movies are good, but really, Mr. Appelbaum, I'm more interested in the technical side of moviemaking. And now they can make people sing and talk in these moving pictures. It's absolutely remarkable to me!"

"Well, you and Lily should come around to the theatre whenever you get a moment. And, if you like, I'll take you upstairs into the projection booth and you can look at all the equipment."

"Oh, thank you very much. I'd really like to do that."

Lil was satisfied that the introduction was going well.

When Esther entered the room and a few pleasantries had been exchanged, she asked, "Murray, may I serve you some tea and cake?"

He was about to say, "Oh, thank you very much, Mrs. Appelbaum," when he glanced at his watch, and realizing it was 3:30, jumped from the table with a startled response. "Oh, my goodness, I'm going to be late at Western Union! I forgot! This is my day for delivering telegrams. I'm sorry I have to leave so soon, Mr. Appelbaum. I hope you and your wife will understand and that I'm not being too rude."

Avner smiled at the flushed young man as he dashed from the room. *Ambition — I like that in a young person!*

Afternoon tea had been brief. However, the initial feeling-out process had gone well for all concerned.

It wasn't too long after the meeting with his future son-in-law that a chance fateful encounter with his long-standing friend took place in front of the Reo. Avner was about to open the front doors of the theatre when, glancing to his right, he noticed a brilliant yellow-and-blue

Pierce Arrow parked about twenty feet away. It was Max Hoffman, whom he hadn't seen for months.

"Avner!" Max shouted.

"Max! Where have you been? Is that your car?"

"Yes, I bought it last year. Isn't it a beauty?"

Avner nodded, impressed. "Obviously things are going very well."

"Oh, yes, they are, Avner, and I notice they seem to be going pretty well for you, too. You know, investing in the stock market has paid off, so now I'm looking at real estate, as well. And that's why I'm here this morning. Somebody told me these old buildings beside your theatre might be going up for sale."

Avner grew serious at this point. "I guess you heard about the Standard? We're losing money there. People don't seem to be interested in Yiddish Theatre anymore. I certainly found that out with the Comedy. You know that I had to sell it at a loss. And that hurt in more ways than one. For as much as I like the movie business, Max, I still really prefer live theatre, and I can't even explain why. It's not just simply a matter of making money for me …"

Max thought for a moment. "Listen, Avner, I think I might have the answer for you. Let me introduce you to a man I've met a couple of times — name of Piton. He owns the Globe Theatre, and I'm told he's looking for a partner. The man drinks a little too much, but I think he has good ideas, and he, too, likes live theatre. Besides, what harm could it do? Perhaps we could meet you for lunch over at Bowles? Esther, Becky, and everybody in good health I presume?"

"Yes, Max, thanks for asking. What did you say his name was?"

"Piton."

"Piton?"

"Yes — Fred Piton. He's Irish or French or something."

True to his word, Max arranged for the two to meet the following week at Bowles Lunch.

"So you're the Avner Appelbaum Max has told me about." The three had just sat down to the day's special of salmon chowder and hot rolls. Avner was surprised at Fred Piton's demeanour. Expecting to meet an aggressive, elder businessman, instead he'd found a rather soft-spoken, suave, and articulate person. Bald, angular, and nattily dressed, Fred Piton was also young, perhaps in his thirties.

"So you like live theatre, music, dancing girls — that sort of thing?" he asked smiling. "Max tells me you lost your shirt with that Jewish stuff. I can certainly understand why." Piton sat back and studied him. "Well, Appelbaum, I can tell you that I, too, like a little excitement on the stage, and I think we can make a buck or two out of it. I'm told you know your way around and have experience operating a theatre. Well, maybe we can do a deal and run a theatre together, one with live performers. But the performers I have in mind will be a little bit different from the stuff you see at the Royal Alexandra or Massey Hall."

Avner was puzzled. "What do you mean?"

"I think the people around here are tired of these touring stock companies that come from the States — all those boring Shakespeare and sad-sack vaudeville acts. I believe there are lots of people who'd like to see burlesque again. What this city needs is a darned good girly show!"

Avner was floored. "Mr. Piton, I know all about burlesque —"

"Please call me Fred."

"Okay … Fred. There used to be a Starr Burlesque Theatre on Temperance Street, I think around 1911 or 1912, but it was shut down. They were running what was said to be a lewd show. In fact, if memory serves me correctly, the case even went to trial. The theatre was found not guilty of producing an indecent show, but as it happened, they were also not allowed to continue to put on these burlesque shows, with all the saucy language and scantily clothed women."

"Right! But did you know, Avner, that the very same reverend who complained about the Starr Burlesque and had it closed down was himself later arrested and convicted of publishing obscene literature? Now what do you make of that!"

"Yes, but Fred, even so, wouldn't it be a bit risky to go into the burlesque business? I can't afford another loss."

"Avner, you needn't worry about that." The self-assured man leaned back and chuckled. "I'm a member of the Orange Order and I've got good connections with both the Toronto Police and the Licensing Commission."

"Well, then, why would you need me?"

Piton studied him earnestly. "I'm looking for someone who's smart, ambitious, has experience running a theatre, and isn't afraid to gamble. Someone to spell me off, and of course, be willing to take some financial risk."

Avner thought for a moment. "Well, as Max told you, I lost a fair bit of money with live Yiddish theatre, but if the situation were right and you could get a licence, I'd certainly give serious thought to a partnership. I've heard about the Minsky brothers in New York. I understand they're making big bucks and irritating all the 'legit' owners in the neighbourhood, but I've heard they're having trouble holding on to their licences."

"Don't worry, Avner. This is Toronto, not New York, and I know my way around this city pretty well. I know how to handle the Jews, the Protestants, and the Catholics. As a matter of fact, I've had a lot to do with Magistrate Jacob Cohen and his son, Arthur, who own a big chunk of the land on the south side of Queen Street. You know, all those pawn shops, gypsy joints, and Chinese restaurants. Well, I'm in good shape with the Cohens — they almost gave me my Globe Theatre. As I told you, I know how to deal with the Jews."

Avner was more than a little surprised at Piton's bluntness and obvious ego. "Fred, give me a couple of days to think about it. We'll talk. This burlesque idea sounds pretty good to me, but I'll have to let you know."

After Piton excused himself, Max leaned over the table. "I told you, Avner. I told you I knew a pretty sharp businessman who knows his way around the city and could help you make a lot of money."

Avner was perplexed. "Well, it certainly sounds good, Max, but to tell you the truth, I'm more worried about Esther than I am about Fred Piton."

"What do you mean?"

"I'm worried what Esther might think. If I told her I was in a business where women take their clothes off on stage, she'd be horrified."

Max's reaction came as a surprise. "Don't worry, Avner. She'll get used to it."

◆ ◆ ◆

Three days after the Bowles Lunch meeting, Avner placed a call to Fred Piton. "You've got a deal, Fred," he said. "Get your lawyer to draw up the papers. I assume, of course, you're going to have no trouble getting the proper licence from the Police Commission."

"No problem, Abe," Piton assured him, employing the first name he always called Avner. "I'll set it up. We're going to make a bundle on this deal. I can smell it! Especially when everybody else in town is obviously afraid to run burlesque." There was a pause before Piton added, "Don't worry, Abe. Just leave everything to me. Meet me at noon a week today in the offices of my lawyer, R.J. Kelly. He's just around the corner from the Globe on Bay Street. We'll make it short and sweet."

So, in early 1929, Fred Piton and Avner Appelbaum entered into a partnership arrangement. For $5,000, Avner was to have a fifty percent share of the Globe, renamed the Roxy, and would assume full-time managerial responsibilities. Piton was to do the booking of live entertainment and supervise the acts, the deal being contingent upon obtaining an appropriate licence to operate live entertainment of a burlesque nature. As additional security, Piton and Appelbaum would each carry life insurance for $15,000, with a double-indemnity clause naming each other as beneficiary.

16

BURLESQUE ON QUEEN

Esther was aghast, and once again, Avner found himself pleading for understanding. "I know what I'm doing, Esther. I think we can make a lot of money with Fred Piton. Don't worry. I won't sell the Reo until I'm sure about this new deal. Just think about it, Esther. We'll have enough money to move into a new home, new furniture, new car, money for Lil and Murray's wedding next year …"

At this point, Esther cut him off angrily. "You're going into business with a Gentile, and you know nothing about him! I've heard he's a drinker and a womanizer. Max isn't always right, you know."

Esther began to alternately hyperventilate and wheeze, a reaction becoming all too frequent of late when emotionally distraught. She caught her breath long enough to shriek, "Your signing a partnership with the Devil. Piton will ruin our lives!" Composing herself somewhat, Esther continued the tirade. "And by the way, I don't know whether you heard from Chanala this morning. Your brother, Harry, has run off."

"He what?"

"He's run off. He left Chanala a note this morning, saying he can't take her temper anymore and he's leaving her for good. Can you imagine? He's leaving his wife and their two little boys! He's a disgrace! What's this world coming to? Naked ladies on the stage, men deserting their families …" Esther had an uncanny ability to associate unrelated scenarios.

Momentarily distracted by the news about Harry, Avner blurted out, "What a calamity! Something must be done about it. I'd better see Chanala straight away and try to sort things out." As Avner headed out the front door, he turned to face Esther and shouted angrily, "I've heard enough from you about Piton, Esther! I know what I'm doing. You've got to trust me."

The deal was closed in R.J. Kelly's law office, and the Globe marquee changed to the Roxy. The theatre's outdoor banners began advertising a new policy of movies and burlesque: "Four Live Stage Shows a Day Featuring Beautiful Dancing Girls."

The Roxy was a success from the day it opened. A well-designed theatre, it already had a proscenium arch, a deep stage, and an orchestra pit capable of accommodating four or five musicians. Located on the south side of Queen Street, the Roxy was within shouting distance of City Hall and two blocks from No. 2 Police Station on Dundas. Its six hundred and fifty seats were nearly always filled for all four shows daily, and Piton, in addition to obtaining the necessary police licence, had even secured permission for midnight shows — a feature that became a great success.

To offset some of their operating costs, Avner made contact with members of the local Chinese community located just west of the theatre on Elizabeth Street. He was able to obtain, with Piton's help, a permit allowing the community to stage ceremonial productions on Sunday afternoons. In the name of economy, Avner also employed members of the family, one of his nieces acting as an usher on her time off from school, another serving as a part-time cashier. He was pleased that the family, in general, seemed to accept his theatre acquisition as a shrewd business move. Esther, however, never once came to the theatre.

17

STOCK MARKET CRASH

For Avner, 1929 was an important year. The Roxy was advertising "Girlesk" and making a lot of money, and the Reo had been sold for a handsome profit. Meanwhile, Lil and Murray Letovsky, having formally announced their engagement, were to marry in August 1930, and Avner and Lou had changed their surname to Appleby, following the urgings of Fred Piton.

"After all, Abe, life is made a hell of a lot easier in Toronto if you use a good Christian name like Appleby. Besides, I don't particularly want people to know I'm in business with a Jew. I know you're someone I can trust, even though you're a member of the wrong faith, but you're an exception. And let's face it, Abe, this is a city run by the Orange Order, a Christian organization! They're not happy with Jews. I don't have to tell you that nothing happens in this town without that organization, and that's right from the mayor on down. Christ, a guy can't even get a job as a cop unless he's somehow connected with the Orangemen."

Avner and Fred were at the Roxy one afternoon, heatedly discussing business in the tiny upstairs office adjacent to the projection booth. Through a window near the desk, they could peer out at the stage and witness their Girlesk cuties and generally keep an eye on what was going on in the auditorium. It was a cozy little enclave reached by a circuitous stairwell leading off the second floor of the auditorium entered through a small, secure, self-locking door. Only Avner and Piton had keys to the door opening to the stairwell.

"Abe, let's have another Scotch," suggested Fred. "After all, it's now six months to the day since we cut this partnership deal."

"No thanks. Fred. One's enough for me." Avner hesitated. "I'm trying to cut back. Esther can pick up alcohol on my breath a block away."

"Christ, you sound like a member of the Women's Christian Temperance Union. Anyway, I want you to meet my newest dame, Loretta Higgins. She's a real stunner, Abe. Wait until you meet her. And I've got some other important people for you to meet." Piton poured himself another tall Scotch and sat contentedly in the hard wooden chair before the office safe. "You know, Abe, the people at City Hall want to know what I'm doing with a guy like you, but I tell them you're a good theatre manager and you're honest. They really don't give two bits about the fact that we're running a burlesque house in the city. What would we care if they did? We're making a pile of dough, and we've got the only girly show in town."

Avner was tiring of this conversation. "To tell you the truth, Fred, people have asked me the same thing about you — what am I doing with someone like Fred Piton?"

Piton looked surprised and annoyed, gulped his Scotch, and reached forward for another refill. "People? You mean that kooky religious wife of yours?"

"Forget about Esther, Fred. You and I both know our partnership is strictly business. You made good on your promise that you'd get a licence and you even got permission to run a midnight show. The money's coming in. What more could anyone ask?"

After his third drink, Piton's speech became slurred, his shiny bald head shook a little, and his thick lower lip quivered. "The reason I wanted to get together this afternoon is to bring you up to date.

You're always talking about the licence, so I'm going to level with you. I bought it."

"Avner bolted from his chair. "You what?"

"I bought it. You see, you get what you pay for in this world, and it just so happens I know a couple of cops on the Morality Squad. When I bought the Globe from old man Cohen and told him I was probably going into burlesque, I knew I'd need a special licence. So I got hold of a couple of cops I know who do inspections for the police, and over a quiet beer just next door here at the Union Hotel, I told them that in exchange for a licence, they'd be guaranteed a little weekly gift."

Avner was upset. Perspiration beaded on his forehead and slid from his face to soil his perfect wing collar. "What kind of gift, Fred?"

"Well, it ain't my girl, Loretta." Piton thought he was being cute, but the joke went over Avner's head. "It's money, Abe, something everyone wants. You and I want it, and let's face it, you and I would have one hell of a time convincing the Police Commission we should have a licence to run a burlesque show. Christ, you've lived in this city long enough. So I guaranteed these two guys a little monetary reward for seeing to it the performances we're offering the good citizens of this city didn't offend public morality. I also told them they could see all the shows they wanted — no charge."

Avner could hardly contain himself. "Fred, isn't that bribery?"

"Calm down, Abe. It's a business expense. Nothing more, nothing less. And we're simply putting it in the books that way. Simple, no?"

Avner was caught off guard by Piton's bluntness and arrogance, even though he'd learned of the man's reputation as a vulpine philanderer, not only from several of the local businessmen but even from Esther! *I don't think you should go into partnership with that goy, Avner,* she'd said. *I've heard stories. A lady who works for Arthur Cohen was in Petrov's grocery store, and I overheard her telling Mrs. Petrov about Piton and the way he behaved in Mr. Cohen's office — flirting with the girls and smelling of alcohol. Just remember I told you.*

Esther's words reverberated in Avner's mind as the business meeting continued. The tiny office seemed to close in on him as Piton's speech became louder and more slurred. The matinee had begun onstage, and the din of Irving Berlin's "A Pretty Girl Is Like a

Melody" sounded from the pit orchestra below. The last thing Avner needed was Piton's cigar smoke billowing in his face. Still, he tolerated the onslaught; after all, this partnership with Piton was proving to be his meal ticket. Business was business, and there was nothing wrong — at least in his own view — in associating with a Gentile.

"Abe," Piton spluttered, "I'll introduce you to the two bulls — the two cops — who get our donation every month. I think you can handle that side personally now that we've been in business for six months, or whatever the hell it is …" His voice trailed off as he strained to peer at the first stripper of the afternoon's performance. "You'll like these guys. They're very easy to deal with. Sergeant Wilder even told me he personally liked the shows and found nothing objectionable in them."

Avner needed to reflect for a moment. "Well, Fred, if you really insist, I'll do it, but I'm leery about it. I've never had to deal with the police personally before and I've never been in trouble with the law."

"You worry too much, Abe. Relax!" Despite his fourth glass of Scotch, Piton was still able to bellow. "Stick with me and we'll make a piss-pot full of money! Just keep on running the theatre and let me handle the other stuff. I'll introduce you to the bulls tomorrow afternoon up here in the office. Say three o'clock?"

Avner agreed to meet their peripheral "partners."

Piton adjusted his spats, his collar, and then rose shakily from the chair. "It's settled then. Tomorrow at three."

Avner was surprised that Piton could drink four Scotches and stand, let alone lucidly discuss business. For his own part, Avner was numbed by the news of his silent partners on the Toronto Police. Good grief! His business partner was an unscrupulous scoundrel! *Maybe I'll have that second drink, after all*, he thought.

Now standing upright, Piton lurched to the left as he attempted to head for the door. "You're doing a good job, Abe. You're my man!" He glanced at the gold watch that always hung by a long chain from his vest. "Christ, it's already four o'clock. I was supposed to meet Loretta a half-hour ago." He opened the office door and supported himself on the doorknob. "By the way, Abe, have you seen my new Packard Six? It's a 1927 Model, and I paid only $2,500 for it. You should consider getting one, too. See ya."

Piton stumbled down the office stairwell, and the self-locking door at the bottom leading to the auditorium quickly closed with a loud click. *How on earth is he going to drive an automobile in that state?* Avner mused. *That insurance policy is a very good idea.*

That evening, when Avner told Esther about his meeting with Piton, she exploded, just as he knew she would. "See what happens when you get mixed up with a man like that? Why can't you be like your brother, Moishe? I'm sure he doesn't have to deal with the police. Only you, Avner, only you …"

Avner frowned. "Piton calls dealing with the police a legitimate business expense. Who am I to argue if it's the cost of making a good living? You, Lil, and Lou have everything you want. It's not such a big issue. Tomorrow's meeting with the two police officers should be no problem."

Esther turned on him. "Avner, I might not know about the law, but I do know that what you're doing with Piton is no good. Those two policemen will only want more." At this point, she was purple with rage. "God will punish you, Avner. I know it!" she shrieked.

At 3:00 p.m. the following day in the upstairs office, the two sergeants made themselves at home around Avner's desk, enjoying the view of the stage and the girls while knocking back several glasses of Jack Daniel's.

Sergeant Wilder finally laid it on the line. "You've got a pretty good show here, gents, but I'm not so sure everyone in this fair city would like it. I can think of a couple of reverends on Jarvis Street in particular who are a little bit unhappy about our good city having a burlesque house again. Can't say I mind it myself, though. I think Fred here has explained the situation to you, Abe. Sergeant Brown and I are happy to put in a good word with the Police Commission for you. In fact, I'm sure the commissioner himself would enjoy the shows." The two cops couldn't restrain their laughter. "We'll just come around once a week — no surprises, right? Nice of you to serve the whiskey, Abe, but it really isn't necessary."

Sergeant Brown was a big, burly man with a churlish manner and a beefy tomato face. Avner disliked his dark, poorly-fitting suit, tartan tie, and grey fedora. His partner, Wilder, was thinner, with a narrow face, pimples, and bags under his eyes. One could spot them anywhere, despite all attempts to be inconspicuous. In Avner's opinion, they'd stand out in any crowd like the sore thumbs they were.

Was it any wonder these protectors of the local morality liked the setup — a line of attractive girls, three strippers, a house orchestra, free whiskey, all just for showing up! As Avner pondered all this that afternoon, he wasn't pleased, especially knowing in his heart of hearts that Esther was right. He was asking for trouble.

But life could have been worse. The 1929 market crash scarcely touched the Appelbaum/Appleby fortunes, at least not directly. Avner, being sufficiently busy managing his theatre on the south side of Queen, held only a few government bonds, virtually no equities. When October 24, or Black Thursday, came, bringing with it financial disaster for tens of thousands, ultimately millions, Avner was scarcely affected. Only later did he learn that his long-standing friend, dear Max Hoffman, had invested heavily in American securities. Using a generous margin, Max had purchased stock in Johns-Manville, General Electric, and Montgomery Ward, as well as a host of other securities.

On that particular Thursday, just as Avner was sitting down for his evening meal, the phone rang. One of the retailers on the street gave him the horrible news that Max had taken his life a few hours earlier, apparently having lost thousands of dollars, his life's investments, in the crash. He'd jumped from the twentieth floor of the Bank of Commerce Building on King Street West.

When Avner went to Benjamin's Funeral Parlour at College and Spadina, he was one of the few who attended, there being no known relatives in the Toronto area. The small shiva was held in the parlour of a local Queen Street haberdasher. A telegram was sent to Poland to notify Max's family of the tragic event. Max, the protector and friend who had entered the orbit of the Appelbaum circle so unexpectedly, had left it in the same fashion.

Avner couldn't understand it. *He was such a quiet, generous man. Who knew he liked to gamble?* Max's tragic ending shook him;

knowing that many others had also killed themselves over their losses was of little consolation to Avner.

"You see what happens when you gamble?" was Esther's response upon learning of Max's death.

"But, Esther," he protested, "all life's a gamble. Didn't I lose money in the Standard Theatre and then the Comedy? So far the Roxy's a good gamble, but who knows? I could walk out on the street and be knocked down by an automobile, no?"

Esther seemed annoyed by Avner's pragmatism. "Well, he must have done something you don't know about. God must have punished him."

Avner was irritated by Esther's rationalization. "What's God got to do with it?"

"Everything!" she snapped.

It was bad enough to lose a good friend, but to have Esther see it as some kind of deified punishment was more than Avner could take. Looking for any kind of excuse to avoid further confrontation, he mumbled, "I'm going back to the theatre to relieve Charlie Mackie, my new man. It's his night off. I shouldn't make him wait." *Thank goodness for Charlie. As soon as I spotted him helping an old man with his coat, I knew right away he was going to be good for the job. In just one short week, he's taken a load of my shoulders, checking patrons for tickets, troubleshooting all sorts of things.*

18

ANOTHER MARRIAGE

Lil Appelbaum and Murray Letovsky were married at the McCaul Street Synagogue in August 1930. The building was a melange of architectural styles. Its large rose window facing the street and lancet-shaped doorways with heavy oak doors were reminiscent of a Gothic cathedral, admixed with the large domed roof of a traditional synagogue. Scenes from the Old Testament depicted in elaborate pane-glass windows and filtering the light gave the interior marble floor and polished wooden benches a mystical, celestial quality. A handsome wooden cabinet standing pre-eminently at the head of the auditorium housed the sacred scrolls or Torah. The elaborate interior seemed to bear testimony to the increasing prosperity of asylum seekers from Eastern Europe.

The sagacious Rabbi Jacob Gordon, a senior rabbi for the Judaic community, officiated as Murray and Lil exchanged vows under the gold embroidered canopy. A traditional wedding dinner was held in the synagogue basement, complete with many speeches periodically interrupted by a spirited klezmer band. The meal was strictly kosher, the after-dinner sweet table a cornucopia of fruit and baked goods. Avner and Esther muddled through the appropriate welcomes and thank-yous as the Letovskys became nestled into the ever-expanding Appelbaum/Appleby branches.

Increasingly, Avner was finding Esther's religiosity difficult to stomach; he was spending more and more time at the Roxy, now a place of refuge from the obsessive rituals practised by his wife. Besides, Lil and Murray had moved in with Avner and Esther, Avner having purchased a house on Grace Street in an area that represented upward mobility, as evidenced by a lot more trees and larger verandahs. For Avner, there was now less privacy.

At first Esther recoiled, feeling the new home was much too far from her synagogue. She did, however, acquiesce when she realized that her sister, Becky, long happily married to Sam Persiko, and Moishe and his family were moving into the same neighbourhood. Besides, if need be, she could manage the extra thirty-minute walk required to visit her place of worship.

Paradoxically, the Depression years that followed the great stock market crash proved to be something of a bonanza in the entertainment business once it was realized that a movie or titillating live theatrical presentation could give ephemeral comfort. Somehow people didn't object to the twenty-five-cent admission charge for fantasy and escapism, and if one wished, a person could stay for all four shows at no extra charge. At Avner's confectionery counter, near the entrance to his emporium of mirth and melody, for five cents patrons could purchase a chocolate bar to munch on as they imagined themselves as Tom Mix astride a wild horse, or Joan Crawford in the embrace of Clark Gable, and then watch the live, in-the-flesh girly show that followed.

Avner continued to employ members of the family when he could. Becky's daughter, Bertha, soon became old enough to act as a part-time cashier; several other nieces showed up on weekends to sell soft drinks and candies. In short, Avner seemed to live a split life, enjoying the camaraderie, and indeed the notoriety, that went with owning a burlesque house, and a home life that was, but for Lil, stifling.

Still, managing the Roxy had its drawbacks. One wet afternoon, Avner received a surprise visit from Sergeants Wilder and Brown. "You know, Abe, you've got a good thing going here," Wilder said, nudging his cohort. "I think our boss might get a kick out of what you guys are showing. Delicious Dora has great tits, don't you think, Abe?" Such was the sort of chatter Avner had noticed went on between the two police officers who regularly showed up to get their jollies — and their money. "You know, Abe, we're really sticking our necks out for you guys. We get a lot of calls at No. 2 Station about your joint, a lot of goody two-shoes calling up to discuss 'moral degradation,' that kind of crap. They want the place closed down. Now, frankly, none of us on the force think it's a big deal, but you know how some of these ministers are. Come to think of it, how come none of the rabbis complain? We never hear a word from your guys. Maybe you boys like tits and asses more than us Gentiles." He chuckled at himself.

Avner wondered again at the conversation he was forced to stomach, the pejorative comments so much a part of the weekly payoffs he'd accepted as a way of doing business … and surviving.

"How about an introduction to that feature stripper of yours?" Wilder suggested with a leer. "You know, the one who can really shake it? What do you call her — Sexy Sal?"

"Boys, you know I can't do a thing like that," Avner responded, trying not to sound dismayed.

"Only kidding, Abe, only kidding."

Avner knew otherwise. Of course, the big cop would like nothing better than an introduction and then some to Sal or any of the girls backstage. In fact, he felt they probably had contact, anyway. Didn't he allow these men free rein of the house? He'd been told by several of the female performers that two guys, obviously plainclothes cops, were backstage. When the two were questioned by stagehands, back when they first showed up, wasn't the excuse given that they were merely doing a routine inspection?

"They do inspections, all right," Jacqueline, the captain of the chorus line, had said when he asked. "One of those turkeys put his hand on my ass and asked me if I'd like to have a good time. Then he had the goddamn nerve to tell me I'd better watch my step when I told him to get lost. Said something about Abe and Fred in the front office, something to the effect that the theatre staff should understand the importance of their presence and maybe I'd be a little bit more accommodating. I told him to take a long walk on a short pier. Curley Posen — you know, the drummer — overheard this little scene and later came up to me. Told me not to worry about these meatballs as long as he's around. I told him I'm used to it, that I can take care of myself. There are always guys around looking for a free piece of ass. But this was a little different because they were cops. Anyway, Curly told me he'd be watching."

Avner had told her to just ignore them. "Tell them you're busy," he'd said calmly. "And tell the other girls to do the same thing. Jacqueline, if the situation gets out of hand, let me know immediately or call Charlie Mackie. He's usually around and he's a hundred percent trustworthy and reliable." Avner was frustrated. "There's no point calling the police because they'd just ask if you wanted to lay a charge. And that could only mean more trouble for us."

AN INTOLERABLE SITUATION

By 1932, Avner could sit back in his office chair and feel like a somebody. He was the successful manager of a theatre, was financially secure, was known as a daring entrepreneur, and was on a first-name basis with many of the city's solicitors, police officers, and luminaries. Esther hadn't changed much — a few grey hairs — but if it were possible, she'd grown even more fossilized in her spiritual life. However, Avner was now a grandfather. With Murray and Lil having given birth to a bouncing red-headed Gerald in May 1931, going home from the Roxy no longer seemed so arduous because he got to play with his grandson, which had become one of his greatest joys.

Avner loved driving his entourage to picnics in his enormous Mitchell automobile. Outings to Casa Loma, high on the hill, were excursions fraught with excitement and some degree of apprehension. When fully loaded, Avner's vehicle didn't always make it up the hill. More often than not, the family were forced to take a circuitous route or go to other picnic grounds, usually High Park with its tall, glorious trees and tranquil Grenadier Pond where they could spend a whole afternoon feeding the ducks.

Still, visiting Casa Loma and other places always made for an exciting day with Lou, Lil, and their cousins. Even as young adults, they seemed to enjoy piling into his car, with several baskets of food, for a Sunday morning outing. Toronto, a pallid, colourless, boring city, where even the residents joked that sidewalks rolled up on Sunday, had at least a few interesting locations that were known, even internationally. And Casa Loma was certainly one of them. The actualization of a strange fantasy of entrepreneur Henry Pellatt's was something positive about Toronto that one could discuss, even though a critic later called the "castle" a mixture of seventeenth-century Scotland and Twentieth Century-Fox.

By October 1933, Lily and Murray had produced a second son, who, in accordance with Judaic tradition, was named after a deceased family member, in this instance Esther's father, Joseph. However, in keeping with Avner's, and daughter Lil's, passion for assimilation, he was simply called Barry. The rambling house on Grace Street, with its enormous Victorian verandah, now seemed to burst its walls with people — Murray and Lil, their two infant boys, and Esther and Avner. And just as in the early ghetto days, the kitchen became the executive cabinet room, while the large, high-ceilinged dining room/parlour served as the reception area for special Sunday afternoon guests and occasional serious family powwows.

The Great Depression had reached its zenith, but Avner, with good luck and some perspicacity, had managed to avoid most of the economic hardships that had infested the planet. "You know, I always told you sex sells," he liked to remind Adolph Frankel and his other cronies on the street. Esther, who would have none of it, was well aware of exactly why the family was surviving — in her mind, naked ladies and the exploitation of men's weaknesses.

Esther, quite naturally, kept in close contact with her brothers and sisters, and on any given day, seemed to know even what they were having for dinner. In practical terms, however, the world outside Toronto's small Jewish community was non-existent. Like so many others, she was unmindful of the growing anti-Semitism in Germany and beyond. She no longer had any contacts in Poland, her mother having died there in 1912, her father passing away in Toronto in 1923. Contact between Avner and his mother and brother, Beryl, in Warsaw had become progressively less frequent as the years went by.

Nazi leader Adolf Hitler became chancellor of Germany in 1933, and virulent anti-Semitism once again — if it had ever disappeared — spread like the bubonic plague. On April 1, 1933, when Hitler proclaimed the Jews were trying to crush Germany, signs were posted everywhere in the country that German people were to defend themselves and were not to buy merchandise or services from Jews.

Thursday afternoons became progressively unpleasant for Avner when, with some degree of consistency, Fred Piton, intoxicated as usual, showed up and demanded to see the books. Not that Avner made any misrepresentations or distortions — he personally had nothing to hide. But Fred, with his now-insatiable appetite for alcohol, women, money, and fast cars — "How's the business treating us, Abey-Baby, and how are the dames?" — teased Avner, knowing his shyness and conservatism when it came to such topics. "That wife of yours, Abe, I never see her around here. What is she, too ashamed, too embarrassed?" Then he usually slathered, "I'll bet your home life's hell!"

More alarming, it was also becoming increasingly difficult for Avner to restrain himself from barking back at his partner. But his partnership agreement with Piton wouldn't expire until 1939, and there appeared to be no way to buy him out. And there was that conjoint insurance policy that would remain — partnership or no partnership. So Avner had to swallow his pride, somehow maintain his composure, and simply do the best he could with his drunken partner. "Yes, we've made a couple of hundred dollars this week, Fred. Here, look at the books if you like. Here's what it comes down to." It was a wonder that Piton could even read anything on those occasions.

Frequently, Piton's girlfriend, Loretta, accompanied him, and Fred had no compunction about discussing his numerous affairs with other girls. Avner noticed that Loretta herself started showing up at the Thursday meetings smelling of alcohol. Even Avner often needed a second Haig and Haig or Jack Daniel's to cope with Fred.

"Why do you stay with him?" members of the family continually asked.

"I have a long-term contract," he answered. "I've got no choice. And except for his once-a-week or so presence at the theatre, he really doesn't give me that much trouble." But, as he confided only to his younger brother, Moishe, "I'm more concerned about the two cops on the take. They seem much too fresh with some of our staff. On a couple of occasions, I've had chorus girls in tears because of improper suggestions made to them. The next thing I know these guys will probably be demanding more money." But complaining to Moishe was all he could do. Or possibly to Charlie Mackie.

"Mr. Appleby, I wonder if I could speak to you for a moment?" Charlie asked him one day, just as the first show was about to open. It was uncharacteristic for Charlie to approach Avner in such a shy, reticent way; he usually came straight to the point.

"Are you aware we had an incident here in the theatre last night, Mr. Appleby?"

Unable to hide his surprise, Avner asked, "What do you mean, Charlie?"

"You know that pretty young cashier, Bessy, who comes in three nights a week?"

"Of course, I do, Charlie. She's a lovely girl. What about her?"

Charlie looked distressed. "Well, I hate to say this — and she doesn't know I'm telling you this — but Mr. Piton showed up last evening, just after she closed the cash box. He grabbed her and attempted to strip her. Fortunately, he was so drunk she was able to get away from him. In fact — I'm embarrassed to say this — she kicked him in the 'you-know-where' and ran into the street. She said she slammed the box office door behind her, leaving Mr. Piton sprawled on the floor with his pants half off. She told me about it this morning, and I thought you'd want to know."

Avner scarcely knew what to say. "Well, thank you for telling me, Charlie. Did anyone call the police?"

"To be honest, Mr. Appleby, I thought we'd better not. Knowing the licensing problems you're having, I had a feeling that if someone laid an attempted rape charge right now, it would get into the press and we could end up having a lot more trouble than we already have."

Avner was impressed. "Good thinking, Charlie. You're certainly right. Piton and his capers are becoming intolerable. The sad part is I can't do very much about it. And having messy publicity, as you say, wouldn't do us any good. What does Bessy think about all this?"

"She's obviously very upset, and she's thinking of leaving the job."

"I'll have a word with her, Charlie, and I'll have to tell Fred I know all about it. Maybe, if we're lucky, we can use the threat of a charge to keep him in his place."

Charlie looked dubious. "It might work, Mr. Appleby," he answered slowly, "but you know as well as I do, Piton can't keep his hands off the merchandise. I know you're not much for gossip, but it must run in his family or something. I heard his brother just ran off with another woman — Dr. Shapiro's wife."

Avner struggled to conceal his surprise. "Well, I can't do very much about the situation. We can't very well report him, and that's it. But I've got to tell you, Charlie, as much as I like this business and the wonderful performers and businessmen I've met, this partnership with Piton's been the biggest mistake of my life. I can't help feeling he must have outside business dealings — drugs, booze — who knows? We sure aren't making that kind of money at this theatre to support his expensive capers. He's always dressed to the nines, pinstripe suits and spats. He drives the latest car. I just don't know, but I don't like it.

Frankly, Charlie, I'd do anything to get out of this fifty-fifty arrangement we have. I'm doing most of the work, anyway — with your help, of course." Avner added the last almost apologetically before continuing. "He's usually too drunk to even look after the bookings. And that was part of our original agreement."

Charlie shook his head slowly. "Well, Mr. Appleby, do you think maybe you should get a lawyer who can get you out of this agreement?"

"I've given that a lot of thought, Charlie. Believe me, I have, but I'm holding off for the time being. I'm terrified of scandal and controversy, as you know, and getting a lawyer wouldn't be cheap. It could get very nasty."

Charlie's response came almost too quickly. "Well, there are other ways."

"What do you mean?"

"Maybe I could get the Carter brothers to have a little talk with him, you know, sort of tell him to straighten up or else. The Carter boys can scare the crap out of anybody."

Avner had to force himself not to smile. "Charlie, you know I'd never get involved with anything like that. I don't need a couple of toughs roughing up my partner. I know you're looking out for me, but that's not going to do a thing for us. I'm just going to have to live with the situation for the time being. But thanks for the suggestions, anyway."

Later, at home, Avner rationalized that his life at the Roxy wasn't exactly unbearable. Despite Piton and the annoying cops, he still enjoyed the delicious notoriety of owning the only burlesque house in town. And he was known and liked by countless downtown businessmen and any number of City Hall types, many of whom he knew on a first-name basis.

The big house on Grace Street had become a beehive of domestic activity, especially after the birth of Murray and Lil's second son. His son, Lou, was living alone and doing a variety of part-time jobs, often filling in as a motion picture projectionist at his Uncle Moishe's theatre, the Regent. Murray, who had such great ambitions to become an electrical engineer, could simply not afford to go on to university. So he, too, had been relegated to odd jobs, including motion picture

　　　　　　　　　　　　　　　　　　　　　　　　　　　　　　　BARRY J. LITTLE

projectionist. Earlier, Murray had a particularly bad experience with the Bell Telephone Company. Hopeful of obtaining even the most junior position, he was told that because he was a Jew he wouldn't be hired; it was simply not company policy to hire "foreigners." Murray told no one, deciding instead to bury his anger and disappointment.

As the Depression deepened, it seemed as though most of the population was out of work or only partially employed. But somehow there were ways of finding enough money to go to the movies and shows, and Avner's Roxy continued to be filled. However, Avner's partnership with Piton deteriorated even further. Despite his lovely Loretta, Fred appeared unable to keep his eyes and hands off several of the chorus cuties, who repeatedly complained to Avner.

"What do you mean I've been fooling around?" Fred growled when confronted again by Avner. "Those babes don't know what they're talking about. Frankly, I think several of those dames have their sights set on me."

Avner could barely contain his revulsion. "Fred, if I hear any more of these disgusting stories, I promise you, I'll arrange to have our partnership terminated."

"Oh, go fuck yourself, Avner," was Fred's reaction as he staggered out of the upstairs office, and resuming the expletives, descended the stairs.

In the week following that altercation with Piton, Avner faced another crisis when part-time cashier Rebecca tearfully confided, with obvious trepidation, that she, too, had been assaulted by Piton.

"It was in the alleyway after work and it was dark — you know, just beside the hotel next door. He grabbed me around the waist and threw me down. It was terrible! I could see he was going to rape me. I screamed as loud as I could, right in his face, and lucky for me, a man passing by on the sidewalk heard me. Then Mr. Piton stopped, and I was able to get up. And he just walked away. It was the worst experience of my life. I'm sorry, but I can't work in this theatre anymore."

Avner was livid. "Yes, you can, Rebecca! I'll see to it that he never comes around here ever again. We won't call the police, even though I know we should. I don't think anything would be done. I'm going to end my contract with him immediately and get him out of our hair. I should have done this years ago!"

The next morning, Avner called his solicitor and told him of his intentions to terminate the partnership.

"Okay, Avner," his lawyer responded. "I'll contact Piton's solicitor. Remember, though, he's one tough son of a bitch and it'll likely not be easy to dissolve your partnership. One thing's for sure. He couldn't run the theatre by himself, so he'll want to be bought out. His Roxy cut is probably all he has going for him at the moment."

In September 1934, Fred Piton finally agreed to terminate his part ownership in the Roxy for $10,000. It was agreed that the conjoint life insurance policy wouldn't be extended beyond the June 1935 renewal date.

Avner was delighted to get out of the unsavoury partnership, and relatively cheaply at that. In October 1934, he became the sole owner of Toronto's only burlesque house.

20

MURDER

On Sunday morning, March 3, 1935, Avner shaved, showered, and dressed in a full business suit. Then, after making himself a cup of tea, he left for work. At about twelve noon, the phone rang at the Grace Street home and Murray answered. On the other end was the agitated voice of Roy Wong, the Chinese community member responsible for the leasing of the Roxy. He was so upset that Murray could hardly make out what he was saying. "What are you trying to tell me, Mr. Wong?"

"We can't get into the theatre. Front door, front door, you know, it's locked! Mr. Appleby always leaves the door open. We can't start the show. Everybody terribly upset."

"I'll be right there, Mr. Wong," Murray answered. "I have a key to get in."

Luckily, Murray was able to catch the Sunday streetcar, just three hundred yards from the house, and within fifteen minutes arrived at the Queen Street emporium. To his surprise, he found the outside theatre lights on. A crowd waited on the street, chattering in Chinese, while a very visible Roy Wong, arms flailing, attempted to placate the noisy throng eager to get in. Of the two doors usually open to provide entrance into the auditorium, only the outer door was unlocked; the auditorium door, some ten feet into the building and across the small entrance lobby, remained locked. Murray had the key to the auditorium door and opened it immediately. Noticing the auditorium lights were on, as well, Murray called out to Avner into an empty theatre. There was no response. Murray ran up the winding stairway leading from the back of the auditorium to the office but found the door locked.

He called out again and tried the door. It wouldn't budge. Wong ran to find a ladder, and together, he and Murray placed it under the office window overlooking the auditorium.

"I'll go up!" Murray shouted. "You hold the ladder. Something's very wrong. He's got to be up there."

Murray quickly ascended the ladder to the tiny three-by-three-foot window. It seemed like an eternity. He looked in and could see Avner in his office chair, immediately below the window, curiously seated with his hands above his head … and motionless.

"He's here, he's here!" Murray shouted. "I don't think I can jimmy open this window. Hand me a broom or something and I'll break it in. He looks very sick."

Murray smashed the window, spraying glass all over Avner and the office floor. But Avner didn't move. Standing at the top of the ladder, peering through the broken glass at his father-in-law so still and motionless, Murray yelled, "I can't get through that window even with the glass out of the way, Roy. Let's trade places."

Wong, a diminutive man, quickly ascended the ladder and crawled through the window into the office, then opened the self-locking office door.

Murray ran up the steps, closely followed by Mr. Chung, one of Roy's colleagues. "He must have become terribly ill and collapsed. I'm going to call Toronto General," Murray said, quickly thumbing through a phone directory and trying not to panic.

"I have a real emergency at the Roxy Theatre at Queen and Bay," he said into the phone. "A man has collapsed. Please send an ambulance." When he got off the phone, he shouted, "Wake up, wake up, Mr. Appleby!" But as he anxiously waited for the ambulance, he noticed the safe and thought, *He must have fallen as he was opening the safe. Maybe he had some kind of seizure or fainted and has a concussion.* Murray lapsed into a state of suspended animation as again time played tricks and it seemed as if the ambulance would never arrive.

Still, within ten minutes of the call, two muscular men in white uniforms and caps ran up the steps with a collapsible stretcher. The first to arrive stopped in his tracks, and as he bent over the supine Avner in the now-crowded little office, he turned to Murray and said, "This man's not sick, mister. He's dead!"

Murray couldn't believe what he'd heard. The taller of the two attendants leaned over Avner's body and grabbed his outstretched arms. "Look, rigor mortis has set in. His arms are as stiff as boards. This man's been dead for a few hours at least. He's not going to Toronto General. He's going to the morgue on Lombard Street. I'm sorry to say this to you, mister, but we'll have to notify the coroner and get the police up here."

Murray's head reeled from shock.

"Can I use that phone over there?" one ambulance attendant asked. "Hey, there's a big bottle of Scotch on the desk. Half empty! What did the old boy do? Live it up from time to time?"

Murray paid no attention to the ambulance attendant's inappropriate comments.

"What do we do about the show?" someone said with a Chinese accent.

"You'd better let it go on," Murray replied automatically. What else was there for him to say? "I'll wait for the policemen and call the family." His vision blurred as tears welled in his eyes. "Oh, this is awful."

Murray then had to make the most painful phone call of his life. After three rings, Esther answered. "Mrs. Appleby, it's Murray." *How can I say this?* "I've got some bad news for you. Something terrible has happened to Avner. He died this morning … I found him in the office … the police have to come."

There was a moment of silence on the line and then a bone-chilling shriek, followed by wailing as Esther dropped the phone. Within moments he could hear more shrieks, more wailing — daughter Lil had obviously been told.

"It can't be true." A sobbing Lil was now on the phone.

"I'm afraid it is, Lil. I'll have to stay here and wait for the police. There may be a lot of questions. No, no, I don't know what happened. Please try to calm down. I'll be home as soon as I can." His mind was beginning to clear. "Just do one thing for me, will you? Please call Lou and let him know what happened to your father, and have him come down to the theatre to help me."

Murray was now aware that the auditorium below was filled with Chinese patrons; the regular Sunday production had begun, albeit a half-hour late. Through the broken window, he could hear the ceremonial singing, chanting, and dancing, the stentorian sound of gongs adding to his mental agitation as he tried to compose himself in the cramped office, his father-in-law now a corpse.

Too distraught to focus on or pay attention to details, Murray still had no idea how his father-in-law had died. Once before he'd been left in a room alone with a dead person — as a teenager shortly after his grandfather had died suddenly in the Letovsky kitchen. Murray anxiously glanced at his watch. Would they never come?

Although Murray had arrived at the theatre around noon and discovered the body at 12:20, it wasn't until 3:00 that a contingent of officers finally arrived. Led by Sergeant Evans of No. 2 Station on Dundas Street West, there seemed to be a barrage of police photographers taking pictures of the office and the body before it was removed for a post-mortem. Murray was informed that the autopsy would be performed in the offices of Chief Coroner M.M. Crawford. Others in the contingent who came that afternoon were Assistant Inspector Moses Mulholland, Sergeant of Detectives Harold Waterhouse, Detective Sergeants Winters and Whitelaw, Detective Hutchison of Police Headquarters, and Detective Sergeant Jones and Detective Keyes of No. 2 Station.

There simply wasn't enough room in the tiny office to contain them all. Murray was escorted downstairs to the lobby where Jones and Keyes pummelled him with questions. "You say you're the son-in-law? When did you get here? What did you know about Avner? Did the man have any enemies? Had Avner said anything to indicate that he might be in trouble?" The questioning took about an hour, and Murray was then faced with the prospect of going home to what he knew would be a scene of emotional chaos.

Just as he was leaving and about to open the outer door of the theatre, Sergeant of Detectives Waterhouse grabbed Murray by the hand. "There's going to be an inquest, Mr. Letovsky. We'll have to wait for the coroner's report, but I think I'd better tell you that your father-in-law is, uh … he was … shot in the head … probably in a robbery. That's how he died. But there may be more questions, so don't leave town."

What's this man saying? Don't leave town? Where would I go? Is this detective accusing me of something? Murray returned to the upstairs office. Earlier, Lou had arrived on the scene, and upon taking one look at his dead father, had fainted and fallen to the floor. When he regained consciousness, he became a bundle of tearful, babbling incoherence. He wasn't much help to Murray or the police. Murray could only muster "I'm sorry, I'm sorry" and help him to a seat in the men's washroom. With the cacophony of the Chinese show in progress, Lou's sobs were hardly audible.

21

THE FUNERAL

As Murray rode the streetcar home to Grace Street, the humiliating interrogation by Detectives Jones and Keyes kept reverberating in his mind. *But why were the police so late in arriving in the first place?* he wondered. *And why did they interview me in the noisy lobby instead of some quiet space away from the theatre? They seemed so casual, so blunt, so without feeling. I think I told them everything.*

The scene at the Grace Street home was one of pandemonium and palpable tension. All the rooms in the house were choked with relatives and friends and filled with a background cacophony of sobbing interspersed with wails and incantations to God. Esther was already dressed in black and seated in a low chair in the front room. A black woollen shawl served as a frame for her pale, sorrowful face. She stared at the floor, muttering, "I told him he'd be punished. I told him not to go to the theatre. I knew I'd be a widow."

Lil was inconsolable. Like her mother, she gazed at the floor continuously, totally oblivious to the surrounding mayhem. She, too, felt widowed.

Murray kissed Lil on the cheek but felt himself completely speechless. Disturbing thoughts and horrible memories reverberated through his mind. It was all he could do to shake Esther's icy hand as a gesture of condolence.

Aaron and Moishe had already arranged for the funeral service; the shiva, the seven-day period of mourning, was to be held at Avner's Grace Street home. For Esther, the diehard mystic, seven days of mourning would be a period when Avner's soul would hover about the house, grieving and mourning for the body it had once inhabited and with which it would be reunited.

The gathered throng peppered Murray with a multiplicity of questions, none of which he felt he could or wanted to answer. Whether out of embarrassment or shame, he didn't want to talk to anyone about the way Avner had died or the police involvement.

When Avner was lowered into the earth the day following his death, Esther and Lil — and for that matter most members of the family — were acutely aware of the presence of strangers at the gravesite. It was realized later that they were reporters from the *Evening Telegram*, the *Globe*, and the *Toronto Daily Star*. At least the Toronto dailies had had the decency not to send photographers. Murray tried to withhold tears as the simple pine coffin was lowered into the ground; the collective sobbing and wailing seemed to be in strange synchronicity with each thud of earth that fell onto the coffin. A chilling early spring rain drizzled as the farewell prayers were recited.

During the seven days of mourning, the immediate male members of the family participated in the obligatory prayers of Kaddish. Along with Esther, Lil, Lou, and Murray sat on low chairs as a symbolic gesture of their humility. The mirrors in the house, in accordance with custom, were covered with sheets so no one could partake in personal vanity during this solemn, remorseful time. Between prayers, family members offered one another condolences, eating bagels and cream cheese and other delicacies in vain attempts to assuage their grief.

By the second day of mourning, Avner's death was a local *cause célèbre*, the story of his robbery and murder being splashed across the front pages of all the Toronto dailies. With the city-wide publicity came, for Murray, a deep sense of shame mixed with a mental broth of grief, horror, sadness, anger, and disappointment. He wondered if others at the shiva were also ashamed.

"I simply don't understand it," Murray said to Lou a few days later. "The police told me not to leave town and said they'd be in touch with me. Already several days have gone by and there have been no phone calls from them. Are you sure they weren't over at the house when we were at the funeral service?"

Lou cleared his throat. "I'm quite certain. Father's gardener, Vil, was here all that time. I asked him if there'd been any visitors, and he said no one had come to the house while we were away." He paused, then suddenly exploded. "Goddamn it, I know who did it! It had to be that Piton bastard!"

Murray tried to placate him. "No, Lou, it can't have been him. Remember? Fred's been in Florida since last September when he left the Roxy."

"Well, he could bloody well have hired somebody," Lou snorted. "Christ, Murray, don't you have any imagination at all?"

Murray was accustomed to Lou's volcanic eruptions but hated dealing with them. "The police did speak to you, though, didn't they?"

"Yeah, for about fifteen minutes. They didn't say they were sorry or nothing. They asked where I was on Sunday and if I knew of anybody my father was in trouble with. They said they'd be in touch with me."

It seemed as though Esther, Lil, and Lou had collectively drowned in a sea of bottomless disbelief. All refused to believe that Avner was gone. Only Murray managed to maintain some measure of self-control. Perhaps it was his failure to bond with his father-in-law that now made it easier for him to achieve a degree of detachment.

Because of the death, the Roxy remained closed for a week. But Murray, the inveterate worrier, knew the family's livelihood depended on the operation of the theatre. There were bills to be paid, staff to be supervised, shows to be booked, and so on. Unwittingly, it seemed he'd adopted the tradition of "the show must go on," even though neither he nor Lou had any theatrical managerial experience up to this point. Both had experience working as motion picture projectionists, but that was as close as they'd ever come to "show biz."

With the shiva ended after sunset following the week of mourning, Murray gathered Lou, Lil, and Esther in the front room. In one corner stood an upright Heintzman piano, and in the opposite corner an outlandishly large Victrola. A bright maroon velvet sofa with embroidered pillows occupied the space in front of the one window in the room, and it was on this sofa that Esther, Lil, and Lou sat like zombies while Murray paced back and forth, preparing to outline future plans for the family. Slivers of sunlight filtering through the venetian blinds reflected off Esther's silver-grey hair, giving her a striking theatrical, if not regal, appearance. Murray hardly knew where to begin.

During the week, he'd read all the newspaper accounts but was well aware that Lou and Lil hadn't, mainly because they were strictly observing the mourning period. Esther, of course, never read the local English newspapers.

"Look," he started, "the police don't have very much to go on, Mother-in-Law. But I'm sure they'll find out what happened. They're investigating all kinds of leads."

Esther sobbed. "What do you mean by leads? What's the difference! It's all the same to me! He's gone, he's gone."

Lil echoed her mother's comments as Lou added, "I'll get the bastard myself!"

How can I be practical with everybody in this state of mind? Murray asked himself. "Look, people, I'm sure the police know what they're doing and I'm sure they're going to get to the bottom of all this mess. Lou, you've got to get yourself together. We have to look after the theatre. I've called Mr. Chung of the Chinese Freemason Society. You remember, he dealt with your father. I've arranged for him to continue with the Sunday afternoon presentations starting next week. I know this is very painful, but we've got a lot of things to look after, Lou —"

Jumping up from the sofa, Lou glared at Murray with penetrating, soulless eyes. "Who needs the goddamn police, anyway? I know who killed my father. It was that Irish drunk, Piton. He hated my father for breaking up the partnership."

Murray could only feel exasperated. "Look, Lou, Piton's been in Florida for six months. I told you that already."

But Lou couldn't be stopped. "I don't give a good goddamn. He hired a hit man."

Murray tried to mollify him. "Don't worry. We'll find out who did it sooner or later. Meanwhile, I want you to have a look at some of last week's newspapers. Charlie Mackie from the theatre brought them around this morning. I think some of the things said in the papers might help us all understand this terrible event, Lou."

"Do you honestly think going over a bunch of newspaper reports is going to help? How bloody stupid!"

"I want you to see what's in the papers."

"For Christ's sake, Murray, what's the point? Do we have to go over this now?"

"I know you, Lou. If I don't go over some of these details with you now, you won't ever look at them. By going over some of the stories, who knows, we might be able to help the police solve this thing."

"You've picked one hell of a time to do this, Murray."

"You know I wouldn't do it if I didn't think it was the best thing for all of us."

Lou stood up smartly, rolled his eyes at the ceiling, and sighed. "Have it your way — shoot!" Then, like a scolded schoolboy, he plunked himself onto the velvet sofa, crossed his legs, and loosened his tie, radiating disdain for Murray's suggestion.

Charlie had left a small bundle of newspapers in the hallway outside the living room door. Murray quickly brought them in and placed them at Lou's feet.

"There's an article here entitled 'Theatre Man Seen Worried E're Murder,' which would indicate your father knew something was wrong, Lou. Unfortunately, the newspaper doesn't identify the friend who spoke to the reporter. But whoever this 'friend' was, he told them he didn't like the look of things. The article states that your father was feeling pessimistic about his immediate well-being, but there's a quote where he apparently said, 'Business is all right, but something isn't right, and I can't say what it is.' Apparently, your father didn't go into any detail, but he was obviously worried about something."

Lou frowned and bit his lip nervously. "He sure didn't say anything to me, and this is the first I've heard of anything like this. I saw him on the Saturday before his death, and he looked and sounded okay to me."

Murray continued. "The newspaper states 'Mr. Appleby took out a life insurance policy for $25,000 about two months ago, naming his immediate family members as beneficiaries.' It goes on to say, 'Mr. Appleby also held a life insurance policy with a double-indemnity clause with his former partner, Fred Piton, who is now in Florida.' So, yes, Piton stands to gain by your father's death, but before you say anything, look at this other article — 'The police state that they have ruled out Piton as a suspect in this case.' I guess it's possible that Piton hired someone to do your father in. But it might be that your father was in trouble with someone else. There's an article here in the *Toronto Evening Telegram* that states that a car was seen outside the Roxy on Sunday morning, a car with Michigan licence plates. Now, they never actually located the car, but apparently border officials were notified by the Toronto Police. Maybe the police were thinking that the Michigan licence plates related to the Purple Gang in Detroit. You must have heard of them — that gang ruled by Abe Bernstein, the mobster who's supposed to be into bootlegging. Does that name mean anything to you, Lou?"

"My father never mentioned anything about gangsters. He would have had nothing to do with them! I've never heard him mention the Purple Gang or Abe Bernstein. Yeah, sure, I've heard of those people. Who hasn't? I simply can't believe my father would be involved with guys like that."

Lil, who had earlier left the room for the kitchen, entered the room at this point with two steaming cups of coffee. It was as though intermission had been called. After a few gulps, Murray continued. "In Wednesday's *Evening Telegram*, there's a report that in a hunt for your father's murderer, a Detroit man by the name of Charles F. Keen, known in the Detroit underworld as The Mustard King, was arrested and charged with the theft of a diamond ring from Georgina Napier, the former wardrobe mistress at the Roxy. He pleaded guilty in No. 2 Police Court and was remanded one week for sentencing. So it looks to me as though the police are following every clue they possibly can. They've now got two lead investigators on the case — Detectives Waterhouse and Storms. They're the ones who located this fellow Keen."

Lou visibly relaxed. Murray had managed to pacify him — for the time being at least.

22

WHO KILLED AVNER?

Eight days after the murder, Murray rose early to meet Lou at nine o'clock in front of the Roxy box office. When Lou failed to show, Murray entered the empty theatre alone with some trepidation. It was difficult to suppress the images that flashed through his mind, still somewhere between disbelief and numbed reality. Somehow he expected to see Avner greet him. Fate, time, occasion, and chance had ripped from him all ambitions of a career in electrical engineering and thrust him into co-management of a burlesque house. He mustered a sardonic smile. *I guess I'll just have to grin and bear it.*

He opened the door to the box office that faced the street and made calls to the projectionist, the orchestra leader Curly, and Charmaine, the featured exotic dancer of the week, letting them know the theatre was back in business. Charmaine agreed to contact the other performers, most of whom were staying at the nearby Ford Hotel along with her. He also called Rebecca, the former cashier at the theatre. In his conversation with Rebecca, he told her, "I hope you can get down here. I've got my hands full."

"Yes, I can get to the theatre, Mr. Little," Rebecca answered excitedly. "I'm glad to help any way I can. I've been reading the newspaper reports. Simply awful! Did you notice the article about the Roxy's night porter getting told he'd get the same as your father-in-law? I remember him. Poor Mr. Kapniki! He must have been scared out of his wits getting a call like that, all alone in the theatre! And the papers also said that your brother-in-law got a threat that if he didn't stop talking —"

"You mustn't believe everything you read in the newspapers, Rebecca. Don't let it upset you."

One week after Avner's death, however, the show did go on with few hitches, though the newsreel was played twice because Curly, the orchestra leader, had to find a last-minute substitute trumpet player, finally coming up with one who didn't read music very well. During the feature striptease, the man blew such a sour note that Charmaine stopped her act just as she was about to remove her stage peignoir, and admonished the unfortunate trumpet player, drawing howls of laughter from the small but enthusiastic audience, which thought it was all part of the act.

Following that first-night reopening, Murray was exhausted. *I'm going to reread those newspapers Charlie brought and buy today's on the way home,* he decided. *Funny, the police haven't called me yet,* Murray mused for a bit. *Well, maybe I just missed their call and everybody's too upset to remember.*

Esther still couldn't and wouldn't read English newspapers, while Lil was much too distraught to pay attention to their presence. "Have you seen Lou, Lil?" Murray asked upon reaching home.

"No," she answered with surprise. "I thought he was down at the theatre helping you. He didn't call here, either. I guess he's just too upset and depressed like all of us."

"Well, we've got to get things going, Lil. See if you can get hold of him, will you? And tell him we could use an extra hand down at the theatre. I'll grab a quick supper out of the fridge and say good night to the boys. I want to have a look at those newspapers again."

Murray's heart pounded as he thumbed once more through the Toronto dailies where, for everybody to see and read, there were pictures and stories of his family — even a picture of him on the front page of two of the dailies. He knew, of course, that his father-in-law had been shot. But now he learned that the chief coroner had revealed that Avner had been shot twice — once in the back of the head and then a second time behind the left ear, leaving powder burns searing the flesh of the scalp and face. The reports went on to say that the nature of the second bullet wound led police to believe the shooting had been deliberately planned, the gun having been fired at close range to make certain he was dead.

Whoever did this must have been in one heck of a hurry, Murray decided as he nervously scanned the papers for more revelations. Saturday night's receipts — $376 — had been taken. But they'd left $75 in silver in the safe and hadn't taken Avner's diamond stickpin, which was said to be worth about $200.

Murray gasped as he read yet another column: "The whole of the homicide detail of the Toronto Police Department was promptly on the scene led by a number of inspectors." This was a flagrant inaccuracy! Murray bitterly recalled waiting for what seemed an eternity, certainly at least an hour and a half before two officers arrived at the scene. And No. 2 Station was only about six blocks away!

Earlier in the day, Murray had gone upstairs to the office where Avner was robbed of his money and life. It appeared to him that the police had left everything pretty much as they'd found it. The rug on the floor was rolled up and the safe was still open, Avner's blood still on it. It was as if the police themselves were in a hurry. They hadn't bothered to return to the crime scene; neither had they contacted him during the week. And there were no messages for him.

Murray couldn't help but notice a very peculiar story in the *Star*.

The newspaper reported that at 9:55 on the evening of the murder, Police Chief D.C. Draper had come to the theatre in his special car carrying a long flashlight and a fireman's electric lantern.

What in heaven's name would he be doing with an electric lantern and a flashlight? And why would he show up so late? The doors would be locked by then. Robbery with killing was never a common event in Toronto. Certainly, Murray knew about the previous Roxy robberies — two in the past three years — but in each case the robbers were caught, one of them while hiding in the theatre building. But no one was hurt. The *Star* also mentioned that Frank Elwood, the regular doorman, had gone on a brief trip to Buffalo with his wife. And he was usually on duty on Sundays. *Was this just a coincidence? And who had given him the day off, anyway?*

Murray went to bed that night of the reopening but couldn't sleep. Images of Avner lying on his back in his chair haunted him. Murray had never been involved with the police, and the more he thought about the newspaper accounts, particularly the inaccuracies, the more agitated he became. *The police hadn't arrived promptly on the scene. And why hadn't they contacted him as promised? Maybe Fred had hired somebody to kill Avner, after all. Perhaps the killer had hidden in the auditorium overnight. One thing was certain: It had to be somebody who knew his way around the theatre and knew where to find Avner. And Chief Draper showing up after 9:00 p.m.?*

The inescapable conclusion, for Murray, was that Avner must have known the persons who killed him. The office door was locked from the inside; Avner wouldn't have opened it unless he recognized the person's voice. No one but Avner had a key to his private office. His father-in-law had even changed the locks after the dissolution of the Piton/Appleby partnership.

The other possibility, of course, was that the killer or killers weren't waiting in the auditorium but rather met Avner at the front door, thus allowing them to come in. And once they were in the foyer, Avner locked the auditorium door. Then he and his killer or killers, whom he might not have known, went up to his office together. *No, damn it! Avner would never let anyone into his office unless he knew him or her well! And he would have been very surprised to learn that someone he knew had spent the night in his theatre.*

Murray decided to speak to Frank Elwood, the doorman. "Frank, did the police speak to you?"

"Well, actually, Mr. Letovsky, the police only asked me where I was on the day Mr. Appleby was killed. I told them my wife and I drove to Buffalo and that I told Mr. Appleby a week before we'd be away. They didn't ask very much else. I still can't believe what happened. He was such a good man. He was so nice to all of us who worked in the theatre. I wouldn't have thought he had an enemy in the world."

Murray had to admit that he hardly knew his father-in-law. As gregarious and ebullient as Avner could be with his downtown cronies and showbiz employees, he'd been, for the most part, strangely inaccessible with Murray, as though he were hiding something. Perhaps he thought Murray knew something no one else knew about him when, in fact, Murray knew very little about Avner's life as a theatrical impresario and even less about his private life.

One little article that appeared in the *Star* during the week of shiva kept surfacing in Murray's mind. Evidently, an eyewitness had seen Avner at about midnight the last night of his life near the Ford Hotel, a few blocks from the theatre. Somehow the reporter was able to establish that Avner hadn't arrived home until about three in the morning.

When Murray accidentally met Esther on the stairwell of the Grace Street home, he felt compelled to ask her the question that burned in his mind. They usually both rose early but hardly crossed paths or had very much to say to each other — until this morning.

"Mother-in-Law, what time did Avner come home that Saturday night?"

Esther could be intimidating with her spasms of protracted silence punctuated by rapier wit and could easily cut down to size even the most heroic. At first she seemed startled but quickly regained her composure to glare at Murray. "I don't know. I was asleep. All I know is that I told him not to go the theatre on Sunday morning."

Murray persisted. "Then you must have been told something by Avner or knew something bad. Why did you tell him not to go?"

Esther appeared rattled. "Sunday morning, after he finished shaving, he had his tea with some toast as usual. It was about ten-thirty and he left for the show, maybe at ten forty-five. I'm not sure.

I asked him not to go. He looked troubled. I knew nothing about his business or friends."

The stairwell conversation continued, perhaps the longest Murray and Esther had ever had. "Did he seem nervous?"

Esther shot back testily, "What difference does it make? He's gone. They killed him."

"What do you mean — they?" Murray asked excitedly.

He watched as Esther retreated, her head withdrawing more completely under her black mourning shawl. She simply stared at Murray, then continued up the stairs to her bedroom to engage in morning prayers.

Murray hurried to the theatre where he now waited anxiously in the upstairs office for Lou to arrive. The phone rang. "Hello, Murray, it's Lou." Murray could detect a slight slurring in Lou's speech. "I'm going to be a half-hour late. I'm sorry. I got tied up."

Leaning back in Avner's desk chair, which was fashioned from an old auditorium seat, Murray had time yet again to take stock of the horrific events of the previous nine days. He looked around the cubbyhole of an office. The door to the safe remained ajar, the dried blood still on one corner. The shattered glass lay undisturbed on the floor beneath the window overlooking the auditorium. On Avner's desk were various papers, a large half-empty Haig and Haig bottle, and a small *Webster's Dictionary*. Even after all these years, Avner had continued to improve his English, though one would never know it. Behind and above the safe there were shelves with miscellaneous papers, a series of office records, and various stamps. The place was a mess, but there were no signs of a struggle. On the safe itself sat two empty whisky glasses. The walls were pictureless, aside from several calendars. An unplugged wall fan faced the desk. Other than himself, it appeared that no one had revisited the death scene since that fatal Sunday.

Murray's musings were interrupted by a knock on the stairwell door below and a familiar voice. "It's me — Lou. I don't have a key. Let me in."

Descending the stairs to the self-locking door, Murray opened it to inhale the alcohol on Lou's breath. Together, they climbed the steps to the office to review, among other things, their respective futures.

"Before you say a goddamn thing, Murray, just remember I'm in charge. Get it?"

"Look," Murray said hurriedly, "I had no —"

"Yeah, yeah, I know, but let's get something straight right now. If it weren't for the fact that you're married to my sister, you'd be out of here, see. So before you start making any fancy plans, you should know you're working for me!"

Murray was stunned by Lou's tone. What had provoked him? He was well aware of Lou's unstable personality, but he really wasn't prepared for such a personal assault.

"For starters, clean up this goddamn mess," Lou growled.

Murray managed to contain himself. "I've got a wife and two kids and one on the way, so it's your call, Lou."

"You bet it is. I'm going to take over the management of the Roxy and you can be my assistant manager. You know — do the day-to-day jobs, the books, the staff, the bookings. I'll make the big decisions."

"Have it your own way, Lou," Murray muttered. *At least for now.* "We'll have to give up our projectionist jobs, of course."

"Right!" barked Lou, reaching for the half bottle of Haig and Haig on his father's desk. "Get on the phone and let those bastards know we're not coming in anymore."

"We should at least give them a few days' notice." Careful not to antagonize Lou further, Murray added, "Charlie Mackie can spell me off. Your father spoke highly of him. I won't be able to be here twenty-four hours a day."

"Good, tell Charlie when he comes that he's running the show on his own next week and then you two will work out a schedule." After a couple of gulps of whisky, Lou seemed a bit calmer. He set down the bottle and focused two red eyes on Murray. "I understand you told Lil you have some ideas about who killed my father."

"Well, not exactly, but I'm pretty sure whoever killed Avner was someone who knew him. First of all, the door to the auditorium was locked. To get to this office and its door, he'd have to come through the auditorium. So it seems to me your father was either met by somebody out on the street he knew and invited in, or he was met by someone who was already in the auditorium and was perhaps hiding overnight.

Your father wouldn't have left that door open, and he wouldn't have let anybody in, unless he knew him or her. It seems to me that whoever killed your father was somebody who knew him, or at the very least knew his habits."

Seeing he had Lou's attention, Murray continued. "Look, whoever killed him could very easily have made it look like a robbery. Your father could've been told to open the safe, or he might have been opening the safe, anyway, for any number of reasons."

"Why don't you go tell that to the cops?" Lou snapped sarcastically.

"Lou, I'm just trying to sort out a few things in my own mind and maybe help you and the police, as well."

"Forget it!" Lou roared.

"Well, there's going to be an inquest, and I'm sure the police are doing everything they can to find out who did this terrible thing …"

"The whole goddamn family's upset and all this isn't helping. I'm still sure that bastard Piton did it!"

"Calm down, Lou. We have to face facts. Let's leave finding the murderer to the police." He looked closely at his collapsing brother-in-law and realized it was useless to persist with any kind of meaningful discussion. It was simply time for Lou to grieve, and how long that would take was anybody's guess. "Go home, Lou," he said gently. "I'll look after things at the theatre and clean up. Charlie will help me."

His brother-in-law glanced at him. "I'll get the bastard!" he repeated as he went down the stairs.

Speechless, Murray could only contemplate his own future.

23

FURTHER COMPLICATIONS

Murray was ranting. "I don't understand it, Lil. Why haven't the police come here to talk to us about their investigation? All I've heard so far has been through newspaper reports! I just noticed this morning that Chief Draper and the Toronto Police are offering a $500 reward for information leading to the arrest and conviction of your father's murderer. Lou tells me nothing. He's hardly ever around the theatre, and when he is, he simply mopes and makes a few grunts." Murray paused for breath. "Of course, I understand why — he's depressed. And who wouldn't be? But you'd think he'd have told me he'd gone to the police and offered a $500 reward himself. Charlie Mackie had to tell me that! Mind you, the reward might help solve the case."

Lil was obviously preoccupied and blurted, "I'm feeling so miserable, Murray. And I can't communicate with my mother. She's spending all her time in her room praying and sobbing. And it's so hard looking after the kids."

"Look, Lil, I know you've got your hands full here, but so have I at the theatre, damn it. But we need to talk about your father. There are all kinds of rumours going around about him, and I think it best if you hear it from me first. There's a story that Jenny, a chorus girl from Chicago, had some kind of fight with your father a couple of weeks before his death. Apparently, Jenny has a gangster boyfriend named Freddy, and some of the girls in the chorus feel Jenny might have had this guy kill your father. No one can find Freddy. He hasn't been around the theatre since March 1. It gets worse. There's also a story about your father having an affair with Jenny, and she's the girl who apparently was identified in the car near the Ford Hotel on the Saturday before his death."

Murray winced when Lil shrieked, "Murray, are you kidding? My father? Involved with a chorus girl? You must be crazy!"

"I'm only telling you what I heard. I don't believe any of these stories. I also heard there was a man backstage trying to sell a gun. I'm not even sure what that means except this guy, who was known to one of the Roxy's chorus girls, approached Jenny with an offer for a gun." Murray paused, fearful of further upsetting Lil, then proceeded, anyway. "I've got enough problems taking care of the theatre. This is all police stuff. Lil, there were a lot of strange things that took place at the theatre on the weekend of your father's death. Somehow somebody unscrewed the light bulbs in the dressing room at the theatre so they wouldn't respond to the wall switches. I can't understand why anyone would do something like that, and I'm not even sure it has anything to do with your father's death. Crazy! Anyway, there's going to be an inquest."

"I've been too busy with the boys, Murray. I've got my hands full with them and I can't talk to my mother when she continues to tell me my father's paying for his sins. What sins? The man was just trying to make a living. He didn't have an enemy in the world. Maybe he tried too hard with his fancy cars and tailored suits from Tip Top. My father always had this need to impress people, to succeed, to be noticed. But running around with other women? I can't even imagine that! I know for a fact that my father never looked at any women other than my mother." She began to sob, her tiny body trembling. "How could anybody even dream of such stupidity about my father?"

Murray knew he'd touch a raw nerve by impugning Avner's integrity, but it was his duty to tell Lil about the rumours swirling around the city and within the Appelbaum family in particular. Murray had never formally studied psychology or read very much about mental issues, and he certainly knew little about Sigmund Freud or his theories. Still, he did sense that his wife somehow had a peculiar, perhaps even an unconscious, tendency to be inextricably attached to her father, irrespective of his behaviour, and somehow managed to submerge her hostile feelings toward her mother.

"Murray, I want you to know that I have my father's diamond stickpin in a small jewel box in our bedroom. To me, the stickpin is like him, a jewel."

"Lil, what's the point of mentioning that to me now?"

"I just want you to know that I need to hang on to something that belonged to my father. Whatever else happens, I want to keep this symbol in the family and pass it along to the boys, who in turn will pass it on to their children."

Murray quickly changed the subject. "Remember I was supposed to talk to a lawyer? I spoke to one today and told him about our problem not finding a will anywhere. He recommended that you, your mother, and Lou meet with him as soon as possible. Your mother will have to sign an affidavit that she's your father's widow, and that no will's been found in your father's papers. He'll also explain to you how your father's estate has to be distributed among you under the circumstances. I've had no luck trying to get hold of Lou to tell him. Could you look after this, Lil? Here, this is the lawyer's business card. Now I have to get back to the theatre."

Lil nodded. "I don't know what my kid brother's up to, but I'll find him. Meantime, I've got to prepare supper for the kids. They've been cranky and irritable ever since my father's death. Barry seems never to stop crying, and Gerry continuously asks for his grandpa. I don't know what to say to him, Murray."

"Just tell him he's gone on a long trip. In the meantime, I've got a million things to do. Thank God the business is holding up." Murray hesitated for a moment as he put on his galoshes. Bending over, he peered up at Lil almost apologetically and whispered, "You know my own father's having money problems. His ice-and-fuel business was once so good. But now, with this darn Depression, people simply aren't paying their bills. He's got my sister and brother working for him full-time. I'm really concerned about Gert and Dave, too."

"Knowing your mother, she'll see to it that her husband and kids won't starve," Lil said sarcastically. Turning the verbal knife a few degrees more, she added, "I can understand why your older sister, Mary, left home at fifteen."

"Mary left for New York because of my father, not my mother. Like your mother, he's too damn religious! Mary hates all that religious stuff." He noticed a faint mocking smile crease his wife's face, knowing there was no love lost between Lil and his mother. Anna Letovsky hadn't approved of him marrying Lil in the first place. He was well aware, too, that Lil found her mother-in-law something of a bizarre amalgam of personalities — a fusion of a Bolshevik dominatrix, a self-taught Florence Nightingale, and Eastern Europe's answer to Auguste Escoffier, the French chef. Knowing that Lil lacked his mother's brassy self-confidence, from the very first meeting he'd tried his best to keep them out of firing range of each other.

A punishing drizzle of wet snow and rain during the months of March and April 1935 turned Toronto's streets into endless corridors of slush, with lawns covered in a patina of ugly grey-and-brown snow. Since the sun appeared to have vanished, the difference between day and night was imperceptible. It was as though everything in the city — people, streets, cars, buildings, horses and wagons, children on their way to school, factories belching smoke — had taken on a peculiar veneer, a blunted, ghost-like, otherworld quality. But Murray paid little attention to Toronto's aesthetics as he trudged daily between the Roxy and Grace Street. The city was somehow turning into his own private purgatory.

One of Murray's great pleasures had always been to bring Lil and the kids over on Sundays to visit his parents on Shaw Street. He particularly delighted in his mother's cheese blintzes and potato latkes.

One Sunday, as he entered the door of her home, his mother's keen eye quickly picked up on the fact that her elder son was depressed. "Have your tea and latkes and have Lil look after the kids. I can see there's something on your mind."

Anna spoke in her usual booming voice, addressing him in a military manner, directly and forcibly, eyeball to eyeball. To a stranger, she could be intimidating; to her husband and children, she was the equivalent of the Oracle of Delphi. "Is it something new, Murray?"

"No, not really." He paused, sensing his mother knew and anticipated further details, so they went upstairs to Anna's private sewing room.

"So get it off your chest already!" she commanded. "Whatever it is, is this something you haven't told Lil?"

"Frankly, Ma, I haven't. She's too upset with everything."

"It looks as though you're the one who's upset."

"Well, it isn't anything new, really. It's just everything piling up." Murray took a deep breath like a schoolboy being reprimanded by his teacher. "Damn it, anyway. If only I'd gotten that job with Bell in Detroit."

"What do you mean?"

"Well, I don't think I'd be trying to run the Roxy with Lil's brother if I had. He's impossible, Ma! He's twenty-five years old, drinks like a fish, and has no idea about running a business, especially a tricky one like the one we have."

"What do you mean, tricky?" Anna asked.

"People in the theatre business tend to be temperamental and unreliable. But Lou's turning out to be the most unreliable of them all. I can't ever get hold of him, and I have to look after everything from the payroll to making peace backstage with the stagehands, chorus girls, and orchestra. And now I hear Pa's having trouble with his business. Pa and Dave and Gert have worked so hard. Dave even delivered coal at three in the morning!"

"Don't worry about us. We'll manage. Any news about who killed Avner?"

"Not a word. No contact from the police whatsoever. No more mention in the newspapers. You know, Ma, I have a feeling something's been deliberately kept from everybody."

24

BIG CHANGES

Esther spent most Saturdays in the quiet isolation of her bedroom, making the occasional foray into the kitchen to ensure Lily wasn't contravening any dietary laws. This Sabbath it was time she spoke out. "Lil, this is the second time I've seen you put cream in your coffee after finishing a meat meal. You should know better. Do you want my grandchildren to grow up as goyim?"

Lil appeared nervous. "Certainly not, Ma. You can see we're trying to keep kosher. What you saw must have been just a mistake."

"Well, I've seen the same thing the last two times I've been in the kitchen."

Lil's response was surprising. "What do you want us to do? Give you a separate kitchen?"

"Maybe that's a good idea!" Esther snapped back.

Lil sighed in frustration. "Fine, fine. There's that small room upstairs at the back of the house. Maybe I'll get Murray to set up a burner and an icebox there so you can have everything one hundred percent kosher — your way." Lil paused, then added, "My father didn't make such a fuss about keeping kosher."

"Your father ate most of his meals downtown. And what he did downtown was his own business." Esther lifted a contemptuous eyebrow. "I'm expecting your Aunt Becky this evening. Isn't that nice? She's grown into such a mensch, always so bright and alert and happy. You know, I think she understands me more than Avner ever did. She always has something nice to say and she listens to my problems. Your father was always much too busy."

"Well, he was never too busy for me," Lil caustically reminded her mother.

Just as the interchange was heating up, the telephone rang. Lil leaped to the phone as though anticipating special news, while Esther didn't flinch. It was Saturday, after all, and in her mother's view, answering the phone constituted work, strictly forbidden on the Sabbath.

"Hello," Lil said nervously. "Oh, it's you, Lou."

Lou's response was brusque. "Tell Murray I'll meet him tomorrow at the Roxy at ten o'clock. I've got good news."

"Have you been drinking, Lou? Are you okay? What do you mean, good news?" Lil had become almost more of a mother to her younger brother than Esther was.

"None of your business. Just tell Murray I'll meet him tomorrow at ten at the theatre."

Lou's been up to something, she decided. *He can't hide very much from me. I always catch his hand in the cookie jar.* Lil prided herself on her perceptiveness.

Murray was now doing Avner's work: going to the theatre on Sunday mornings to do the bookkeeping on the week's take, opening the doors to the theatre to admit the Chinese Freemasons for their presentations.

Early the Sunday morning after Lou's phone call to Lil, Murray arrived a little early, and to his surprise, found the front doors unlocked. He then discovered the door to the stairs leading to Avner's office was unlocked, as well. Murray felt a chill as he climbed the stairs, calling out, "Who's there?"

"It's me, Lou," came the familiar voice. "Come on, get up here. I've got important news for you." Murray quickly entered the little office to find Lou standing beside his late father's desk in a somewhat Napoleonic pose. "Here, have a chair, Murray." Lou quickly reached for a large bulky brown envelope on the desk and cavalierly flung it at Murray. "Ten thousand bucks." He hesitated. "Ten thousand smackers. That's what I've been doing the past couple of weeks."

"Lou, that's marvellous! But how did you get it?"

Lou caught Murray's apprehensive look. "Never mind. And, Murray, for Christ's sake, I didn't steal it!"

"All right, I won't ask any questions." *Whatever Lou's done, it surely isn't legitimate*, Murray thought.

"We're going to fix up this joint. Put in new seats, new curtains, add a few more strippers to the show. I'm going to be running the most profitable, successful live theatre in the city. And I'm going to make a fortune."

What do you mean "I'm"? Murray wondered. *Aren't I a partner in this theatre? Who does he think he is — a new Billy Rose?* Aloud he could only say, "Sounds good, Lou."

Then before Murray could utter another word, Lou interjected, "I'll make out a list of things for you to do."

Lou dropped into his father's chair, arched his back, and folded his arms in self-satisfaction. "I'll be the prince of vaudeville and burlesque. Yep, Murray, my old man would be real proud of me now. There's only one other job I've got to do and that's to find that bastard Piton."

Murray was stunned by all this sudden bravado. "Lou, leave it up to the police."

His brother-in-law looked at him in disbelief. "Well, have you heard anything? Because I bloody well haven't!" Lou took out one of his favourite Camel cigarettes and dangled it in front of Murray as he leaned over the desk, outlining the future of Toronto's only burlesque house.

◆ ◆ ◆

Within a week, renovations had begun in the Roxy Theatre. Lou's decor turned out to be a cross between American whorehouse and art deco. A new red velvet curtain replaced the tattered purple drapes that had hung from the small proscenium arch. Plush green seats replaced the former stained, gum-ridden, cigarette-butted ones, and stucco walls received a fresh coat of amber paint. Outside, a new marquee was built — a half-moon-shaped structure of steel and glass fringed by a hundred brilliant lights hanging from the front of the theatre and partially straddling the street below. This enormous construction was capped by a convoluted web of neon tubing that at night lit up the south side of Queen Street with flashing, high-kicking chorus girls.

"Didn't I tell you?" Lou repeatedly bragged to Murray. "Business is bigger and better than ever!"

And I have to do more and more work, Murray mused.

Murray was never again contacted by the police following his initial interview on March 3, 1935. Nor did the police visit Avner's home to question Esther or Lil. The Toronto dailies reported that the police had some clues but no suspects were ever found, no charges of murder laid.

And no inquest was ever held.

25

UNCLE HARRY RESURFACES

On April 6, 1936, Lil and Murray welcomed their third son at Mount Sinai Hospital on Yorkville Street — a busy series of houses strung together to form a clinic serviced almost exclusively by Jewish physicians unable to obtain hospital privileges elsewhere in Toronto. After a week's rest, Lil returned to Grace Street.

"We'll name him after my father," Lil said. "Alan sounds close enough to Avner, don't you think?"

Murray grinned. "Yes, of course, it's a fine name, and I know your mother will approve."

Lil, like her mother, was clearly out of her element as a homemaker. Nevertheless, she made a valiant attempt to mother her baby boys. At least Murray thought so, even if Esther had her reservations. One evening, Murray came home from the theatre early to find Lil breast-feeding Alan in the master bedroom.

"Murray, you're home early!" Following her natural instinct to assume there must be trouble if Murray were home early, she added, "Is there something wrong?"

"Oh, no, Lil. I just wanted to come home and spend a little more time with you and the kids. I thought maybe I could help out at home. Charlie's looking after the theatre this evening. You know I still can't rely on Lou. But to be fair, he is coming around the theatre a little more often and is a little easier to talk to now. He simply can't get over your father's death. And, in fact, Lil, I don't think he ever will. He seems to be lost without him."

"We're all lost without him, Murray."

Infant Alan began to cry in Lil's arms. "Murray, would you get a couple of spare nappies out of my top dresser drawer? I placed them in there in case I ran short nursing Alan."

What an odd place to put diapers, Murray thought. *She always seems to be stuffing things into drawers and cupboards.* "Here they are, Lil," he said, opening the drawer. But as he did so, his eye caught sight of an envelope underneath a little jewel box at the back of the drawer. Murray impulsively picked it out and opened it. "Lil, there's a telegram here. I couldn't help but notice it." He handed her the diapers, noticing her trembling hand and flushed face. "Can I read it?" he asked, sensing something was amiss.

"You might as well know, Murray. It's from my Uncle Harry."

"You mean your Uncle Harry who deserted Aunt Chanala and the two boys?"

"Yes," Lil answered tersely.

Murray was stunned. "Lil, everyone thinks he's dead! He's been gone almost ten years and nobody's heard from him. How did you get in touch with him? Why haven't you said anything to anybody?"

"Well … about six months after Uncle Harry disappeared I noticed a letter in the mail tray addressed to my father postmarked from Mexico. Father didn't say a word about who sent it, but I had a hunch it was from Uncle Harry. So I decided to write to the British embassy in Mexico City to ask if they knew the whereabouts of a Harry Appelbaum. I didn't tell anybody, of course, because everybody was so angry with him for deserting Aunty and the kids. But sure enough, I got a letter from the British embassy giving me an address for a Harry Appelbaum in Monterrey. So I took a chance and sent a telegram. Sure enough, it was Uncle Harry. We exchanged letters for quite a while. He didn't say very much in the letters except in one when he mentioned he'd met a wonderful lady called Luce. I got the impression he wanted to marry her, but I'm not sure. His letters stopped coming after that. I've written many times since, but there's never been an answer, even after I wrote to tell him of Father's death. I'm sure he would have answered me if he'd received that news. That telegram is the first I've heard from him in years."

"Lil, I can't believe you've kept this a secret all these years!"

Lil clutched infant Alan a little tighter and took him off her breast. "Murray, please understand. Uncle Harry begged me to tell no one. He did a bad thing deserting Aunty Chanala and the boys. But he's still a decent human being. He just wanted a new life for himself away from Aunty whom he couldn't stand."

"It's unforgivable, Lil. Nothing justifies desertion, particularly the way he did it, walking out cold, not telling anyone where he was going and not caring about those two boys. I know he was your favourite uncle and your father's brother and all that, but I have little respect for him. Your mother won't even mention his name she's so disgusted over what he did!" He paused to read the telegram. "'Dearest Lily. Will be in Toronto over Passover. Meet noon Sunday Royal York lobby. All my love, Uncle Harry.' Lil, Passover's only three days away, and he's coming here to Toronto now after all these years? I don't believe it!"

"Murray, you have to keep this a secret. Let me hear what he has to say. Hopefully, he's planning to see Chanala and the boys. Maybe he's returning to Toronto. I can hardly wait to see him."

Discreetly tucking the telegram back under the jewel box, Murray said, "Look, Lil, I didn't come home to discuss such matters. I just wanted to see you and the kids. I guess they're asleep by now, but I'll go upstairs and poke my head in."

Murray stood outside his sons' room for a few moments, trying to reflect on all he'd just heard. *Lil can be very secretive, even devious,* he thought, *but she can also be very loyal.* He could foresee only tremendous family tumult if or when news that Harry was alive and in Toronto was revealed. A *murder, a lost career, a brother-in-law with whom I can't work, three kids, my own parents in financial trouble, and a wife who never ceases to surprise me. What next?*

Certainly, more was to come.

Murray and Lou were well aware they'd soon be facing competition. Just two hundred feet to the west of the Roxy, a new vaudeville theatre had been built.

"Lou, aren't you worried about the competition?" Murray asked one day. He could have predicted Lou's response.

"Are you kidding? Our striptease is every bit as good as Minsky's in New York, if not better. Besides, I hear they're going to have mainly vaudeville acts. Don't be such a goddamn worrywart. They're trying to compete with Shea's across the road, not us."

Murray wasn't reassured by Lou's confident explanation. "I don't know. It looks like they've got a pretty fancy theatre. I know that Caplan and Sprachman are expensive architects. They've built a number of new theatres around town. Who do you suppose is behind all this, anyway?"

"Rumour has it that it's the Allen family. You know, the ones who own Premier Theatres. They've got a lot of good cinemas — and a lot of loot."

"But what are they doing in live theatre?" Murray paused reflectively. "They don't have any experience in vaudeville, do they?"

Lou's look was penetrating. "I don't know, but they sure as hell know how to make a buck! Maybe they just like vaudeville or girls. Who knows?"

Murray, always more cautious, responded, "Lou, hand me that

paper over there on the desk. Maybe we can find something." Murray quickly scanned the amusement section of the *Star*. "Ah, here it is — 'Toronto's new amusement palace, the Casino.' They're advertising a cast of thirty-five people with twenty beautiful girls. Look, their prices are even cheaper than ours — sixteen, twenty-seven, or thirty-five cents, depending on the time of day. Our morning show is twenty-five. They're advertising 'Lovely ladies in Paris nights with four vaudeville acts and other personalities.' But no strippers. And here, in the bottom of their ad, they've got what can almost be interpreted as a moral disclaimer — 'Informality and fun without loss of good taste.' I wonder if that's a dig at us, Lou."

"Who cares? We're selling tits and ass and that's what works." Lou, a little more loquacious than usual, added, "We'll beat the pants, or should I say the panties, off them. So quit looking as though the world has ended, Murray. You're such a goddamn pessimist."

"I suppose you're right." Murray went on, reluctantly. "I still worry that our shows are a little too raunchy for this city. And frankly, with the extra strip acts and spicy comics, I think we're taking a bit of a gamble. But I'm prepared to wait and see. I thought that even your father and Piton had gone too far with their Girlesk show, and I always thought they'd get into trouble and have their licence cancelled. I don't know how they got away with it."

Lou's face paled, and once again Murray had that sense Lou was hiding something. "Well, they managed somehow. And we haven't been bothered by anybody, have we?"

"I haven't heard anything." Murray wanted to sound empathetic, though privately he wasn't reassured. He also still wondered how and where Lou had obtained $10,000 so quickly after his father's death. *I hope he didn't do anything illegal. That old rag peddler who used to come around our house was always talking about money.* He recalled what the old man had told him, "If possible, make money honestly, if not, make money somehow." He could only hope Lou didn't subscribe to that. He had this terrible feeling that Lou had placed a big bet and won. Those sharpies he hung around with sure threw around a lot of money.

Could Lou have used the Roxy as collateral?

26

AN ALARMING LAWSUIT

"Have a look at this, Murray!" shrieked an angry Lou. Murray had just come up the stairs into the office to report on the previous week's earnings — his usual custom on Monday afternoons when Lou arrived.

"What a goddamn nerve. This letter is from Fort Lauderdale, from the offices of a Mr. O'Brien, a lawyer! Can you believe this?" Lou banged his fist on the table. "We've got a lawsuit on our hands. The Roxy Theatre Management Company, me, you, Lil, my mother, we're all being sued! And guess who by? Mr. Fred Piton!"

Murray wasn't ready for this outburst. "All right, Lou. Take it easy and calm down. What does it say in the statement of claim? Here, let me read it." He fumbled with the paper and got to the paragraph that had so upset Lou. Murray was shocked. "He says your father promised him fifty percent of the Roxy should he die. Is he crazy? Their partnership was dissolved six months before your father was killed. Your father owned the theatre outright! There's certainly no record of that kind of agreement in the papers we have. And your father didn't make a will, as you well know. But, anyway, why would he promise such a thing? It makes no sense! I'll get hold of Joe Sedgwick and we'll get this matter straightened out."

A well-respected lawyer, Sedgwick had acted for Avner in several business dealings. The tall, angular, hawkish man with twinkling green eyes had a razor-sharp mind to match his razor-sharp features.

Lou took a shot of whisky, and his contorted face flushed. "Christ, I thought my father's estate was settled long ago. It was bad enough finding out that Piton was a beneficiary of that crazy life insurance policy. Now that killer wants more blood? How can he make such a claim?"

"Look, Lou, I'll get Joe on the line right away."

A sweet young voice with a Yorkshire accent advised him, "Mr. Sedgwick is in court, but he'll be back this afternoon. Whom should I say called?"

"Please, just have him call the Roxy Theatre and ask for either Lou Appleby or Murray L ... Little." Murray stumbled over the surname he'd legally adopted recently, he and his father, Samuel, having found the name Letovsky much too cumbersome in an English-speaking city. The name had branded them as foreigners and was, at the very least a nuisance in business, its frequent misspelling producing chaos at the bank when cheques were processed.

Murray glanced at Lou. "He's in court right now. I'm sure we can settle this matter, but let's wait for Sedgwick's call. I have to go backstage. There's a bit of a ruckus there. Seems one of the musicians came in late for the first show."

Lou was taking another drink as Murray went downstairs. At about 5:00 p.m., Murray was in the box office when Sedgwick called and the cashier handed him the phone.

Murray told him about the lawyer's letter. "So it seems Fred Piton, Avner's former partner, is claiming he's entitled to fifty percent ownership of the Roxy. He says it was promised to him."

Sedgwick responded brusquely. "All right, Murray. I'll look into it for you. I'll need to get hold of Avner's papers first. Then I'll set up a meeting with you and Mr. Appleby at our Bay Street office. We're just three buildings south of the bank, near the corner of Queen and Bay."

Two weeks later, Murray and Lou met in Sedgwick's well-appointed office. The lawyer got right down to business. "Mr. Appleby, I've reviewed all the estate papers, including your father's conjoint insurance policy agreement with Fred Piton. I must confess that I find it hard to believe your father would agree to the terms of that agreement, but there's no doubt Piton was entitled to the money he received on Avner's death. It was paid out by Pilot Insurance, which confirmed the money was issued to him at a Fort Lauderdale post office. However, there's no mention in any of the papers I have about an agreement to transfer half the Roxy ownership to Piton in the event of your father's death, which is no surprise. According to Piton, this was a verbal agreement." Sedgwick smiled before adding, "You'll forgive me for joking, but a verbal agreement isn't worth the paper it's written on."

Lou was livid. "That bastard didn't even send a letter of condolence when my father died. Where did you say he lives?"

Sedgwick smiled again. "All I have is a post office box number in Fort Lauderdale. He's acting through this attorney, O'Brien, who has an office down there. But not to worry, Mr. Appleby. This man Piton has no case. I'll send a letter to O'Brien to that effect."

"I could kill that bastard!" Lou said angrily. "How dare he!"

"Lou," Murray pleaded, "if you keep making threats like that, you could wind up in the can. Just forget about him. Everybody knew what he was like, and you know a man like that will try anything. I don't want to be hurtful, but I think your father was extremely naive with this guy. I also can't believe your father would ever make such a promise. Certainly not half the Roxy ownership."

Choosing to ignore his brother-in-law, Lou looked hard at the lawyer. "Sedgwick, why don't you put in your letter that we're going to sue Piton for making such a false and outrageous claim?"

He'd barked the order, but Sedgwick was ready for him. "I'll do no such thing. I gave you my advice. He has no claim and we'll leave it at that. You won't have a hope in hell with a countersuit. It would just cost you a lot of money. You'd be chasing your tail."

Murray could see Sedgwick was getting irritated with his brother-in-law. "Lou, listen to Mr. Sedgwick," he counselled. "God knows, we've had enough trouble. Must we go looking for more?"

Lou, about to utter another expletive, obviously thought better of it and settled for a cigarette.

Fred Piton was never heard from again.

27

A HUGE DEAL

In mid-June 1937, Murray stood in front of the bathroom mirror, his face covered in shaving lather. *Another day with Lou and the Roxy.*

He felt tired before the workday had even begun. "Lil, is that you? You're up very early."

She stood in the doorway, bleary-eyed and pale, wearing her favourite peignoir, a gift from her father, nervously clutching a piece of paper in her hand.

Murray turned in shock. "Lil, what's the trouble?"

"It's terrible news. My mother received a letter from Poland yesterday. I don't know whether you know that she's been writing to her mother and her brother, my Uncle Beryl. Beryl has died, only fifty-four, and they don't know how or why. He's left behind five children and a wife and his mother. They're all living together in a big house in Warsaw. This letter is from the eldest daughter, Faga. She also writes that life for Jews in Warsaw has become miserable."

"Well, why don't they leave?" asked Murray.

"Apparently, they can't get the necessary papers to come to the United States or Canada. They've got lots of money, but they seem stuck and they're very worried. So is my mother, and of course, I am, too, even though I've never met any of them."

Murray scarcely knew what to say. "What terrible news! I'm so sorry to hear about your family, Lil. My mother and father hardly ever mention their parents. As far as I know, they're still alive and living near the Latvian border. I wish I could stay with you and talk more, but I have to get to the theatre."

"Oh, by the way, Murray, I got a call last night from my cousin, Sam, Uncle Aaron's son. He said he'd call either you or Lou at the theatre today."

Sam Appelbaum was a strange little man. Short, squat, oily, and a lousy dresser, he somehow managed to pass himself off as a person of accomplishment and believability. Lil always referred to him as "my cousin, the charming rogue."

Later that morning, Sam phoned the theatre and was put through to Lou. "I finally got hold of you, Lou. What the hell's wrong with you? Why haven't you answered my calls?"

"I'm a busy man," Lou barked.

Sam quickly retorted, "Yeah, yeah, I know you're very busy, but doing what? I hear it's Murray who's doing all the work at the Roxy.

Listen, Lou, I've got something that might be good for all of us, so just calm down. I'm your cousin, remember? You can trust me."

Lou was skeptical but also intrigued, and he couldn't resist the prospect of getting in on a money-making scheme, even if it was with his less than favourite cousin. "Meet me upstairs in the office with Murray tomorrow afternoon," he said. "And just make sure you're not wasting my time."

The following day, Murray and Lou met with Sam, who opened with, "I hear you're doing very well here."

"Yeah, we're making a living," Lou said.

Murray couldn't resist the opportunity to qualify Lou's statement. "Truthfully, Sam, we're doing very well at the box office. What's up?"

Sam couldn't wait to deliver the news. "Here's the deal. The Roxy's doing well, the Casino next door and the Allens aren't. Arthur Cohen isn't very happy with the kind of business they're doing. He's their silent partner and owns the land the Casino's built on."

"What's that got to do with us?" Murray asked, puzzled.

Sam straightened his tie and wiped his mouth with a soiled handkerchief. "The Allens and Cohen know you're taking business away from them —"

"Yeah, I know!" Lou cut in. "They advertise burlesque, but it ain't the real thing. They've got some big names, too, like Joey 'Gabby' Faye, the radio comic who's usually with Bert Lahr in his vaudeville act, but it isn't enough. I hear they're losing a bundle."

Sam raised his hands in a gesture for attention. "The deal is this. They want you to sell your theatre and become partners with them and have you run the shows. Whatever they're doing simply isn't working. Frankly, I just think they have too many cooks over there. But you guys seem to know how to sell burlesque, and that's why they want to cut a deal with you."

Lou could hardly contain himself. "They want us to sell our theatre and join them to run their shows?"

"Yeah, no doubt about it. The Allens have known me for years and know I'm your cousin. That's why they've asked me to approach you guys."

Lou frowned. "What's in it for you, Sam?"

His cousin smiled smugly. "Let's just say I get a commission."

"You'll have to show us the figures, Sam," Murray insisted. "It might be a slick deal, but we'll need more information. Wouldn't you agree, Lou? Besides, Sam, you have to understand that Lil and her mother, Lou and me, we're all part of the Roxy Theatre Management Company. And all our signatures are needed for any transaction."

"You can trust me, boys. I'll get you the figures. Between you and me, I think the Allen family, especially Herb and Jules, might like the idea of owning a girly palace. And sure as hell, the Allens and Arthur Cohen don't like the idea of losing money. Maybe they want their own little amusement centre. Who knows? They're all a little crazy. They'd just like you guys to run it and make a profit. Cohen will go along with anything that makes a buck. I'll have the papers for you in a week's time. Just give me the word."

Upon hearing the news from Murray, Esther was naturally suspicious of yet another theatrical venture. "My husband and my children are always getting involved in show business and look what it's brought me. Nothing but troubles." She softened her tone to add, "Look, Murray, you do what you think is best. I'm sure Lou and Lil will listen to you."

A week passed until Murray approached Esther again cautiously. "I think it's a good deal, Esther. Lou and I have met with the Allens and Cohen and we think we could do well together. And we've had a good offer for the Roxy."

"Fine, fine," Esther said. "If you and my children want to stay in a business with naked ladies, how can I stop you? I'll sign whatever agreement I have to. I don't need to be troubled by the details."

Murray nodded. "Good, Esther, and you're quite right. You don't have to read the fine print. The Roxy Theatre Management Company will now own a third of the Casino Theatre and be responsible for its management through Lou and me as co-managers. Lou, being the largest shareholder of our company, will have the biggest say in how things are managed, of course. I'll be looking after the day-to-day jobs, just like I did at the Roxy."

"Enough already!" exclaimed Esther, now somewhat annoyed. "You're making a living looking after my daughter and my grandchildren. That's enough."

By the end of 1937, Lou Appleby, Murray and Lil Little, and Esther Appleby had become part owners of the Casino Theatre at 87 Queen Street West, with Lou and Murray as co-managers.

28

THE CASINO THEATRE

The Casino Theatre was quintessentially art deco by design, its marquee festooned with neon chorus girls and hundreds of light bulbs lighting up an otherwise drab and dreary Queen Street. The theatre shared the street with the broken-down Union Hotel, with its entrance for men only, an assortment of small restaurants oozing pungent cooking odours, a selection of pawnbrokers advertising wares using the time-honoured three brass balls, discount clothing stores, and several seedy, mysterious-looking establishments — drapes drawn over the windows — promising fortune-telling.

Immediately to the west of the building was a rickety two-storey, turn-of-the-century claptrap with a sole occupant — an aging ex-chorine — the building having been left to her by its original owner, Jacob Cohen, the first Jewish magistrate in Toronto. Rumour had it this was a gift for being his special female friend.

The grand City Hall was no more than several hundred yards away, and to the northwest stood venerable Osgoode Hall, the fountainhead and headquarters of the Ontario judicial system, with its law school, courtrooms, and great library. Surrounding the property was an ornate iron fence, complete with peculiar cow gates, all that separated the hall from the realities of Queen Street West.

The Casino itself, though attractive in the architectural fashion of the day, had some serious limitations as a theatre for the conventional performing arts. There were some good points, though. It seated twelve hundred and fifty patrons in seats that were plush and comfortable. There was also a second balcony. The sightlines and acoustics were exquisite — from the stage a whisper could be heard at the back of the house. There was a small tiled and mirrored lobby, and along the east side of the building a very long alley led to the backstage entrance.

The stage itself had very little depth, no more than twenty feet or so, and most of the sets had to be "flown" — hung — from above. The stage should have had greater depth and capacity, but the purchase of sufficient neighbouring property to allow that wasn't possible, belonging as it did, to the Liquor Control Board of Ontario, which wouldn't relinquish its lucrative site. No matter what the policy of the theatre might have been, the Casino was destined never to be a fully workable theatre because of its foreshortened stage. It had an adequate orchestra pit, but lacked the runway one might expect, in keeping with the conventional burlesque houses of its day. The theatre's air conditioning was a feature not too common in the 1930s. Murray liked to say it was important for the theatre to cool off its customers, so to speak, in more ways than one.

Using a small office on the ground-floor auditorium level, Murray got to work immediately, while Lou, curiously, chose an upstairs office, an almost exact replica of his father's in the Roxy, only larger. Reached via a small door adjacent to the second balcony, it, too, had a winding stairway and a window through which to view the performance onstage. It was also immediately adjacent to the motion picture projection room, just as Avner's had been at the Roxy. The office was Lou's domain, his command post and retreat, a place to entertain and be entertained. It was a cloistered refuge in downtown Toronto where he could entertain the curious and not so curious from City Hall and Osgoode Hall, along with selected visiting performers, business associates, "gofers" requiring access to after-hours whisky, a motley disarray of supposedly well-connected racing touts and bookies, and occasionally members of the family whenever something of a very personal and intimate nature needed to be discussed.

"Lou, you buzzed me?" Murray had taken his time arriving at Lou's office one afternoon, irritated by what he felt was another of Lou's gimmicks. Lou was very proud of the set of buzzers on the side of his desk — one to summon Murray, or a surrogate, from the downstairs office; another linking him to the ticket collector, usually to allow free entrance to a guest; and a third connected to the stagehands' cue panel backstage.

"You see, Murray, we've been here at the Casino just a couple of months and my idea of tits and ass is paying off — three quality strippers, four shows a day, and lots of rowdy comics." He downed his first Scotch of the afternoon.

"You were right, Lou. The raunchier the better. I can see from the figures already. As soon as we have three strippers, business picks up. Straight vaudeville doesn't seem to work. Not anymore. They're dying at Shea's. I have to admit getting onto the Minsky brothers circuit and linking up with Milt Shuster in Chicago was a great idea of yours. I've got to hand it to you, Lou." Murray had learned how to stay on his brother-in-law's good side. "You certainly know our customers. Nothing sells like sex."

"And what do you think of Helen?" Lou asked with what seemed like an embarrassed grin.

The question arrived from out of nowhere.

"Helen … Helen who?" Murray replied over his shoulder, about to leave the office to run backstage.

"The cute little redhead in the chorus line, or don't you notice these things, Murray?"

"Of course, I do." Lou's interest in the recent addition to the chorus line their choreographer had brought in made Murray very uncomfortable. "Oh, you mean that new girl Lester Montgomery just hired?"

"Yeah, that's her. If you're going backstage right now, I have a little note I'd like you to take to her."

This is unusual, Lou asking me what I think of a chorus girl and wanting me to deliver a note to her! a flustered Murray reflected. *Best not to ask any questions.* He hustled down the stairway, took the side aisle to the exit door, and was soon in the stage door alley where Carl Steiner, the chief stagehand, hovered anxiously by the door.

"I've been waiting for you," Carl said. "Didn't you get my message?"

"Oh, sorry," Murray answered. "I did, but I got tied up with Lou."

Carl's face seemed pained. "Phil Silvers isn't here for the four o'clock show!"

"What?" Murray's stomach twisted into a knot. "It's five minutes to four. Where the hell's he gone! He'll miss the show. Where's Alda? Maybe he knows something."

Bob Alda was the resident house singer and master of ceremonies at the Casino. Soft-spoken with jet-black hair, he had a matinee idol appearance and romantic singing voice. The girls were crazy about him, and within a few short weeks, he'd become a good friend of both Murray and Lou. Bob was standing in the nearest stage wing, ready to go on and announce the four o'clock performance. Murray hustled over to him. "Where's Phil?"

"Likely at the Dufferin racetrack. He runs out in between shows to place bets. He tells me he can't help it."

Murray reacted quickly. "Look, Bob, go on without the comic bits. I'm going to have a word with Phil. We'll dock his pay."

Murray had no sooner finished talking to Bob behind the curtain when suddenly the stage door was flung open and in flew Phil Silvers, headed toward the metal stairway leading to the dressing room. Spotting Murray out of the corner of his eye, Phil offered his usual cheery "Gladdaseeya!"

Trying not to raise his voice across the backstage, Murray snapped, "Phil, this is no joke. You almost missed the show. Go get dressed. I'll tell the band to hold everything for five or six minutes." Murray swung around to his right, spying Bob just as he was about to pick up the stand-up mike and walk onstage. "Hold it, Bob. I'm going to run downstairs to the orchestra and tell them to wait until Phil gets ready. I'll speak to him later."

It had been an exhausting day for Murray. When he arrived home at one in the morning, Lil was still up. Baby Alan was running a fever, and Lil appeared anxious.

"Murray, he's been crying all day, and I finally called the doctor. It looks like he's got chicken pox, and I think Gerry and Barry have it, too. I tried to reach you all day. Didn't you get my messages?"

Murray fought down his annoyance. "No, I didn't, Lil. We've got a new cashier, and I don't think she knows what she's doing. Besides, I've been busy with the performers. Lester Montgomery wanted some new scenery painted and Percy Grisewood, our new scenery painter, told him quite flatly he couldn't do it because he was too busy, and then an argument followed and I had to settle it. And Phil Silvers nearly missed the four o'clock show. We should fire him, but he's part of the circuit and the audience seems to like him. The guy keeps telling me he wants to get out of burlesque, but it's the only way he knows how to make a living! And that gambling habit of his is going to ruin him. He's either placing a bet with one of the bookies on the street or down at the racetrack between shows. Honestly, I worry about him. Maybe he should have stuck with the clarinet. At the rate he's going, he'll never amount to anything in this business."

He took a deep breath. "Then, after the last performance, Sherry, our headline stripper of the week, came to the front of the house crying. When I asked her what the trouble was, she told me she couldn't do her exotic strip act because of the music the band was playing. I pointed out that it was the same music she gave Archie Stone and the boys when she arrived two days ago, but she said it wasn't the same. It turns out she couldn't take her clothes off because the band was playing in the wrong key! Can you believe that? She took an hour of my time, and I had I to go backstage and grab Archie and show her that no one had changed the music. I ask you. What difference could it possibly make what key the music is in when she's taking off her clothes! Is everybody in this business crazy?"

Lil's response did nothing to help. "Well, you seem to like Bob Alda and his wife, Joan, and their little boy, Alan. And isn't he the cutest little thing you ever saw? I thought they seemed quite normal."

Murray remained unsure. "I don't know, Lil. Bob's very nice, everyone likes him, and he's a very reliable guy. But you know, I was backstage last week and there was little Alan with a cigar in his mouth, and he's only three years old. Bob was showing him off. You call that normal?"

But Lil wasn't persuaded. "I'm sure it was all in jest, Murray. Besides, don't you think that's kind of cute?"

"Just don't try it on my kids, Lil, okay? Anyway, I'm too tired to argue. I'm going to bed."

Lil seemed about to say something else but didn't. As he headed off to sleep, Murray wondered what more she could possibly add but then dismissed the thought.

29

SUFFERING PHIL SILVERS

The next day, after Lil finally told Murray his mother had called, he phoned his father, sensing something wasn't right. "Pa, what's wrong? Ma called yesterday, and Lil didn't tell me until this morning."

"Murray, I hate to tell you this, but our Lakeshore Ice and Fuel business has gone into bankruptcy and I can't meet the payments on the house. The mortgage company's going to foreclose on us. We have to move."

"Pa, this is terrible! Why didn't you tell me sooner? I might have been able to arrange something at our bank. How's Ma taking it?"

"You know her, Murray. She has an answer for every situation. She wants us — her, me, and Gert — to move in with you on Grace Street. Dave's going to get a room somewhere else. Ma thinks there's room for the three of us, especially now that Avner's gone."

"Pa, that's crazy. Yes, there's an extra bedroom on the second floor, but what's that got to do with Avner's death? The kids are all upstairs on the third floor. That's nine people in the house, Pa! Lil will never go for such an arrangement."

"Look, Murray, this'll only be for a short while. Gert's sure to get married soon. She's going around with a very nice man. And Ma and I won't need to stay too long. I hope to get a job as a night watchman at Swift, and Ma plans to take in sewing. So we'll soon be able to pay off our debts and move into our own place."

Murray's head was spinning. "You know I'll always help you and

Ma, of course. But I think coming to live with us on Grace Street might create problems. I'll have to talk this over with Esther and Lil. After all, it's Esther's house, Pa."

As Murray expected, Esther was indifferent while Lil was outraged. "Murray, you must be crazy. This is my mother's house, and she and my father, may he rest in peace, left this house to her. And it's through the goodness of my mother that you and me and the kids are still here in this lovely big home. But *your* mother's another story. She's going to take over! I know she's a marvellous cook and I'm not, but this is our home!"

Murray was disheartened by her angry response. "What am I supposed to do? Leave them out on the street?"

Reluctantly, Lil finally agreed, and at the end of September 1938, Anna and Samuel Little and daughter, Gert, moved into the Grace Street home. The house soon became a battlefield with territorial challenges, alliances, secret meetings, domestic espionage, and few victories.

Lil continued to worry Murray. "I told you your mother would take over the kitchen, Murray. But she's actually taken over the entire house! And everything she says is acceptable to you! I feel like a scullery maid!"

"Wouldn't you help your parents if they were in trouble?"

"Of course, I would."

"I thought my mother might be a help to you, not a hindrance ..." Murray knew he was stretching things.

"You must be kidding. She not only bosses me around but your father's like a puppet. Frankly, I don't know how such a sweet guy can cope with her. She even tells me how to dress the boys. Murray, if your mother doesn't leave soon, I will!"

"Look they're not going to be here permanently. As soon as my father gets on his feet again and pays off some of his debts, they'll get their own place and be out of here. Besides, I don't hear your mother complaining." Another stretch, but he wasn't fooling Lil.

"Murray, I know my mother doesn't like it, either, but she's too depressed to put up much of a fight. She's in her bedroom most of the day, as you well know. And now that she has her own little kitchen at the back of the house, she's really in a world of her own."

Murray was about to defend his parents once again as the temperature of the verbal interchange continued to rise when the phone rang, startling Lil.

"It's only the telephone," Murray said. "Stop being so edgy and answer it."

"Murray," Lil told him, her voice softened, "it's the theatre."

Glancing at his watch anxiously, Murray thought, *My God, it's almost one o'clock in the afternoon. I hope Charlie Mackie is there.*

"Hello. Oh, it's you Charlie. What's the trouble? Phil Silvers called in sick? Again? He's at the Ford? Okay, tell him I'll be right down. The show will have to go on without him. Rags Raglan is on the bill, and he can sub with a couple of his own bits. I'm leaving right away." Murray fumbled for his car keys. "Trouble again, Lil. These performers!"

Murray drove his newly acquired 1938 Buick to the hotel as quickly as he could. *Did Charlie say room 604?* No matter. He'd find out the number at the front desk. Why didn't Lou ever help out when the performers gave them trouble? Too busy entertaining in the upstairs office no doubt.

Hurriedly parking beside the hotel, Murray entered and found out from the clerk that Phil was indeed in room 604. When he got to that room, he anxiously knocked on the door. A feeble, hoarse voice answered from within. "Come in. Door's open."

There was no "Gladdaseeya." Instead, Murray saw an ashen, pudgy-faced man lying in bed, perspiring and obviously short of breath. The room was a mess. Phil's black horn-rimmed glasses were off to the side of the bed beside a pitcher of water and a foul-looking glass.

Murray could only say, "Phil, you look terrible!"

"Do I need your one-liners, Murray?"

"I didn't mean it that way. You look very sick. Have you called a doctor?"

"No!"

"Why not?"

"I can't afford to."

"What? Didn't I just give you an advance on your salary two days ago?"

"That money went for the ponies. I'm cleaned out — broke. I can't afford a doctor."

"You must be kidding. Look, I'm going to call Doc Parker, and we'll straighten out later."

"Murray, you're a good friend and maybe the best theatre manager I ever worked for, but I hate this goddamn burlesque." Phil coughed a few times, wiped his forehead, and took a gulp from the glass beside him. "Murray, if there's one thing I'm going to do — mark my words — I'm going to get out of burlesque. I'm going to be a real star. I'm tired of being the bottom banana."

"Phil, first things first. Let's get you better. I'm sure one day you're going to be a much bigger star, and between you and me, I understand your feelings about burlesque." Murray placed a call to Dr. Parker who, obligingly, often took care of performers at the Casino. "Phil, he'll be here within the hour. In the meantime, you need some food and I'll see to it that something's sent up. Now I told you, if you're broke, we'll look after the bill. Just get better."

"Murray, you're a real pal. I'll never forget that you came over. What I told you about burlesque is between you and me. It's not that I don't like Harry Conley or Rags Ragland or Bobbie Morris and all the other guys and gals. But I just know I'm cut out for bigger things."

Murray was growing tired of such explanations. "Phil, I've heard enough. Please, just get better. I've got to get back to the theatre."

Quickly leaving the room, Murray thought, *He'll never make it — first of all, he has to stop gambling, and I'm not so sure he can do that. But all the same, I have to admire his chutzpah.*

When he returned to the Casino, a crowd of performers greeted him as he entered through the stage door. Feature stripper Maxine DeShone, wrapped in nothing but a see-through kimono and still wearing her pasties and G-string, and Red Marshall, with his baggy pants and floppy shoes, confronted him.

"Murray, is Phil okay?" Red asked.

Murray cleared his throat and smiled. "He's going to be fine. Doc Parker will see him and will hopefully convince him to get some food into himself. He's likely got the flu or something like that. Parker can give him one of those new sulphur wonder drugs."

Maxine turned to him. "Everything came off perfectly at the last show."

Unable to resist the pun, Murray shot back, "I hope it did!"

Several of the stagehands and Bob Alda had gathered to hear the news. "Murray, you have nothing to worry about," Alda said. "I did the bits with Red and Bobbie, and I don't think the audience knew the difference."

"He'll be back in a few days," Murray said reassuringly. "Let's everybody get back to business."

On Thursday mornings, Murray always met with partner Arthur Cohen at the Premier Operating Company's head office on Carlton Street. Highly intelligent, Cohen was a tiny man who oozed a prickly arrogance and was well known for his penny-pinching. Murray found these Thursday morning sessions at head office his most difficult encounters of the week — far worse than the performers and his own circus at home.

"Mr. Cohen," he reported, "the receipts are good this week. In fact, ever since we hooked up with Shuster in Chicago and Minsky in New York, business has been great."

Cohen, being his usual thorny self, quipped, "In business, Murray, you can always do better."

"Well, yes, I suppose we could do better. But frankly, I think we're getting away with blue murder, with three strippers on the bill and some fairly spicy dialogue."

The man stared at him icily. "Personally, I never watch that trash, Murray. It's really quite beneath me."

What arrogance! It was all Murray could do to resist a reply. *Well, you certainly don't seem to mind the money.* Instead, he said, "We try to get the girls to exercise restraint and limit the bumps and grinds and suggestive movements, Mr. Cohen. And I tell the comics when I think they've gone too far, but I'm never quite sure. You know, of course, some of their skits are really funny — great parodies. I actually like them."

Cohen surprised Murray with his response. "Well, I'm glad you see some redeeming merit in burlesque, Murray. You do what you have to do. Just keep it legal."

30

WORLD WAR AGAIN

Murray met Cohen the following week, still ruminating about the previous encounter. God, he hated meeting this guy. He never really knew what the man was thinking except that money always seemed to be on his mind. Murray wondered what Cohen would do if the books didn't balance or he thought they were losing money at the Casino. What a crazy setup — Lou, Arthur Cohen, the unpredictable Allens, and him running a burlesque house. What a circus!

"It's always good to see you, Murray," Cohen said in his squeaky, high-pitched voice with mock enthusiasm when the two sat down together in Cohen's office.

"Well, Mr. Cohen, it's good to be here and show you we're still making a profit despite all the bad war news."

"Bad news? What do you mean? The English and French will kick the ass of this maniac, Hitler. Mark my words, Murray, the war will be over in weeks."

"I hope you're right, Mr. Cohen. My parents and Lil have relatives overseas, and who knows what's already happened to them."

"Stop being such a worrywart, Murray."

He was surprised at Cohen's naïveté about the war Canada had recently entered alongside Great Britain. Hadn't the man read about the massing of German forces for months? Hitler's takeover of the Sudetenland, *Kristallnacht*, the German American Bund? And what about the Jewish refugees aboard the Hamburg-America liner MS *St. Louis* and how no country, including Canada, would grant them asylum? Cohen was either very poorly informed or so preoccupied with his own business that he didn't have the time or concern for anything else.

Still, the man always intimidated Murray. "Well, sir, here are last week's books. I have a question, though, with one of the items. In fact, I've noticed it regularly over the past three or four months."

"What is it, Murray?" Cohen snapped in irritation.

"Sir, I know we have a Mr. French on the payroll, but I'm unaware of who he is and I'm not sure why he's receiving $100 a month."

The vulpine little man abruptly changed complexion from pale to paler. "Do you really want me to tell you, Murray?"

He mustered some inner resolve. "Well, if I didn't want to know, I wouldn't have asked. It's a bit of a mystery to me who this person is and why he's on our payroll. And why I, as manager, have been asked by both you and the Allens to pay $100 a month to him and send it to a box number."

"Murray, if you really must know, Mr. French is a prestigious lawyer. And you're obviously very aware that the kind of theatrical enterprise you and the Allens are engaged in, or should I say we, doesn't exactly measure up to community moral standards, at least in the minds of some. Mr. French sees to it there's no pressure to bear on the Casino. In short, he keeps our licence to operate a burlesque house viable."

So I'm the one who's naive! My God, we're holding on to our licence by paying a lawyer to pay someone off at City Hall! A penny suddenly dropped. *I'll bet my late father-in-law kept his licence by paying someone off!*

Cohen was still talking. "Murray, you should know I'm very straightforward when it comes to business. I make no bones about it. Mr. French is an integral part of our theatrical enterprise, and I don't want any further questions about it. You'll simply have to accept the realities of business. And, by the way, if I'm wrong and there's a prolonged war, just remember that war means a lot of servicemen. And guess what a lot of servicemen will want to do?"

Perplexed, Murray remained silent.

"Well, I'll tell you," continued Cohen, a slight nervous twitch appearing on his upper lip. "Men of a certain type like to see good girly shows. War or no war, we're going to be winners on Queen Street."

What a bastard. Always reducing a conversation to money.

Cohen could see that Murray was upset by the topic and the reve-
lation about Mr. French's role, so he tried to lighten the conversation.
"I see you have Rose LaRose featured this week under the heading of
'Pretty Babies.' Sounds pretty enticing."

Was that a touch of ridicule in his speech? Murray knew Cohen
rarely, if ever, came around to the theatre — probably wouldn't want
to be found dead in it. "Yes, we're getting the very best burlesque
performers, Mr. Cohen. The very best from the Minsky and Shuster
circuits. They all seem to like Toronto because they don't have to work
Sundays. So the show business end is doing well. And don't forget,
the Chinese Freemasons rent the theatre on Sunday afternoons, just
like they did at the old Roxy. And we're starting to rent out to chari-
ties most Sunday nights. So, in short, we're utilizing the theatre seven
days a week and making money." *That should please him.* Murray had
begun to tire of this interchange with Cohen.

"Sunday nights, you say, Murray? You're renting the theatre to
charitable organizations?"

"Yes, we are, Mr. Cohen. Organizations like B'nai Brith don't seem
to mind coming to a burlesque house on a Sunday evening. Some
of their performers are quite good, too. One of their comics — Lou
Jacobi — is as funny as any of the people we hire. A couple of weeks
ago they had an amateur night, and a young Black teenager named
Sammy Davis, Jr., brought the house down and won the dance contest."

"That's all very interesting, Murray. I'm glad to see you and Lou
are running a good show. Or should I say a series of good shows?" he
added almost derisively. Then quickly glancing at the bookkeeping
records Murray had brought, Cohen signed them off with diplomatic
authority.

Murray couldn't wait to leave the office and return to the Casino.
He hoped Cohen was right and the war would be over soon. He and
Lou had young families. And, fortunately, the army wouldn't take him
because of his bad eyesight. Nor would it want Lou due to his poor
hearing.

Putting on his grey fedora, Murray neatly folded the weekly reports
and placed them in his shiny black leather briefcase. He sure as hell

didn't like this war, but somehow Hitler had to be stopped. Surely, the British and French could do it.

Murray took the streetcar just outside on Carlton Street, then transferred south on Bay, heading toward the theatre. He'd no sooner made himself comfortable in his seat when he overheard a shouting match between the conductor and a woman carrying a load of parcels. She spoke poor English, and the argument seemed to centre on her not paying enough, with several Yiddish curse words evident to all in the trolley. The argument seemed to go on for several stops before finally terminating. Seated in front of Murray was a young couple, and he couldn't help but overhear the woman turn to her companion and say, "I think Hitler's right about the Jews, don't you?" The utterance wasn't a particularly new one for Murray's ears, but on this day, with the terrible news from overseas that Germany and the Soviet Union had invaded Poland, the comment shook him.

I guess there's no sanctuary for us. We're Jews no matter what!

Murray arrived about a half-hour before the 1:00 p.m. stage show, and as he walked past the Casino Box Office, the cashier waved to him. "What is it?" he asked.

"There's an Adolph Frankel here who wants to speak to you, Mr. Little. He told the doorman he was a friend of the Appelbaums, so he had one of the ushers show the man to the office. He's waiting inside for you."

Still perturbed by what he'd heard on the streetcar, Murray went to the cashier's window. "Tell him I can't see him now. Tell him I'm tied up backstage. Perhaps another time."

31

FIRST TASTE OF BURLESQUE

By the end of June 1940, the war in Europe was going badly for the Allies: British forces had been evacuated from the beaches of Dunkirk, and the French had signed an armistice with the Germans at Compiègne in the very same railcar where Germany had suffered its own humiliation following its defeat in 1918. Much of Western Europe was now in ruins.

The summer of 1940 saw the beginning of the Battle of Britain. Luftwaffe pilots bragged of oceans of flames over England; even Buckingham Palace had received a direct hit. For Murray, though, it was warfare at home that was far more immediate and relevant. As soon as his parents and sister had moved into Grace Street, his mother had immediately dominated the home. Lil had taken to referring to his mother as the Field Marshal, and the quality of Murray's relationship with his wife went from bad to terrible. Working with brother-in-law Lou was also becoming increasingly difficult because of Lou's tardiness, drinking, and penchant for using his upstairs office as a secret hideout for some of Toronto's seedier characters and politicians.

Lil looked for any excuse to get away from Anna. "Murray, why don't you take Barry with you to the theatre today? I think he's old enough to see one of the shows. He'll enjoy that, especially the music. I'll take Gerry and Alan shopping with me at Simpson's. I've got to get out of the house. Your mother insists on doing all the food shopping and cooking. I can't get a word in edgewise, let alone get into the kitchen. So I've got to get out of here — for the day at least. But the boys need looking after." Lil's exasperation was tangible.

"Okay, Lil," he agreed. "You go shopping at Simpson's with Gerry and Alan. Why don't you buy them some new clothes for the High Holidays? I'll take Barry backstage and show him around, treat him to lunch somewhere, and let him see the afternoon show. I'll bring him home just before supper. I think he'll enjoy his trip to the theatre. We'll consider it a birthday treat."

Lil nodded, then said, "Just give me some idea how long this is going to continue. Your mother's been here only a few months and already I feel like a prisoner."

"I think you've made that very clear, Lil. I can't change my mother and I can't throw her out, but I'll do what I can to soften the impact of her presence. In the meantime, I'll help get the boys ready. I can hear the three of them fighting upstairs in the attic."

But Lil wasn't finished. "Listen, Murray, my mother's been pretty good about all this, but she's beginning to feel oppressed, too. I think she could use a vacation. She's mentioned it to me several times, and I know she wants out of the house, too. She has a cousin in Miami, and I'd like to make arrangements for her to visit Florida over the winter."

"All right, Lil. That sounds good to me. Please try to understand the pressure I'm under, particularly at the theatre."

Lil nodded again. "You know I don't interfere with anything you and Lou do at the theatre, Murray."

"I know, but between your brother, Arthur Cohen, and the Allens, I've got my hands full. Not to mention handling the performers and dealing with the stagehands, the musicians, the projectionist, the front-office staff —"

"How many times do I have to hear your list of complaints?" Lil snorted, ending the conversation abruptly.

Murray was very proud to take his shy seven-year-old son backstage. "Carl, this is my middle son, Barry," he said, introducing him to the man who effectively ran things backstage. Known for his short fuse and mercurial temper, Carl could be very off-putting to the performers. However, he seemed to take an instant liking to the young boy.

"If you'd like, Murray, I can show him around backstage," Carl offered. "Nobody's going to object, and I'll bet he'd like meeting the girls."

Murray was surprised at Carl's enthusiasm. Perhaps he had a son of his own. Or maybe he was just trying to make up for some of the bad reports Murray had received, about the times he'd lost his temper.

"Carl, I think I'll introduce him to some of the performers myself. And if you don't mind, maybe he can stand behind the curtain and watch one of the shows while I go out front. I know Barry particularly likes music."

"That's just fine with me, Murray." Carl was being more than conciliatory. "Anything you want."

Murray led Barry to the dressing room off stage right. "Barry, I'd like you to meet Red Buttons. He's this week's featured comic and a great favourite with everybody."

Red was sharing the star dressing room with Roxanne, the featured stripper of the week, and he called to her to come and meet the young boy. "Roxanne, this is Murray Little's boy, Barry. Murray told me that someday Barry would like to be a musician."

"A musician, eh? Lots of good musicians around this place." She put a delicate finger on Barry's cheek. "You must stay and watch the whole show, if that's all right with your daddy."

"Fine by me," Murray said. "I'm sure Barry won't mind. Right, son?"

Barry blushed, and Murray figured his son had just realized that watching the whole show would mean seeing Roxanne remove her clothing during her exotic dance. "I'd like to stay, Dad."

Lil was probably right, Murray concluded. It wouldn't do the boy any harm to watch the entire performance, including the strippers.

"Tell me, Murray, are all your boys as cute as this one?" asked a smiling Roxanne.

"Well, yes, but each one's a bit different. Barry seems to be the most musical, so I thought he'd enjoy coming backstage as a birthday treat." Murray's "middle son" beamed.

Father and son left the dressing room and climbed the metal stairway to the upstairs dressing room where Murray rapped on the door. He could hear the cackling and squealing of the chorus girls. "Everybody decent?" he called through the door.

A strident voice replied, "Most of us are. Come in, anyway!"

To Barry, Murray figured, it must all seem bright and dazzling. Seated in front of mirrors, surrounded by what appeared to be a galaxy of light bulbs, were perhaps a dozen doll-like faces with red lips, long eyelashes, and glistening white teeth, as well as a seemingly endless line of shapely bare legs.

"Barry, this is Mrs. Haley," Murray said. "She looks after all the costumes for the performers. She's from Scotland."

Mrs. Haley gave the boy a warm hug and proceeded to make a fuss over him, perhaps reminding him of his grandmother, Murray's mother, with her silver hair, thick glasses, and apron.

"Okay, Barry, we'd better let the girls finish getting ready," Murray said. "I'll take you downstairs and you can stay backstage with Carl."

After the show when the curtain finally closed and Archie's band played "Little Girl," Carl grabbed Barry's arm gently and pulled him back to reality from behind the curtain. "Your dad's here, kid, I hope you weren't embarrassed by what you saw."

"Gee, no, Carl. I thought the whole show was kind of neat, especially the girls!"

Carl threw back his head and laughed. "Well, I can see you're going to be a regular customer back here, young man. Your dad's at the stage door waiting for you. See ya."

When Barry joined his father at the stage door, Murray asked, "What did you think of your first taste of show business, son?"

"Great, Dad!" Barry replied enthusiastically. "When can I come back?"

32

A SHADY PROPOSITION

Murray took Barry home following his burlesque baptism, then quickly wolfed down one of his mother's specialities — potato latkes followed by beet borscht with sour cream and black bread — and prepared to duck back to the Casino. But as he was putting on his coat, Lil stopped him in the hallway.

"Murray, I've purchased Mother's train ticket to Miami, and she'll be leaving in two weeks. She's feeling so dispossessed and so anxious to get out of this house."

Why is she still on about this? Murray wondered. "Lil, do what you have to do and make whatever arrangements you have to — whatever it takes." Again, he was running short on patience. "Lou wants me back at the theatre. Apparently, he's got something important to tell me, so I've got to run."

Back at the Casino, the doorman whispered to him, "Mr. Appleby's been looking for you, Mr. Little."

When he entered Lou's upstairs office, his brother-in-law was holding court. "I'd like you to meet a couple of gentlemen from City Hall, Murray. This is Willie Anderson. He's a City of Toronto solicitor."

Murray was surprised by the lawyer's appearance. Short, stout, plethoric, he had a strikingly red bulbous nose and a face riddled with pustules. *This man represents the city in legal matters? What a presentation!*

Lou continued. "And this is Frank Mitchell, who's also a lawyer at City Hall."

Mitchell was tall, strikingly handsome, and immaculately dressed, a man with smiling russet-brown eyes and thick bushy eyebrows that somehow seemed manicured. All three men — Willie, Frank, and Lou — reeked of alcohol.

Lou seemed unusually cheerful. "Before we get into the discussion, you guys, let's catch this chorus number that Montgomery, our choreographer, has put together. He's featuring Helen."

Mitchell turned to Anderson, and they exchanged knowing glances.

Murray, more than a little confused, was content to sit on the sofa at the back of the office until the viewing was over. Glancing around the room, he noticed a picture of Avner hanging above the filing cabinet. He'd been upstairs dozens of times, but for some reason hadn't noticed that picture before. Something else he hadn't observed until now was the long-barrelled hunting rifle stashed in the corner of the room behind the sofa.

The final strains of Cole Porter's "I've Got You Under My Skin" wafted faintly as Lou closed the viewing window when the chorus line number finished. "Wasn't she great, guys?"

Murray was becoming more and more uneasy.

"Yeah, just great!" Anderson and Mitchell replied together. "Terrific!"

Then Mitchell added, "Let's get down to business."

"Christ, Ollie isn't here yet," Lou groused.

Ollie? Murray wondered. Where on earth did Lou find all these people? They were obviously here for the booze and girls. So what did his brother-in-law need him for? Murray watched as Lou, Mitchell, and Anderson toasted one another with more Johnnie Walker, perhaps to calm their nerves.

About twenty minutes had elapsed when suddenly there was a loud thump at the door and a strange voice bellowed, "Hey, Lou, you son of a bitch. It's me, Ollie. Let me in!" A swarthy, muscular man with straight black hair plastered to his scalp lumbered into the office. "Sorry I'm late, guys. I got hung up at the hotel with some broad."

No questions were asked.

"Who's that stiff sitting in the corner, Lou?" Ollie asked. "He doesn't seem to be enjoying himself."

"Ollie Baskin, this is my brother-in-law, Murray Little. He helps me run the place."

"What's wrong with him? Doesn't he drink?"

Lou grinned. "Don't worry about him, Ollie. He's okay. So let's get down to business, gentlemen. Ollie, as most of you know, owns the New Statler Hotel on the north side of Queen just east of Osgoode Hall. He wants to upgrade the hotel, needs cash, and is willing to take me in as a partner, provided I put up some of the money. Ollie and I thought that Murray here might want a piece of the action, you know, to keep it in the family." Lou smiled sardonically. "A few years ago, Premier Mitchell Hepburn very kindly changed the liquor laws in the province to allow hotels to serve beer and wine by the glass in their beverage rooms. Frank and Willie here think more big changes in liquor laws are on the horizon and a piss-pot of money can be made in a place like the New Statler, especially with improvements to the beverage and dining rooms. However, what's worse at the moment is Prime Minister Mackenzie King's intention to ration the supply of beer and wine hotels can get. Frank and Willie, with their federal and provincial connections, think they can help us with those restrictions if they come so we can get the usual beer and wine the Statler receives, upgrading the liquor licence in the process."

"Yeah, we stand to make ourselves a killing if we do all that," Baskin interjected, and Mitchell and Anderson nodded.

All eyes turned to Murray.

"So what do you think, Murray?" asked Lou. "Are you in?"

Murray wished the floor would open up and swallow him. "Well," he ventured cautiously, "I'd have to hear a lot more of the particulars."

"I can see already you're too goddamn conservative for this!" blurted Baskin. "What are you — a dry? Don't you know a once-in-a-life-time deal when you see one? Don't you trust your brother-in-law? What the hell's wrong with you?"

Murray was about to respond when Lou interceded. "Look, Murray, basically the deal is this. Ollie's going to keep majority owner-ship of the New Statler and he'll cut us in as partners. All we have to do is put up $50,000 for renovations. I said I could get $40,000, so we're just asking you for $10,000." Lou finished his glass of Scotch.

Murray was puzzled enough to ask Baskin, "Why do you need me? Why can't you, or Lou for that matter, go to the bank for a loan?"

Baskin snorted, obviously irritated, while Lou poured himself another Scotch. Mitchell and Anderson seemed interested only in the events onstage, glancing repeatedly through the viewing window and stretching their necks like a pair of ostriches.

Lowering his voice an octave to where it was low and grav-elly, Baskin turned with black piercing eyes to Murray. "Listen, you goddamn chicken, you gotta know the banks won't give me or Lou any money, at least not right now. We've been told two or three times by them that they don't like the kind of people we associate with. We also know we'd be turned down if we applied to the province for an upgraded liquor licence."

Gesturing to Mitchell and Anderson, Baskin added, "These two guys will do what they can to fix the federal restrictions if they come and any interference from the province, but what we really need is a front man who's clean. So we want to set you up as the nominal manager. And with a nice respectable guy like you doing the asking, we shouldn't have trouble getting liquor permit upgrades when they're available. What's more, you can help us with the bank. Lou says he can raise forty G's without the bank. All we're asking from you is a lousy ten G's to make up the difference."

Where in God's name can Lou raise $40,000 without a bank? Murray wondered. And for that matter, what bank's going to give me $10,000 for renovations to Ollie's hotel? "Don't you think it's a bit of a gamble renovating the hotel in the hope you'll get an expanded licence sometime in the future?" he asked. "You all know how strong the drys are in this province. You might be able to sell beer and wine as much as you want, but if you're expecting to add hard liquor, cocktails, as well, that might be a very long wait."

Baskin crouched like a wrestler, his stout body about to leap on his opponent. He snarled at Lou, "What kind of a brother-in-law you got here, anyway? Doesn't this son of a bitch understand there's a fortune to be made? With the dining room improvements and other renovations and a secure supply of at least beer and wine, we'll still be rolling in money. And believe me, Premier Hepburn loves a drink himself. We're all confident he'll let us serve cocktails damn soon."

Murray was annoyed and embarrassed by Baskin's invective. He certainly liked the idea of making more money. Who wouldn't? But he had no stomach to be a puppet or yes man for either Baskin or Lou!

Then he noticed the office had become silent except for the purr of the projectionist's machine in the room next door. Ironically, Archie Stone's band had begun playing again, this time, "Brother, Can You Spare a Dime?"

Loosening his tie, Murray gulped down a mouthful of ginger ale. The quiet continued until after Murray had lit a cigarette. "All right, I'll make an appointment with Walter Blenkenship at the bank and see what I can do."

"Good, Murray," Lou slurred.

"Yeah, great!" grunted Baskin.

Mitchell, standing at the viewing window, turned to the inebriated Lou. "That's one hell of a stripper you've got this week, Lou."

"You must be looking at Joan Lee. We're doing 'Stripsody in Blue' this week," Lou replied.

Mitchell leered. "That's quite a dish, Lou. How about an introduction?"

Murray sensed his opening; the party was obviously going to get rowdier. "Nice meeting you, gentlemen," he said quickly. "I'm sure we'll meet again. I've got to run."

Lou yelled after him as he descended the circular stairway,

"Murray, don't forget to tell the doorman that Frank, Willie, and Ollie are to get free passes always."

How many free passes had Lou given away? Reflecting on this, Murray hustled out as fast as he could. Who knew what his brother-in-law would give away next!

33

AN AGREEABLE BANKER AND AN ANGRY REVEREND

"Good morning, Murray. Nice of you to come by."

It was a typical welcome from Walter Blenkenship at the Dominion Bank at Queen and Bay, just east of the Casino Theatre. Having banked there since his early days with the Roxy Theatre, Murray and Blenkenship had developed a warm working relationship. He was a typical bank manager at least in appearance — poised, always splendidly decked out in a dark pinstriped suit, wavy grey hair immaculately trimmed. The banker even wore small spectacles at the end of his nose.

"What can I do for you, Murray?" Blenkenship asked pleasantly.

Murray cleared his throat. "I need to borrow a fair amount of money — $10,000, in fact."

"What on earth for, Murray?"

"I want to acquire a part interest in the New Statler Hotel just down the way."

Blenkenship adopted an almost grandfatherly tone. "I know that place. It's basically a beer hall, isn't it? What would you want to do there?"

"To begin with, the building needs an upgrading. My brother-in-law, Lou Appleby, is going to come up with $40,000. Our combined contribution would give us a forty-nine percent interest in the place."

"Who has the controlling interest?"

"His name's Ollie Baskin. He's had the hotel for several years and is doing pretty well, particularly during the day with the crowd from Osgoode Hall. Ollie feels that with Lou and me as part owners, we'll be able to upgrade the liquor licence. If we can serve hard spirits and cocktails, business will boom."

"Can't Mr. Baskin do this on his own?"

"I think, regrettably, Ollie has a bit of an uncertain reputation, if you know what I mean. He's concerned that on his own he won't get an upgraded licence. In fact, he's been unable to get an improvement loan in general, even though the hotel's been making a small profit."

"Murray, I know you're an honest person, and you know you have good credit with me, but why would you want to become involved with someone like that?"

"That's a good question, Mr. Blenkenship. First of all, I'm stuck with my brother-in-law as a partner at the Casino. And not to join in would almost certainly cause more trouble with him. To be honest, this is a gamble ..." Murray knew he was vacillating. "Still, it looks as though we can potentially turn a good profit at this hotel. It's perfectly located for business, what with the crowd from Osgoode Hall and City Hall, and as you know, the Casino's very, very busy these days. The hotel could pick up a lot of business from our theatre customers. It's just across the street. And if it had that upgraded liquor licence ..."

"Your weekly deposits are certainly excellent, and the theatre's turning a good profit."

"Since the start of the war in September last year, business has quadrupled. I'd say that half our audience is now made up of servicemen. Many come down from Camp Borden, just north of the city, on their way to being shipped out to Montreal and overseas to the U.K. I think the Casino represents to many of these young fellows their one chance to have a look at a real live girly show."

Blenkenship smiled. "What you say makes sense. Mind you, Murray, the Casino's getting quite a reputation around the city because of its striptease acts and blue comics, if you know what I mean."

Murray nodded. "I know all too well what you mean. Working in burlesque isn't easy. I'm certainly aware of the reputation the Casino is getting, and it's one that affects both my family and me. But it's a job and an excellent source of income at that. And we're not doing anything unlawful." Murray paused, aware he must seem overly apologetic. "Yes, I know some say we're selling smut and sex, but we're not really. I like to think we're selling fantasy and that people come to the Casino for a good time."

Obviously aware of Murray's discomfort, the banker came to his rescue. "I didn't mean to offend you, Murray. Personally, I've enjoyed the occasional show myself. As far as the loan goes, I'll draw up the necessary papers. Of course, I'll have to clear it with our head office, but I don't expect we'll have any difficulties. Give me a call in a couple of days or drop by when you have a moment."

"Thank you, Mr. Blenkenship." Murray put on his grey fedora and walked briskly out of the bank building, heading back on the south side of the street toward what had been euphemistically labelled the "Emporium of Mirth and Melody" by local newspaper hacks. His eye caught the headline in a corner newsstand: "Coventry Destroyed by Reich Bombers in Worst Raid of War — 1,000 Dead."

It's going to get much worse over there before it gets better. I can only thank my bad eyesight for not being there in uniform. But those poor bastards ... and people make such a fuss about a burlesque show!

He hustled along the street past the Roxy, now renamed the Broadway, and couldn't help but recall the horrifying events of March 3, more than five years earlier. Each time he passed, the same thought ran through his mind: *Who the hell would fire two bullets into Avner Appelbaum's head?*

As Murray arrived in the maroon-tiled, glass-panelled foyer of the Casino, he noticed two men in overcoats leaning against the wall adjacent to the auditorium entrance.

"Are you Murray Little?" asked the chunkier of the two.

Murray was startled. "Yes, I am. What can I do for you?"

"I'm Detective William Teasdale, and this is my partner, Detective Peter Miles. Could we have a quiet word with you, Mr. Little?"

Have they learned something new about Avner? "My office is just down the way if you'd like to step in, gentlemen."

Their massive frames seemed to fill the tiny downstairs office where there was hardly room to swing a cat — just enough space for a desk, a small safe, one filing cabinet, and a swivel chair.

"I'll get right to the point, Mr. Little," the chunky officer said. "You're the manager of this organization, I understand?"

"Yes, that's right," Murray answered anxiously, waiting for the detectives to get to the point.

"You're also a part owner, are you not?"

"Yes, yes."

"Well, I have to tell you Mr. Little that we've received a number of complaints from Toronto citizens about the nature of your theatrical productions in recent months, and more recently in a letter from a Reverend James Mutchmor."

"You received what?" queried Murray.

"You heard me," Teasdale answered gruffly. "Some of our citizens and the reverend have been complaining about the public nudity, the display of vulgarity, and the bad language in your theatrical productions. Reverend Mutchmor has been here several times and has fully documented his observations. He's filed a letter of complaint with the police commission and particularly objects to the use of the word *hell* by your so-called comics. Here's a copy for you. The other complaints, basically, are the same — expressing disgust at women removing their clothing in public and making lewd and suggestive movements while doing so." Teasdale paused. "Speaking personally, I don't find your presentations all that objectionable. I've seen worse public displays on the beach at Sunnyside."

Miles, the other detective, nodded approvingly and stuttered, "Y-yeah, it ain't so b-bad really. But we've g-got to answer to these complaints, so we've b-been checking out your theatre."

Murray recoiled in shock, remembering he'd seen a minister in the theatre on a number of occasions. But the reverend certainly hadn't come to his office and complained. And none of the house staff had said anything. He recalled a man of the cloth looking as if he were enjoying himself, even munching a hot dog at the snack bar. "What would you like us to do here, gentlemen?" asked Murray, regaining his composure.

"Well, we're going to have to serve you with a summons," Teasdale said. "You'll have to appear before the Police Commission. Do you mind if I smoke?"

"No, not at all," answered Murray. He stared at the wall, pondering his next move. The detectives were obviously impatient. "What if I preview and censor these shows myself before they come to Toronto? Since they all come through our circuit, the performers usually appear at the Palace Theatre in Buffalo before they come to Toronto. It's only a three-hour drive, so I could see to it that any objectionable material is removed before they come to Toronto. If not in Buffalo, I can still monitor their first show at 1:00 p.m. Thursdays. Dewey Michaels is the owner of the Palace, and I know I'll have no trouble with him or the performers. They know that Toronto, the city of churches, has a reputation to protect."

Teasdale butted his cigarette in the airplane ashtray on the desk. "Well, if you think that's going to work, that sounds fine. In the meantime, we've got a summons to serve you and here it is. You should review it. Hopefully, the Police Commission can resolve this issue. Oh, and by the way, Mr. Little, if you don't mind, would you leave our names at the door? You know — for free passes?"

Murray wasn't a fool! Who did they think they were kidding? *These fellows don't want passes just so they can follow up on my proposed cleanup!* He smiled. "That won't be a problem, gentlemen, and once I see what the specific objections are in the letters of complaint, we'll modify the performances accordingly. Perhaps Reverend Mutchmor would like to give me a call."

The two detectives grinned at each other. Miles stuttered, "N-not b-bloody likely!"

Murray had hoped these two might have some news about his father-in-law's death. And now this! Theatre manager, hotel manager, home peacemaker, and now official censor. He wished he could trust Lou. At least getting out of town for the day once a week might be nice. And if he took Lil, she could enjoy the shopping. And what had happened to Arthur Cohen's "Mr. French"?

PHOTO ALBUM

Avner Appelbaum/Appleby in his thirties.

Esther Appelbaum/Appleby in her early fifties.

Lou and Lil, Avner and Esther's children.

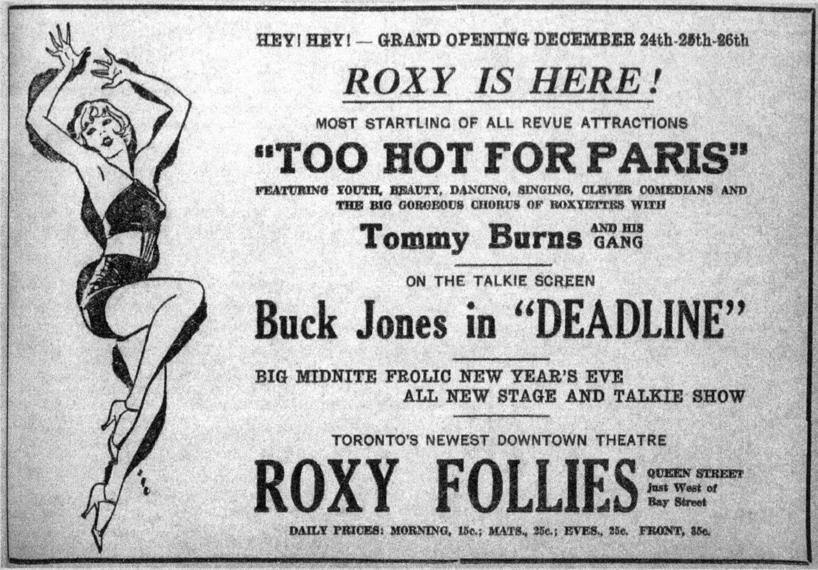

First advertisement for Avner's Roxy Theatre on the south side of Queen Street West, published in Hush, a popular Toronto tabloid, on December 24, 1931. The Roxy began life as the Globe Theatre in 1918. Credit: Courtesy Toronto Public Library.

The Roxy Theatre's name was changed to Broadway in 1937.
Credit: City of Toronto Archives, Fonds 1488, Series 1230, File 1143.

Avner in his early fifties.

Police photos of Avner's office at the Roxy Theatre after his murder on March 3, 1935.
Credits: City of Toronto Archives SC266, Item 36045 and Item 36044.

Murray Letovsky/Little at the scene of his father-in-law
Avner's murder at the Roxy in 1935. He found the body.
Credit: City of Toronto Archives, SC266, Item 36043.

The Casino Theatre circa 1940. Credit: City of Toronto Archives, Fonds 251, Series 1278, File 11.

The first Casino Theatre advertisement in 1936.

A selection of Casino Theatre advertisements from the 1950s.

Lil Appelbaum/Letovsky/Little.

Lou Appelbaum/Appleby.

Murray Little circa 1940.

Barry Little and his mother, Lil, in Miami, Florida, in 1940.

Murray and Lil in 1955.

Lou, Esther, and Lil in the mid-1940s.

34

TWO SISTERS

Becky was paying one of her many visits to Esther. "You're going where?" she asked her sister. "This isn't like you, Esther. Travelling to Florida on your own yet! I know you. You won't eat food in a restaurant because it's not kosher. I can't imagine you travelling alone on a train."

"I'll manage somehow," Esther assured her. "I just have to get out of the house. It's no longer my own home now that Anna and Samuel have moved in. Lil feels the same way. With Avner gone all these years, I still feel deserted. Lil keeps busy with her boys, who are growing up nicely, thank God. Murray's so busy at the theatre that he's hardly ever home. I think a little change won't hurt, and, Becky, as I get older, winters in Toronto are becoming more difficult for me. I fell on the ice twice last Saturday on my way to the synagogue. So don't worry. I'll be staying with cousin Sarah, who has a nice apartment in Miami. I'm told it's right on the ocean. And, of course, she keeps kosher."

"Have you made all the arrangements then, Esther?" asked a surprised Becky.

"I think so. Lil bought the tickets for me. I take the overnight train from Union Station to New York. Then from Grand Central in New York I take the Empire Express to Miami. And Sarah's going to meet me at the station."

"Well, if that's what you want to do, it's your business. But before you go, you should tell Anna and Samuel what your real feelings are about having them in the house. That might produce a little heat at first, but if you and Lil let your feelings about them be known, they might be encouraged to move out faster."

"More easily said than done," quipped Esther. "I'm hoping that when I return from Miami I'll feel a little better about the home situation."

"And what about Lou? Can't he help? I hear he and Murray are doing very well at the Casino."

Esther's face sagged. "To tell you the truth, Becky, I'm a little worried about Lou. Avner's death took the *sitzfleisch* out of him. He's not the same person. Even five years on, he's constantly depressed and drinking more and more. Avner used to try to hide his drinking from me, but I could always smell it on his breath when he came home after work. But at least he was able to work back then. Lou turns up late for work every day, and I overheard Murray telling Lil several times that Lou drinks at the office. And in the late afternoon he even has one of the ushers go out and buy him a bottle of Scotch. He's just too depressed and too drunk to be effective. I'm ashamed to admit it, but I know Murray's doing all the work. I just have to see how exhausted he is when he comes home at night. Lil doesn't want me to mix in, but Lou's my son. So I say nothing to him. It wouldn't help, anyway. And to make matters worse, Becky, Lou's hanging around with a bunch of nogoodniks he knows from his school days — bookies, prizefighters, ball players … If Avner were still here, Lou wouldn't behave this way."

Becky could see that Esther was very close to tears as she talked about her late husband and only son. Her usual aloofness and composure had evaporated.

The perennial optimist clutched her older sister's hand. "Everything will work out for the best, Esther. You have a nice holiday in the warm weather, and I'm sure, in time, Lou will make some kind of adjustment. He'll have to. Just try to be positive. I'm sure his drinking's just a phase."

Esther reverted to her usual cold cynicism, so familiar to Becky. "I think this family's cursed. The two main men in my life are no longer part of it."

How could Esther think she was being punished? Becky wondered. Knowing that her sister's marriage with Avner had been arranged, she knew Esther had never been completely involved with her husband. Still, Becky had to admit Lou was another matter. Esther did care deeply for him. She desperately wanted to change the subject. "Have you heard anything from Avner's mother and brother Beryl? Are they still in Warsaw?"

"I've heard nothing, not a word. Avner's brothers tell me they haven't had contact in nearly eighteen months. Thank goodness you and I and most of our families got out when we did! This Hitler is the devil incarnate, and the Jews are receiving God's punishment for the sins they've committed. And I don't mean the killing of Christ. Their sins are their failure to observe God's commandments."

"Esther, let's not get into that again," Becky pleaded. "Let's change the subject." She refused to surrender her happy optimism. "What about Chanala and the boys? And have you ever heard anything about Harry?"

"I don't even want to think about Harry," Esther snapped. "For all I know, he could be dead. And rightly so, deserting his two boys! But now that you ask, I did see Chanala just last week on College Street on my way to the synagogue. She's had a terrible time without money or resources. She's scrubbing floors and waiting on tables in a restaurant on Spadina several nights a week. Her two boys, Maxie and Morris, are growing up fast and help out by doing odd jobs after school. Chanala tells me the boys are very good to her and never ask about their father. She's lucky — they're very involved with their mother. I wish my Lou was as involved with me."

"Esther, stop feeling sorry for yourself," Becky implored. "I've got to hurry home to make supper for Sam. Don't forget to drop me a card from Florida."

She kissed Esther on the cheek and walked out into the cold, wet Toronto night. *That poor woman. She still thinks God especially singles her out, watches her every move, and is quick to punish her for any non-observance. Will she ever learn?*

35

GRILLED BY THE POLICE COMMISSION

"Murray, you must be joking," howled an angry Arthur Cohen. "Who the hell's this Mutchmor, anyway?"

Cohen's fury caused Murray to flinch. "He's a well-respected Toronto minister with a lot of clout with municipal and provincial politicians. He's very outspoken and influential and has made a name for himself as a moral crusader. However, to hear about a complaint that the Casino's undermining community moral standards comes as something of a surprise. We take care that our acts don't offend. Even more of a surprise, we've noticed a minister attending performances in recent months. He's never complained to anyone, and in fact, he always appears to be enjoying himself. We've come to the conclusion that he and the Reverend Mutchmor are one and the same person!"

"Well, what exactly did he say? Where's the letter?"

Murray fumbled nervously for the letter, which he'd crumpled and stuffed into his pocket. "Here it is! When I got this thing, I was so upset I wanted to tear it up."

"That's not like you, Murray," Cohen observed, taking the document from him and smoothing it out.

"Complaints like this impugn my integrity and reflect upon my family," Murray said. "Besides, what's his evidence that what we're offering is doing harm to anyone?" With each utterance, his indignation intensified. "Who is he to act as judge and jury? And if the whole theatrical production is so very distasteful to him, why does he keep coming back for more — and apparently enjoying it?"

"I wouldn't worry too much about it, Murray."

"Well, Mr. Cohen, you don't have to appear before the Police Commission. I do. That piece of paper is a subpoena to appear before them at a meeting in a week's time. It's easy for you to say not to worry, but I'm the one who has to sweat it out before that commission, not you."

"I'll choose to ignore that last comment, Murray. We'll get hold of Mr. Sedgwick, and he can appear before the commission with you. I'm quite certain Mutchmor is merely a nuisance."

"I hope you're right. In any event, I have a contingency plan. I think we can censor our own shows. I don't believe we have to change very much, if anything, but I'm willing to go down to Buffalo and preview Dewey Michaels's shows at his theatre on Main Street."

"Well, that would be very good of you, Murray. It's unfortunate that none of the Allens or Lou are capable of relating to the performers, at least not in a business manner, if you know what I mean. Besides, I don't trust any of them!"

Was Cohen referring to Lou and his chorus girl acquaintance, Helen? Maybe this sly fox knew a lot more than Murray gave him credit for.

"Fine, Mr. Cohen. I'll call Dewey and start censoring the shows as soon as I can. He might have to speak to Milt Shuster in Chicago about our situation, but I'm confident our performers won't mind."

Without warning, Cohen snapped back to business as usual. "Leave the week's figures on my desk, Murray. I'll review them and have one of the staff deliver your copy to you rather than have you wait."

Cohen appeared particularly accommodating today, seemingly not quibbling about the figures, Murray mused on his way out the door. In fact, the man seemed somewhat anxious to have him leave …

The following Thursday, Murray arrived with lawyer Joe Sedgwick at the Toronto Police Commission on the second floor of City Hall on Queen Street West. Murray knew he must be noticeably overanxious when Sedgwick told him, "Calm down. You're not going to lose your licence. We'll find out what their problem is and I'm confident we can make an appropriate arrangement."

When Murray opened the big oak doors of the hearing room, he was immediately greeted by a uniformed officer who directed that he and his counsel should sit in the two wooden chairs in front of an imposing desk. Within moments, three starchy-looking, moustached police commissioners in dark blue uniforms marched into the room from a side entrance and quickly sat behind the high desk.

God, they remind me of the Gestapo, Murray decided. *They look so stern and unemotional. Their shoes even made a clicking sound on the floor, almost as though they were saluting.*

"Which one of you is Murray Little?" barked the commissioner in the middle.

"I am." Murray raised his arm in a motion that must have looked like a *Sieg Heil*. He quickly rose to his feet and cleared his throat.

The middle commissioner continued. "Well, you know why you're here, Mr. Little. We've received a number of written complaints. In particular, the Police Commission has taken special notice of a letter written by Reverend Mutchmor regarding the antics going on at your theatre. We take these complaints seriously, as you can appreciate. This licensing body is accountable to the city and its citizens. It's our responsibility to see that the moral standards of the community are upheld."

The commissioner was about to continue pontificating when Sedgwick jumped to his feet. "My client and I, with all due respect Mr. Chairman, would like to know specifically what's been found objectionable."

"So you're the solicitor, are you?" the chairman said almost mockingly. "To be specific, many of the complaints pertain to the bad language used by your comics, Mr. Little. Reverend Mutchmor, in particular, objects to the use of the word *hell*. He cites in his letter that the comic Bozo Snyder used that term."

Flustered, Murray turned to Sedgwick and whispered, "Bozo's a pantomime comic. He never utters a word onstage!"

Sedgwick nodded and smiled. "With all due respect, Mr. Chairman, my client informs me that the particular comic mentioned doesn't speak onstage and is, in fact, a pantomime artist. Perhaps the reverend has mistaken this comic for another in some other stage production."

It was now the chairman's turn to become rattled. "Well, that's a technicality." The other two commissioners fumbled through their papers. "Look, I don't give a good goddamn who said it. If the word *hell* was used onstage and the reverend said he heard it, that's good enough for the commission and me." He glanced to either side, and his fellow commissioners nodded. "Listen, Little. See to it that in future none of your baggy-assed comics use *hell* or anything else that's profane. If this comes up again, your theatre's going to become a parking lot." The chairman hesitated, straightened his tie, and glancing upward as though having an epiphany, pronounced, "I'll let this appearance before the commission stand as a warning to you, Little. You can keep your licence provided you clean up your act."

Murray allowed himself to collapse farther into his chair, and wiping beads of perspiration from his forehead, muttered, "Thank you, sir."

"Thank you, gentlemen," Sedgwick added.

Six soulless eyes glared at him and abruptly turned away as the three officers marched out of the room.

"Thanks, Joe," a relieved Murray managed to say. "Do you think they didn't pursue the issue because they themselves made a technical error that we could have appealed?"

"I don't know," said Sedgwick. "The big thing is the licence stays."

"I'm going right back to the theatre and speak to Pinky Lee, this week's comic. Frankly, Joe, I don't know what to tell him other than to stop using the word *hell*. I guess I'll also have to watch what the girls do onstage a little more carefully, but I haven't seen anything too suggestive. At times we have as many female customers as male, and so far I haven't heard anybody come to the office personally to register a complaint."

"Well, Murray, it only takes one or two goody-two-shoes to make trouble. The main thing is your licence is secure, at least for the time being."

Murray was puzzled. "What do you mean 'for the time being,' Joe?"

"Well, you know this city as well as I do. It's Toronto the Good. It's always possible that some frustrated troublemaker could get his way. There's always some son of a bitch who wants to take the moral high ground for self-aggrandisement."

Murray found himself speaking with less surety, almost meekly. "I'll do what I can to see the comics don't use profanity. I'm shocked that some people object to the word *hell*. And it might not be that easy telling the strippers to change their acts. After all, burlesque is strip and tease! But I guess I've got no choice and I'll have to act as a censor of sorts."

Sedgwick sighed and slapped Murray on the back. "Looks as though we've dodged another bullet, Murray."

Murray was still confused. *That must have been the shortest hearing ever. A brief formality, that's all it was. And what about that fellow French Cohen told me about? Has he played some kind of role here?*

The two men quickly left City Hall just as its enormous clock tower struck three. Murray turned to Joe. "I'm exhausted. I need a coffee and a bun or something before I go back to the theatre. How about joining me over at Bowles just across the street? I need a breather and maybe you could give me some understanding into what's going on here at City Hall and with the Police Commission."

Sedgwick peered at his watch. "I have clients at four, but a coffee on a miserable afternoon like this would be welcomed. I have to tell you, Murray, I'm not a real insider. I might know less than you do about the inner workings of City Hall."

Once inside Bowles, the two men sat beside the window in the white-tiled cafeteria, long accepted as an enclave of male patrons only.

"Look, Murray, I have to tell you: You're obviously a very nice guy, but I think you're terribly naive." Sedgwick was stern-faced, deadly serious. "I have no inside information about the Police Commission, how it works, and what it does. Or who's on the take and who pulls the strings. I don't even know what motivates our mayor for that matter. Or City Council or the aldermen. Who knows why they run for office in the first place? But you can bet your bottom dollar that not all of them are lily-white. And from what I've seen with my many years of experience, I think the same thing applies to our esteemed judiciary."

Murray wasn't looking for a sermon but listened attentively as the lawyer waxed on. "But I do know this. You and your bunch over at the Casino aren't the first to try to make a buck out of selling fantasy sex, or theatrical sex or whatever you want to call it, in this supposedly pristine city of ours. The Star Theatre would have been the first, I guess, back in 1907, located appropriately enough on Temperance Street. And its specialty? Can't you guess? Burlesque, of course! And probably a lot more risqué than your kind of stuff. But there used to be a Toronto Vigilance Committee back then, and it ultimately succeeded in closing the theatre. So, being Toronto, we continue to have a street named Temperance."

Murray felt obliged to defend himself. "Hey, I don't have any high-minded moral pretensions here. I honestly don't think that what we're presenting at the Casino is in any way corrupting anyone. I just think people should be able to attend what they want — and that includes everybody. Our patrons come from everywhere, even men of the cloth and from over there ..." Murray pointed with agitation toward City Hall. "And there are some of your colleagues, too. We see them walking over from Osgoode Hall! If what we're doing is so bad, why do the patrons keep coming?"

Sedgwick smiled. "Murray, you've got a point. A lot of people like to say one thing and do another. Still, you're a straight shooter, and personally, I don't like to see a guy like you in the burlesque business, even if what you say is true and it's strictly speaking legal. But I'm sure not fussy about your partners."

Murray gulped down his coffee. Sedgwick seemed to know the situation at the Casino pretty well. "I want to thank you for helping us once again, Joe. But I have to get back to life's seamy side now," he added with a laugh.

The two men left Bowles, shook hands just outside the door, and parted, Murray to make his way briskly along Queen Street West toward the Casino and Sedgwick to descend into the dark canyon of Bay Street.

Once back at the theatre, Murray reviewed previous bookings and noted that on February 15, 1941, in the amusement section of the *Toronto Daily Star*, they had advertised Maria Cord, Bozo Snyder, and Red Marshall as the feature attractions.

Mutchmor must have gotten his comics mixed up, Murray thought. Bozo and Red were on the same bill and it would have been Red who used the word *hell*, not Bozo. The commissioners obviously hadn't done their homework. Murray began to tap his fingers on the oak desk. In fact, he mused, the commissioners hadn't really seemed all that interested in the complaint process. Were they perhaps merely trying to show off their civil duty by putting up a good front responding to the complaints? In any case, his licence was still intact!

Murray pulled out a Sweet Caporal cigarette and continued his reverie. *I still don't trust them, even though it may all have been a bit of a joke to these commissioners. I'm still going to have to monitor the shows. The safest thing is to always play ball with the police.*

He called Lil and told her the good news. She was pleased, especially when he suggested they celebrate with a light meal after the last show. No sooner had he replaced the receiver than the buzzer from Lou's upstairs office rang. What did Billy Rose want now, or should he say Little Caesar? It was all right for Lou to strut around the place in his Adler elevator shoes and well-tailored suit, hair slicked down and a smelly Cuban cigar in his mouth, but Murray was the one who did the dirty work. *I suppose he simply just wants to know how we made out at the commission*, he speculated as he hustled upstairs to his brother-in-law's office.

Lou snorted "Good" upon learning of the commission's decision and promptly toasted the theatre's longevity, raising a glass of Scotch in company with Anderson and Mitchell, his two loyal City Hall cronies.

"I knew you guys wouldn't have any trouble," Mitchell burbled enthusiastically. "Those cops like tits and ass just like everybody else."

Anderson's usually red face appeared even redder.

"Ain't that right, Willie?" Mitchell added. "You know those guys over at City Hall like I do. And you sure as hell know the cops, having to bullshit in court with them every day."

Murray cut in. "Lou, it looks as though I'm going to have to go to Buffalo and check out the shows each week. Lil may wish to come along with me to do some shopping in the States. I don't have to tell you how crazy your sister is about buying American clothes."

Anderson lurched over to Murray and belched in his ear. "Eaton's and Simpson's ain't good enough for your wife?"

Murray knew it was time to leave but remained long enough to add, "I'll put in a call to Milton Shuster's group in Chicago, Lou, and to the Minskys, and tell them what we intend to do. I'm sure they won't be offended. Oh, and by the way, I've got a meeting late this afternoon with the man we talked about the other day, that Dave Sherman who used to be the chauffeur for the Allens. Apparently, he's very reliable. You remember, I introduced you to him briefly about a week ago. It was the Allens' idea that I get some help in the office and you agreed to it."

"Yeah, yeah, I remember. A sullen son of a bitch, as I recall. But anything to help you, Murray," Lou added sarcastically. "Anyway, me and the boys here have a lot of serious things to discuss. Oh, and by the way, be sure to drop Sedgwick my personal thanks."

What were these three guys up to? Murray wondered. And how much work did Willie and Frank do over at City Hall, anyway?

Murray's meeting with Dave Sherman later that afternoon proved to be just as Lou said it would likely be. He could see that his new assistant wasn't going to be easy to work with. The man was sullen, depressed, a fellow of few words. But the Allens had insisted that their former chauffeur have a job at the Casino. *Maybe they've had enough of him*, Murray concluded. *Still, if I can handle Lou, I'm sure I can deal with Sherman.* Still, he remained concerned about how Sherman would treat his theatre staff and worried what the performers might think about the strange fellow. But it was what the Allens and Cohen wanted. So that was it — carved in stone!

36

ENTER SAM APPELBAUM

Lil came to the theatre earlier than planned, having decided to catch the last show before meeting her husband. The presence in the house of her mother-in-law, Anna, and father-in-law, Samuel, as she was coming to realize, wasn't all bad. The move had provided her with devoted built-in babysitters other than her own mother. She was now also driving the family car, and with the boys getting a little older, was able to get out of the house more often. Lil was beginning to feel more independent. Besides, she really enjoyed live theatre, even if it was burlesque.

She had arrived just in time to catch the feature attraction of the show that week: "Stripsody in Blue." Lil had no scruples about watching a striptease, and that evening she saw Joan Lee, a curvaceous blond, mince around the stage to the music of Jerome Kern's "All the Things You Are," teasingly peeling off another piece of apparel every eight bars and ending up under a baby-blue spotlight dressed in nothing more than pasties and a G-string.

To Lil's surprise, there were no catcalls or wolf whistles, only generous applause from an audience composed mainly of uniformed servicemen perhaps getting their last looks at a semi-clad female before being shipped overseas to God knows what. She gasped inaudibly when, in one final gesture of titillation, a bare, beautifully shaped leg emerged from behind the curtain for a brief moment as Archie Stone's pit orchestra blasted out the final chord.

◆ ◆ ◆

Murray poked his head out the office doorway and spotted Lil standing at the back of the theatre, all gussied up like Lady Godiva's pet horse. Where did she think she was going? Hadn't she come down just to pick him up? The scent of Evening in Paris reached him while he was still yards away from her. "Lil, you're all dressed up! I thought we were just going out for a bite to eat at Bassel's."

"So what, Murray? When I go out, I like to get dressed up. You know that. And besides, who knows who we'll meet at Bassel's? I like to look my best when I meet people. It makes me happy!"

"So let's grab some food then."

Bassel's Restaurant at the corner of Yonge and Gerrard had evolved into a popular Toronto meeting place, since it was open almost twenty-four hours a day, seven days a week. The Bassel brothers served good food and lots of it, so their downtown location was the ideal venue to see and be seen. Many of the Casino performers preferred the Chinese cuisine readily available on Elizabeth Street, no more than a few hundred yards from the theatre; others enjoyed the added attraction of the not-so-legal gaming rooms hidden behind the general eating areas at several of the establishments. Still, Bassel's was also a favourite of the performers, and one could always count on spotting Casino comics, strippers, or chorus girls mingling with the eclectic throngs of chatty, enthusiastic customers.

This evening was a particularly busy night at Bassel's. Murray was a great fancier of Bassel's club sandwich served with mounds of hash brown potatoes followed by Boston cream pie.

"Look, Murray," Lil suddenly said with muted enthusiasm, "there's my cousin, Sam Appelbaum, Aaron's son."

As it turned out, Lil and Murray had been seated at a booth immediately adjacent to Sam and his wife, Eva. Murray couldn't help but notice Sam's Cheshire cat grin and frequent glances their way. Finally, Sam got up from his booth, and with a mouth half full of cheesecake, leaned over to extend a handshake to Murray and Lil. Wiping his lips, he smirked. "Well, hello there, cousins, hello partners!"

Murray's head snapped back, and Lil choked on her coffee. "Why, hello, Sam. Cousins, yes. But what do you mean by *partners*?"

Sam regarded them gleefully, and oblivious to the stares of the customers within earshot, said, "We're partners! Take a good look at the Casino contract. You people took me on." He peered at Murray owlishly.

Few things would stop Murray from his Boston cream pie, but now he put down his fork and spoon. "You must be kidding. You're no partner in the Casino Theatre, if that's what you mean! What are you talking about?"

"Have a look for yourself. Meanwhile, enjoy the rest of your meal, and maybe in other circumstances we can discuss our new business relationship." Smugly, Sam returned to an indifferent Eva, who seemed oblivious to her husband's conversation with Murray and Lil.

Is Sam crazy? Murray thought, anger and confusion mounting in him.

"Relax, Murray," Lil said, touching his hand. "Maybe he's just being a tease. Still, you have to admit he has a certain charm."

"Charm, schmarm! I'm going to get our contract tomorrow and see what he's talking about! I hope it isn't something else Lou's cooked up. The last thing I need is Sam interfering in the operation of the theatre."

Murray and Lil quickly left the table, and as they walked through the crowded restaurant toward the door, Sam called out, "Have a nice evening, partners!"

The following morning, Murray checked his copy of the Casino agreement. As he expected, there was no mention of Sam Appelbaum anywhere. He then called Gersten Allen, who managed financial affairs for the Allen Group.

"Gersten, I need to compare your copy of the Casino agreement with ours. I think there might be a problem. I'll be at your office at two o'clock, if that's convenient for you."

Sounding a bit surprised, Gersten said, "Certainly, if you insist, Murray."

Later that afternoon, when Murray and Gersten sat down in the Allen head office on Carlton Street to examine the Allens' copy of the Casino contract, sure enough, attached to the final page was an addendum signed by Esther Appleby, Lou Appleby, Murray Little, and Lil Little, naming Sam Appelbaum as a new partner of the Roxy Theatre Management Company. As such, the man was entitled to share in the company's interest in the Casino. Murray couldn't believe his eyes! "Where the hell did this addendum come from, Gersten?"

"I don't know, Murray. It's been there from the beginning, hasn't it?"

"It sure hasn't!" Murray shouted. "The Casino's lawyers should have the original version, shouldn't they?"

"Yes, of course, they will. Let me get on the blower to Sidney Rosenthal."

Gersten's secretary put him through. "Sid, could you dig up the Casino contract? I need to check something. It's very important. I'll hold the line while you're searching."

While Gersten was on hold, Murray paced the plush office carpet.

"You've got it?" Gersten said. "Look at the last page. Is it an addendum naming Sam Appelbaum as a new partner of the Roxy Theatre Management Company?" There was a slight pause. "It is?" Gersten turned to Murray. "It's confirmed, Murray. Sam Appelbaum's listed as a partner in your company."

Hot with anger, Murray addressed Gersten, who seemed surprised himself. "Somehow Sam Appelbaum, who brought us into the Casino in the first place, has managed to cut himself in through us! None of us — Lou, Lil, Esther, or myself — have ever set eyes on this addendum. He's forged our signatures and managed to stick this addendum onto the original contract. I can't imagine how!"

Murray returned to the Casino and immediately went upstairs to

Lou's office where he found Lou seated in the small sofa at the back of the office polishing a Winchester hunting rifle.

"How do you like my new baby," asked Lou, grinning broadly. "Just got it today, and I can't wait to go out with Willie and the gang from City Hall. Before we know it, it'll be deer-hunting season!"

"Look, Lou, I've got more important matters to discuss than your deer hunting."

Lou seemed disappointed. "How so?"

"I've just been with Gersten Allen and guess what? Your cousin, Sam Appelbaum, has forged our signatures — yours, Lil's, Esther's, and mine — and made himself a partner of the Roxy Theatre Management Company!"

"He did what?"

"He's made himself a partner of ours through forgery. I've just checked the original contract and the Allens' copy and each has an addendum naming Sam a Roxy partner. There's no such addendum on our copy. It's unbelievable, but somehow he's managed to pull it off."

Apoplectic with rage, Sam leaped from the sofa, grabbed the Winchester, pointed it at the door, and screamed, "I'll kill that bastard, cousin or no cousin!"

"For God's sake, Lou, this isn't the time for emotional threats. Put that rifle down! We need to get started on a plan of action so we can straighten out this ridiculous situation."

Lou dropped the Winchester on the sofa and reached for his Johnnie Walker on the desk.

Murray continued. "We'll have to get hold of Joe Sedgwick first, of course, and we'll probably want to get a handwriting expert to prove the signatures are forgeries. This could turn out to be a very messy business, Lou, especially since Sam's a cousin. There could be one hell of a family ruckus over this!"

Lou's eyes were ablaze with anger. "Some cousin! And some partner he'd make! That sneaky son of a bitch. How dare he?" Lou huffed. "I don't care what the family says. I say put him in jail and throw away the key!"

"Let's see what our lawyer has to say first. I'll call Joe right now."

Lou regained his composure long enough to ask, "How the hell did you find out about this?"

Murray described the encounter in Bassel's Restaurant, then repeated, "Let me talk to Sedgwick to see what action we should take."

"Okay, do that. But then let's skin him alive! And who cares what the family says."

Lou sat on the sofa and resumed polishing his Winchester as Murray quickly departed the office.

37

TRIP TO BUFFALO

Esther wasn't pleased. "You're going to Buffalo every Saturday and taking Lil and Barry with you? What you and Lil do is your own business. If you want to disobey God and ride on a Saturday, well that's up to you. I've about given up on you both. But to take young Barry, my father's namesake who I hope and pray will someday be a rabbi, how could you? He should be attending synagogue and doing his Hebrew studies! I just don't understand your godlessness, Murray."

Having half expected this confrontation, Murray was ready for his mother-in-law this time. "Listen, Esther, it's very important for business that I go to Buffalo. And as for Barry, as soon as he heard our plans, he insisted on coming along. Gerry's too wrapped up with Boy Scouts right now, but I expect he'll want to come with us sometimes, as will Alan when he's old enough. You must know by now that Gerry and Barry haven't shown an interest in attending synagogue. They don't understand what's going on there and don't like the atmosphere. Lil and I won't be dragged into a synagogue against our will, either. You must understand that you don't have to go to synagogue to be a good Jew!"

The Sunday morning parlour debate was heating up dangerously.

"The boys must have bar mitzvahs. Murray. It's unthinkable that you'd even consider they wouldn't."

Murray stood his ground, aware he was close to shouting. "When have I ever said that? You know full well that Gerry and Barry are attending religious school after regular school during the week and are also going there on Sunday mornings. But you must understand that they're not attending because of any great interest in Judaic studies! They're preparing for their bar mitzvahs to make everybody happy, truth be told. And I'm sure the same will be true for Alan later on."

Esther was shaking. "I never dreamed my daughter would marry such a godless man!"

It was time to tone things down. "You needn't worry about the boys," he said softly. "They're going to grow up to be good men, synagogue or no synagogue. Of course, our boys will have bar mitzvahs. But taking them to Buffalo will be an educational experience for them, and I'm not trying to be funny, Esther. I want them to have good educations, but I also want them to see the real world. If they attend synagogue, it will be their decision — not mine, not yours!"

"Murray, you've created a house of sin here." Clearly unable to say more, Esther stomped out of the room and slammed the parlour doors with enough force to rattle the Passover plates and dishes shelved in their separate cabinet at the back of the parlour. She stormed down the hallway and poked her head into the kitchen where Anna and Samuel were having their Sunday morning breakfast. "Can't you do something about that son of yours?" she demanded. "Our household's godless enough as it is!"

Anna and Samuel were caught off guard. Rarely had they seen such an explosion from Esther.

"You speak to him," Esther goaded. "He's your godless son. Tell him how important it is to have some *Yiddishkeit!*"

Just finishing his tea out of a saucer, Samuel looked up half apologetically at Esther. "Well, we did try with Murray. And as you know, we also tried with our older daughter, Mary, but she simply ran away from home."

Esther retreated upstairs.

Lil stared out the front-room window. "You'll never change my mother."

Murray paused before responding thoughtfully. "There's no changing that entire generation."

The following Saturday, Murray, Lil, and Barry left for Buffalo, taking the recently opened Queen Elizabeth Highway extending from Toronto to the Peace Bridge at Fort Erie, Ontario, allowing a quick, comfortable, scenic drive. The family's newly acquired Plymouth sedan made the excursion all the more enjoyable.

"We won't have time today to look at Niagara Falls," Murray explained to Barry, who was riding in the back seat. "I'll be busy all day. But while I'm at the theatre, you can go shopping with your mother if you like. Next time I promise you we'll see the Falls."

"Oh, no!" Barry retorted. "Do I have to go shopping? I'd rather go with you, Dad."

Lil glanced at Murray curiously. "Do you think it's all right, Murray? The Palace isn't the Casino, you know."

"Sure. Barry's almost nine and mature for his age, don't you think?"

Lil was less enthusiastic. "Well, if you say so, Murray, but I'm a little concerned about what his grandparents might say."

Murray almost laughed. "Your mother's a prude and out of touch with reality. I don't care what she thinks."

"Well, what about *your* parents?"

Murray grabbed the steering wheel more intensely and accelerated somewhat, trying to contain his annoyance. "They're a lot more open-minded about nudity than you might think, Lil."

The family arrived at the Peace Bridge around noon.

"Can you tell me how to get to the Palace Theatre on Main Street?" Murray asked a U.S. customs officer at the far end of the bridge.

A broad smile spread across the officer's face. "Oh, yeah, sure, everybody knows the Palace! Just take Niagara Street over to your right and keep going until you hit Main Street, then make a hard left. You can't miss it. It's about five blocks up."

"There it is!" Barry yelled a little later as Murray cautiously made his way north on Main. What the place lacked in size it made up for in magnanimous gaudiness. The exterior of the narrow building was framed by two Doric pillars, while its facade was plastered with pictures of half-naked women in seductive poses. This week's feature attraction was comic Bob Ferguson along with stripper and "talking woman" Mary Murray.

When Murray and Barry entered Dewey Michaels's office, they found a man who looked more like a Bay Street broker in Toronto than a burlesque house manager. Michaels was immaculately turned out in a tight blue suit complete with bow tie and spats. His office wall was covered with eight-by-ten glossies of some of the performers, while his desk was neatly stacked with papers and numerous pencils and pens, all placed compulsively in a series of rows.

Dewey greeted them warmly. "It's a pleasure to meet you, Murray, and you, too, sonny. Lou Appleby called and told me the troubles you're having back in Toronto. Those churchmen are too much, aren't they? You know, we've had our troubles here in New York State, but so far in Buffalo the church types have left us alone."

He sat down, leaned back, and started reminiscing. "Back in 1937, it wasn't the church that put the kibosh on burlesque. It was the Shuberts who wanted the Minsky brothers out of New York. The Minsky boys with their striptease were cutting into the Shuberts' theatre business. So the New York mayor at the time and still the mayor, Fiorello La Guardia, and his licence commissioner then, a guy named Moss, ran the boys out of town. Would you believe, it got so bad that across the river in Jersey, several theatres began running burlesque and had shuttle buses operating from Times Square to Jersey. You've got to give those Minskys credit!

"Have a look at the show, then come backstage and I'll introduce you to the performers and you can go over what you think is appropriate. Here in Buffalo we don't think we're corrupting public morals … unless exotic dancing is immoral. We think we're running a pretty classy theatre here. Bud Abbott and Lou Costello have played our theatre a number of times, and look at them now. Movie stars no less!"

Murray almost envied him his location: Buffalo was a pretty slick place. "Well, Dewey, Toronto's known as a city of churches, as you've no doubt heard, and it's a lot stuffier than Buffalo."

Michaels smiled at him sympathetically. "I have to admit, Murray,

I don't know very much about Toronto. People here are more worried about the war these days, even though right now the town's booming. Many think we're going to find ourselves involved in that stupid war with Hitler and Mussolini. And a lot of people are angry with FDR and his dumb Lend-Lease plan for England. Mind you, they're not unhappy with their paycheques from Curtis Bell and Bethlehem Steel, are they? Personally, I think those companies are just merchants of death, but who am I to talk morals."

"The war has changed things as well in Toronto," Murray said. "We're doing terrific business! A lot of our patrons are servicemen on leave or going overseas, passing through Toronto on their way to Montreal and then by boat to England."

Michaels seemed uncomfortable. "Enough politics, Murray. Why don't you and your son go upstairs and catch the show and I'll pick you up later and take you backstage to say hello to Bob and Mary?" Dewey was about to open the door of the office when he stopped short. "By the way, Murray, Appleby told me some time ago about his father's murder years ago. Have they found the killer yet? Lou seemed to think it was his dad's partner who did it."

"No, the murder remains a mystery. I doubt they'll ever find out who did it. And Avner's death and the way it happened has had a terrible effect on Lou, as well as on Avner's wife, Esther, and on my own wife, Lil. I don't know whether any of them will ever recover from it."

"Don't the Mounties always get their man up in Canada, Murray?"

Michaels's clumsy attempt at humour wasn't appreciated by Murray. "That's only in the movies. If it weren't for the murder, my life would certainly have been a lot easier."

"I'm sorry, Murray. Them's the breaks. I have to tell you, though, that the performers all tell me they have no problems with you when they're playing Toronto, if that's any consolation."

"Well, it's a job and quite frankly only a few of the performers are a problem. It's the pressure from my partners that's the real headache."

"We seldom have trouble with the performers here, either. Most are real pros, hard-working, decent, just in a different kind of business from most people. Occasionally, one of the strippers might get a little racy and suggestive … a bit too much of the old bump-and-grind. I think the girls do it as a joke. Problem is, the audience doesn't always get it. So we have to get them to tone it down. And the occasional comic goes over the top, of course. Some of the lines are quite funny, clever even, but we try to keep them respectable." Dewey emphasized this with some pride. "Look, I'll meet you in the lobby after the show. How's that? It begins in a few minutes."

Murray and Barry made their way to the back of the theatre. The house lights were still up, and walking up the two aisles were candy butchers holding trays at their waists containing a variety of items the two men were hawking to the predominantly male audience. "Candy bars, cigarettes, exciting potions from the East, postcards you'll be sure to enjoy."

Barry turned to his father. "How come we don't do that in our theatre?"

Murray wasn't surprised by the question. "We're not allowed to sell in the aisles in Toronto. And we're certainly not permitted to sell magic potions … things like that."

"Dad, why don't you buy a couple of those potions? I'd sure like to know what they are!"

Murray frowned. "I don't think so! It's enough having you here in the theatre."

"Do you mean there's something I shouldn't see, Dad?"

"Well, not exactly …" Murray wondered how best to put it. "Between you and me, I think if your mother saw we'd bought any of those items, she'd be upset."

And that ended the conversation for the moment.

There were three strippers on the bill — and lots of hooting and shouting from the audience as the dancers paraded their wares. So unlike Toronto patrons, Murray thought. The strippers seemed to be having fun as they minced and gyrated around the stage to an overly loud four-piece band. Each of the performers seemed to have some kind of gimmick. The first one was able to quiver her torso, twirling tassels in opposite directions on each breast. The second offered a prolonged Eastern-style belly dance. It wasn't until the final stripper appeared that Murray became uncomfortable. The striptease was performed in the dark, with each item of clothing removed by a pair of phosphorescent hands. The act ended with the stripper apparently totally nude except for two glowing hands on her breasts.

There were no vaudeville acts, either, just a small chorus of half a dozen girls who performed two "production" numbers. Bob Ferguson and Mary Murray and the house singer did three fairly straightforward burlesque skits.

Listening carefully for any profanity, Murray was pleased. The word *hell* wasn't used at all, not even in the sketch in which buxom Mary strutted across the stage, dropped her purse, and Ferguson, returning it to her, said, "I beg your pardon," trying to be polite.

Mary then turned to him and asked, "What are you begging for? You're old enough to ask for it."

At that juncture, Ferguson turned to the audience. "What the hey!"

Murray could tell that Barry loved every minute of it.

After the production, Murray and Michaels went backstage, leaving Barry to sit through another session of the candy butchers and a third-rate B movie.

Backstage, Murray and Bob Ferguson greeted each other. Ferguson used his standard line. "You know, Murray, if Bob Hope had my material, he'd be playing the Palace and the Casino."

Murray, who always enjoyed Bob's company, said softly, "Look, Bob, I'm kind of embarrassed being here, but I'm here for a reason. Recently, we had trouble in Toronto with our goody-two-shoes clergy and the Police Commission. They're putting pressure on us and threatening to cancel our licence because we're supposedly offering the public filthy material ... corrupting public morals."

Ferguson nodded understandingly. "They're doing a La Guardia on you."

"Looks like it. But as far as I could see, none of the comic sketches here were filthy. Even the potato masher scene seemed acceptable to me."

Ferguson laughed. "You mean the one where the punch line was 'You know where you can put that potato masher'?"

"Yes, that's the one. I did have a little trouble with the last stripper on the card, though. The hands on the breasts are out of line for Toronto. That act could turn our place into a parking lot."

"Hey, that's a good line, Murray. Mind if I use it sometime? The strip in the dark? That's Joy you're talking about. She isn't coming to Toronto with us. So you don't have to worry."

Satisfied, Murray said, "So we'll see you and Mary up in Toronto next Thursday then."

Saying goodbye to Ferguson and Michaels, he hurried back to the auditorium to retrieve Barry. "Well, how did you enjoy the show?" he asked his son. Barry's answer surprised him.

"It wasn't as good as the ones I've seen at the Casino."

"Why not?"

"There wasn't enough singing and music and the jokes were kind of corny. But I'd still like to know what those guys were selling."

Murray attempted to skip over the last issue. "The potions and little packages are for older people, Barry."

"Even the postcards?" the boy asked in mock innocence.

Murray sighed. "Let's meet your mother and have a nice evening at the Town Casino."

Lil was loaded with shopping bags when they found her at the front of the theatre. She had a broad smile on her face, but Murray soon erased that. He was extremely annoyed. "Just how much did you buy? It looks like you've bought out all of Berger … and Adam, Meldrum & Anderson, too!"

"I just needed something to cheer me up," Lil retorted.

Murray tried to mollify his snap response to Lil's shopping spree. "Just how happy do you want to be?"

Lil chose to ignore the question and turned to Barry instead. "Here, Barry, give me a hand with the packages. Let's head for dinner and the early show at the Town Casino. I'm hungry and really looking forward to seeing Sophie Tucker!"

When they finally left for home, the drive to Toronto seemed endless, despite the smooth new highway. To make matters worse, it had started to rain, so visibility was no more than twenty feet. Murray, ever cautious, drove his Plymouth at the minimal speed. The three occupants being exhausted, conversation was sparse. Lil was still smarting over Murray's terse comments about her shopping excesses, while Barry ruminated about his experience at the Palace Theatre. "Dad, are the same people coming to our theatre?"

"No, not all of them. They're not all on the circuit. For example, that lady who danced in the dark …"

Barry ventured with obvious disappointment, "I really liked that lady with the gloves who shone in the dark. I hope she's coming to Toronto, Dad."

"Well, she's not!" Murray snapped.

Barry knew well enough to change the subject. "That big lady at the Town Casino, Sophie Tucker, what was she saying that was so funny? I couldn't figure out what the people were laughing at."

"Her material is for grown-ups, Barry," Murray replied. "It's what we consider *sophisticated*. She's a very well-known performer and has what we call a *class act*."

Barry hesitated for a moment before asking, "Dad, will our theatre ever have class acts?"

Murray glanced at his son sadly. "Probably not, unless something changes dramatically."

The car continued its crawl, and there were no more theatrical post-mortems.

38

LIQUOR MACHINATIONS

Several weeks later, Murray learned that he had become the de facto manager of the New Statler Hotel. Money from the bank now being available, along with Lou and Ollie Baskin, Murray was working almost around the clock. The war in Europe was a planet away; the real war was on Queen Street, with its second front at the Grace Street homestead.

The New Statler Hotel at 112 Queen Street West was a ramshackle three-storey cube of nondescript design with a large dining room managed, paradoxically, by a first-class international European chef, a culinary maestro who had escaped to Canada from Germany just before the outbreak of war. Excellent food, nightly dancing, and a very busy beer parlour quickly turned the hotel, as expected, into a meeting place for a heterogeneous array of customers, including Osgoode Hall professors, law students, civil servants, hustlers, street bookies, servicemen, and the occasional hooker.

Each of the twenty tiny rooms was neat and tidy, many being booked twice a day, servicing, as it were, the needs of the local clientele. Sprucing up the hotel's atmosphere and clientele was, of course, a necessary step toward acquiring from the Liquor Control Board of Ontario a beverage licence allowing them to serve cocktails. And more specifically, currying the favour and good graces of the LCBO's chairman, Judge Walter Robb, the man about whom Ollie joked, "Don't you mean *robber*?" when referring to the man.

Murray enjoyed the occasional gourmet meal prepared by Hans Freed, the master chef of the New Statler. Once Murray learned that his $10,000 loan was approved, he arranged to meet Ollie and Lou in what was now his favourite dining room.

Ollie greeted Murray with a forceful slap on the back. "How the hell are you, you son of a bitch? I hear you got the money. Lou's got the cash, and we're all set to renovate this joint."

The three men sat at the table as Ollie nursed his still-illegal noon-time martini, prepared for him by Shoozie, the hotel's bartender.

Murray eyed the martini with dismay. He was feeling tired and knew he appeared haggard. "Look, Ollie, don't you think you're taking a bit of a risk using the name *Statler*. The Statler hotel chain is big in the States, and they could come after you for using their name."

"What the hell's wrong with you, Murray?" Ollie snarled. "Can't you read? I've got *New* in front of *Statler!*"

Murray's exasperation increased. There was no talking to this guy. "Have it your way, but just remember that I warned you, and I'm a partner in this enterprise. I've already got enough responsibility on my plate. I don't need any additional aggravation."

Ollie gulped down the remains of his first martini of the afternoon.

"Listen, Four Eyes," he growled, pushing himself back from the chair and standing to assume his best pugilistic stance, "you ought to consider yourself bloody lucky to be part of this deal at all. I told you we're going to make a lot of money in this hotel, so quit being so goddamn negative."

"Fine, have it your way, Ollie."

Baskin sat down and grabbed a passing waitress by the buttocks. "Sweetheart, get Shoozie to bring me another martini."

Getting involved with this character may have been a very bad move, Murray mused. *I don't know whether he's more attracted to the smell of money, perfume, or resin liniment.*

Murray was in no mood to argue, but Ollie was on a roll. "Do you realize that those sons of bitches at the LCBO have got everybody in this town by the short and curlies? Just a couple of months ago, they banned the dancing and floor show at a joint on King Street. So now there are only five hotels in this entire city where dancing and floor shows are allowed. That's the kind of authority this board has!" Ollie pounded the table with a meaty fist. "So we've got to look nice and clean."

The best place to start is with you, Ollie, Murray thought, considering the man's personal disregard for the province's liquor laws.

The waitress returned with the men's luncheon orders. Ollie grabbed Murray's hand as he was about to savour his eggs Benedict. "You see? This ain't no greasy spoon. Just look at the classy way Hans puts together your eggs!"

Murray remained controlled. "Yes, I can see, Ollie. Now may I be allowed to taste."

"Hey, hey, listen to him," said Ollie as he munched on his own Dagwood sandwich.

No wonder they need me as a front man, Murray mused. *With behaviour like this, Ollie can never appear before a licensing commission. He's so rough and tactless! The sooner I finish my lunch the better.*

As Murray pondered his fate with his ill-conceived New Statler trinity, a pretty young face appeared seemingly out of nowhere. "Hi, Lou, I just dropped in to grab a quick bite before the first show."

Lou turned crimson. It was his friend, Helen, one of Lester Montgomery's fourteen Casino chorines. Caught off guard, he stammered, "You … you know Ollie, of course, and Murray Little. Pull up a chair and join us."

Have I stumbled into some kind of tryst? Murray wondered. *I think the best thing I can do is get out of here.* He bolted down his lunch as swiftly as he could and excused himself from the table.

Scurrying across Queen Street, Murray took pleasure in scanning his theatre's marquee. This week they boasted a stage show offering a new high in entertainment, featuring Stella Mills, the Thrill of Thrills, and Pinky Lee, the Ambassador of Mirth, as well as the Fourteen Montgomeryettes and a grand cast of thirty-five. It was just before 1:00 p.m., and there was already a lineup of servicemen anxious to catch the first show of the day.

At least we're making some people happy! he reflected.

39

NEW YORK BOUND

It was Monday morning, and with the kids at school and Murray already at the theatre, the Grace Street home was quiet. Esther stood in the front living room with Lil, awaiting a taxi to take her to Union Station, the first step on her trip to Miami via New York.

The taxi pulled up at the house. "Let me help you with the bags, Ma," Lil insisted. "Remember, it's gate 3 at Grand Central Station at 12:30 tomorrow, the special express to Miami. Here's your ticket. I'll come down to Union with you." Lil glanced at her watch, then did a last-minute check, first in the front living room, then in the hallway, realizing something with a shock. "Ma, you've only got the one bag packed!"

"I'm going to Miami, not the North Pole!" Esther shook her head before adding sarcastically, "I'm sure I've got enough *schmattas* for

Miami, and if not, Sarah, for sure, will lend me anything extra I might need."

At the station, Lil waved goodbye to her mother as the redcap picked up Esther's valise. Her mother was wearing a black shawl, and Lil couldn't help but think, *She looks more like one of those war refugees in the movies than a vacationer! But I envy her. How I wish I could go, too.*

With her mother safely on the train, Lil focused on the voice of a newspaper boy in the distance, shouting the day's headlines. "Duce ship sunk, crowded Duce ship sunk."

Puzzled by this, she approached the lad, who was busy negotiating change and handing out papers at the station's main entrance. She handed him three cents for a copy and whispered to him, "What does Duce mean?"

"Don't you know, lady? Il Duce. That's what they call Mussolini, Hitler's pal in the war." He continued advertising his wares. "Read all about it — Duce ship sunk, crowded Duce ship sunk."

That night, Lil told Murray she had a strange foreboding when she left her mother. "I don't know, Murray. I had the weirdest feeling when I left my mother at the train station. I can't explain it, but I had a sense that something bad was going to happen. I don't know why. It was just one of those odd feelings."

The following morning, at about eight o'clock, the upstairs phone rang in the hallway, just outside the main bedroom at the top of the stairs. Lil leaped to answer it with some trepidation. A voice with a New York accent was at the other end. "I have a collect call for Mrs. Lil Little from an Esther Appleby," he said. "Will you accept the call?"

"Yes, of course." Lil was flustered, even though she'd told her mother to call her when she arrived in New York. "Hello, Ma. Are you all right?"

"Of course, I am! I'm calling from Grand Central just like you asked. I'll be boarding the train for Miami at gate 3 at nine o'clock. You see? Could be I'm more independent than you thought."

"I'm not surprised you're managing. Just call me when you arrive in Miami."

"Give your brother a call, look after the boys, and tell Murray not to work so hard." There was a slight pause. "And don't forget to see that Gerry and Barry attend their religious school. Passover is soon and the dishes have to be changed."

"Fine, Ma. I won't forget. Let me know if you need anything."

In the bathroom, Murray poked his head out the door, face slathered in shaving cream. "Everything okay with your mother?"

"So far so good," Lil answered tersely.

The clerk behind the desk snatched the ticket from Esther's hand. "The Empire Express leaves in half an hour at one o'clock, and you're in coach 10, Pullman first class."

That's my daughter, thought Esther. *So like her father — buys me a first-class ticket.*

Esther made her way to the well-upholstered seat that Lil had reserved. A porter saw to it that she was comfortably seated and placed her valise in a special storage compartment at the rear of the railcar.

About five minutes before the train was to depart on its southern journey to Florida, a balding middle-aged man and his companion, a much younger female with platinum hair, seated themselves directly across the aisle from Esther.

She stared at the couple. The man seemed oddly familiar to her, but she wasn't certain who he was. She thought she'd heard his voice before, perhaps over the telephone.

"Put your bags away, Loretta," the man said. "Let's head for the club car."

As the train pulled out of Grand Central, the couple left their seats, and Esther focused her attention on praying. Her oft-repeated morning prayer words seemed distant somehow, almost hollow and meaningless, as she wrestled with the notion of the identity of the passengers across the aisle. Who were they? Why did she recall that voice? How would she know anyone like him, anyway? He didn't look Jewish. She must be mistaken. Esther tried to get her mind off the intrigue, but the sound of the stranger's voice reverberated in her mind. *It'll come to me. He'll be back and I'll give his voice a real good listen.*

Esther buried herself in her prayer book, occasionally glancing out the train window at the passing American countryside but more often looking toward the door leading to the club car. She dozed intermittently as the Express churned its way down the Eastern Seaboard. Eating non-kosher food in the dining car would contravene dietary laws, so Esther had brought along some Hershey chocolate bars and a thermos filled with tea, which she felt would sustain her for the two-day journey.

When Esther retired to her Pullman bed shortly after sunset and her evening prayers, the two strangers still hadn't returned to their seats. Sleep was held in abeyance, though, as she continued to ruminate about the couple's identity. *They couldn't have got off the train. There have been no stops since we got on. That's not until tomorrow morning.*

In the morning, Esther breakfasted on a chocolate bar and a cup of lukewarm tea out of her thermos as the redcap disassembled the Pullman compartment. Much to her surprise, the mysterious couple were already dressed and seated across the aisle. She listened attentively, but they spoke in whispers, so she couldn't make out what they were saying. Esther's curiosity was palpable. She searched for some pretence to hear the man's voice once again. Finally, unable to restrain herself further, she leaned across the aisle. "Excuse me, sir. Do you have the correct time?"

The man turned to his right, and their eyes locked for what seemed to Esther like an eternity. He glanced at his watch. "It's 7:30 in the morning, lady."

Esther fumbled for words. "I'm going to Miami and am due to arrive at nine o'clock at night. I guess I'll have to get my wristwatch fixed when I get there."

The man seemed annoyed. "Yeah, I guess you will."

It was early afternoon before the train reached the Georgia-Florida border and the porter announced that the train would be stopping at Jacksonville at three o'clock. The announcement jarred Esther from her dozing state.

The man across the aisle turned to his companion. "Loretta, we're getting off very soon. Have you got everything?"

A soft voice answered, "Of course, I have, Fred."

It couldn't be! A startled Esther heard her pulse pound in her ears. Fred Piton! She was sure of it. Esther was consumed with shock and rage. The man who had murdered her husband was sitting right across from her! She struggled for several minutes to regain some control, then turned to the couple again. "Are you people from Toronto?"

The man looked at his lady companion before answering, then stared at his pesky inquisitor. "We've been there …"

"Did you ever hear of the Roxy Theatre?"

"The what?"

"The Roxy Theatre."

"Never heard of it!" The man returned his attention to his partner, making it clear he was in no mood to answer any more questions.

"Jacksonville, Florida!" the conductor bellowed as the train slowly approached a station platform. With that announcement, the couple quickly leaped up and headed toward their stored baggage near the car exit. Neither looked back at her.

To Esther, following their every movement with eagle eyes, it seemed as though the couple flew off the train when it finally stopped at the platform. She peered out the window to see if she could keep track of the departing couple. *I can't see them. God has arranged for this meeting and has asked me to do something! It's that goy, Piton, and a no-good shiksa friend. I should have challenged him about Avner. He was lying about Toronto and not knowing the Roxy.* Esther quickly glanced at her watch. *I've got five minutes. I'm getting off the train and deal with him face to face.*

Esther got to her feet, but no sooner had she stood than the train suddenly lurched forward, hurling her to the floor. She screamed in pain. "My leg, my leg!"

Several passengers rushed to her as she lay on the floor clutching her left thigh. "You okay, ma'am?" the conductor asked, arriving on the scene almost immediately. "We have a doctor on board. I'll get him to come immediately." The conductor glanced at the small crowd that had gathered. "If the folks here can give me a hand, we can put you onto this seat until he arrives."

Esther was in double agony. *First, I miss my chance to confront that monster, Piton, and now this!*

Within minutes, a small man who identified himself as a doctor from New York on his way to Miami arrived. He even spoke some Yiddish.

"Tell me where it hurts and let me have a look," the doctor said in Yiddish. He touched the left thigh gently as Esther lay motionless and half anaesthetized by the events that had just taken place. "Missus, this could be just a bad bruise, but I suspect you've broken your hip bone. We can make you comfortable until we get to Miami, which I think would be the best place to get an X-ray. We won't have to stop the train and take you off here. I'll arrange with the conductor to call ahead and have an ambulance ready at the station for you."

Esther couldn't believe her bad luck. What had she done to deserve this?

When the train pulled into the station, two ambulance attendants boarded it, and Esther was quickly taken to Miami General where X-rays revealed a fracture of the left hip.

"You won't need an operation," the surgeon told her, "but we'll have to put your hip in a plaster cast for six weeks. And you'll have to stay in bed while it heals here in hospital."

◆ ◆ ◆

Cousin Sarah, who had been waiting patiently for Esther at the station, had no idea that the ambulance she'd noticed in passing had been arranged for her cousin. Failing to locate Esther, she placed a call to Lil in Toronto. "I'm worried, Lil. Your mother wasn't on the train as arranged."

"That's impossible!" cried Lil. "I spoke to her just before she boarded in New York."

Sarah had a sudden recollection. "Wait, Lil, there was an ambulance at the station."

"For goodness' sake, Aunty Sarah! Check the hospitals and call me right back."

About an hour transpired before Sarah called again. "Lil, I've got some bad news. Your mother's in Miami General Hospital. She broke her leg and they've put her in a big cast. She's going to have to be there for six weeks. She's very uncomfortable but says, God willing, she'll be fine."

"Oh, my God! Tell Ma I'm taking the next plane out of Toronto."

Lil quickly called Murray at the theatre to tell him the news. "I'm going to try to get a flight to New York tonight and hopefully I'll be in Miami by tomorrow evening. Your mother and father can look after the kids. I'll call Lou and start packing, so if I'm not home this evening, you'll know why."

Arriving in Miami the following evening, Lil took a room at the elegant art deco Blackstone Hotel. With great trepidation, the next morning she visited her mother. "You know, Ma, I'm not really that superstitious, but I had such a strange feeling before you left that I actually told Murray about it. I felt something awful might happen, and I guess it did." She glanced around the room. "But it could be much worse. You're obviously in very good hands now. I'm staying at a lovely hotel not far from here, and I'll leave you my phone number so you can call me any time if you need anything."

"Well, God willing, I'll get better. But you know, on the way down, I was sitting across from a couple, and I'm absolutely sure it was Fred Piton and his girlfriend. I wanted to let him know how I felt about your father's death, but I missed my chance. He got off the train, so I decided to go after him. But when I stood up, the train suddenly started, and that's when I fell. My luck!"

Lil tried to comfort her. "You would've been wasting your time, Ma. Even if it was him — and I'm not saying it wasn't — he would've just denied anything you would've said to him. And besides, the police were never able to find any evidence against Piton. So what could you do, anyway?"

Esther sighed. "Maybe lay the guilt on his soul, if he has one."

"Oh, before I forget, how's Aunty Sarah?"

"She's visited me three times already after finding me here. She's fine. I'm the one with the problem."

Lil returned to her hotel to find a small note slipped under the door. She picked it up anxiously and read: "Call Murray as soon as you can. Barry's ill."

Lil dialled the telephone, hands trembling. *My God, what next? What's going on?*

"Operator, I wish to call collect to Mr. Murray Little at the Casino Theatre in Toronto in Canada. Please, operator this is an urgent call."

The voice sounded disinterested. "I'll do what I can, ma'am. Do you know the number?"

"Yes, yes, of course, it's Waverley 5880. Please hurry, Operator!"

It was late afternoon, and the evening cashier, Honey, was on duty. "Casino Theatre," Lil heard her answer. "Yes, of course, I'll accept a collect call for Mr. Little." There was a pause, then Honey, who was usually unflappable, returned to the line, flustered. "Mr. Little's gone home. Hello, who is this?"

"It's his wife, Lil."

"Hello, Mrs. Little. It's Honey, the cashier. Mr. Little went home a few hours ago. Do you want to speak to Mr. Sherman?"

"No, honey, thank you. I'll get a hold of him at home." Lil could feel her heart pound as she asked the operator to redirect her call to Grace Street.

Anna answered the telephone. "Murray's upstairs with the doctor and your son." Her voice was tense. "Hold on. I'll get him."

When Murray came to the phone, he sounded breathless to Lil, having likely flown down the stairs to grab the telephone. "Lil, Barry's been running a fever and complaining of a sore throat ever since you left. I had Dr. Shaul see him this morning, and he thought he heard a faint heart murmur. He's called in Dr. Hepburn, a heart specialist from Toronto General. Dr. Hepburn's here right now. He thinks Barry has a mild case of rheumatic fever and wants him to stay in bed for at least six to eight weeks. When I told him you were in Miami, he suggested that rest in a warm climate might be even better for Barry."

"Is he going to be all right?" Lil asked anxiously.

"The doctor thinks his chances are very good for an excellent recovery."

"But can he travel?"

"The doctor says he's not that seriously ill and can travel. He just doesn't want things to get worse and doesn't want to take any chances. You know, develop a serious heart murmur."

Lil knew what she had to do. "Murray, bring him down here. I'll rent a larger apartment and look after him. How about Gerry and Alan? Are they okay?"

"Yes, they're in great shape. I think my parents can handle them by themselves. If Barry has a better chance in a warmer climate, he's better off with you. As soon as you've found an apartment, let me know and I'll bring Barry down. And as far as the theatre's concerned, my absence for a few days or a week won't make any difference. Dave Sherman's very reliable. The place isn't going to collapse without me." Almost parenthetically, Murray added, "By the way, how's your mother doing?"

"She's comfortable and seems resigned. Give my love to Barry, Alan, and Gerry."

Lil found a large apartment — a perfect spot, quiet, and right on the beach at the corner of Ocean Drive and Fourth Street in Miami Beach.

Murray and Barry arrived in Miami a week later. Prior to this, the farthest Barry had been from home was Buffalo, so Murray knew the train ride down the U.S. East Coast was a great adventure for him. When they arrived in Miami at night, Barry said, "It's just like the Land of Oz." Ensconced in the back of the taxi on the way to meet his mother, Murray could tell his son was in awe at the plethora of colours and lights of the magical city.

"Look, Dad, so many white buildings! And look over there!" He pointed to the Blackstone Hotel. "I've never seen such a big neon sign!"

"That's where your mother was staying before she found the apartment you'll both be living in."

"Will I have to stay in bed for a long time?"

"It will only be for about six weeks, and I'm sure the time will pass very quickly. Your mother and I have discussed getting you into school here as soon as the doctors give us the okay, and we're pretty sure that will be in early spring. I'm going back to Toronto as soon as you're settled. I've got Gerry and Alan and my businesses to look after. Mother, of course, will be with you. I don't know how long Grandma Esther will stay, but I'm sure she won't leave until you're in school. After all, she did come to Florida for a vacation, and having a grandson around would be viewed by her as a bonus, if not a blessing."

40

BACK TO TORONTO

The lonely train trip homeward to Toronto gave Murray a sense of temporary respite from the mental maelstrom in which he'd found himself. He could actually read a newspaper without being interrupted by a call from the theatre or a report from Grace Street that the boys were fighting. And being away from Arthur Cohen and Lou Appleby was a holiday in itself.

Murray retired to the plush smoking car, lit a Sweet Caporal cigarette, and watched the American countryside whip by his window: patches of cotton fields and peanut crops dotted with dilapidated shacks, poor people in ragged clothes seated on porches. Still, it all seemed so peaceful out there. And yet he couldn't help feeling he was in the eye of some kind of mental hurricane.

A tall waiter in a white jacket and black cap interrupted Murray's musings. "Can I get you yesterday's *New York Times, sir? And how about a Canadian Club or Scotch on the rocks?*"

"You can bring me the *Times*, thanks very much, but I can do without the drink."

Canadian Club and Scotch — both reminded him too much of Lou and his cronies. Murray leisurely scanned the newspaper that advertised "All the news that's fit to print." Things seemed to be going from bad to worse: the Balkan countries had joined the Axis, and FDR had signed a Lend-Lease Act authorizing war supplies and materials to the

Allies. This war was very depressing. He could only hope the United States didn't get further involved. *God, we could have a world war!*

Nervously, Murray folded the *Times* and slapped it on the table in front of him. Barry was sick, and he sure didn't like the idea that he and Lil were thousands of miles away from home, especially with the war going on. And God only knew what awaited him when he returned to Toronto. Murray tremulously lit another cigarette. Well, maybe he should be thankful they were on this side of the Atlantic.

He found it strange that his mother-in-law, Esther, never made any reference to her husband's family left behind in Poland. The whole world knew how this maniac Hitler was treating Jews. For all he knew, those Appelbaums in Europe were dead.

Murray pondered that for a moment. Esther was odd and mysterious all right, but come to think of it, his own parents never talked about the family they'd left behind in Russia. His father never spoke about Murray's grandfather, though he did admit once that the man was a grocer and butcher. Murray's mother had once, very reluctantly, told him that her father was a flax dealer. But he'd had to be told by his sister, Mary, that Mother's maiden name was Hillel. Murray sometimes got the feeling that they simply wanted to permanently cut themselves off from the kind of life they'd led in Tsarist Russia. But if that was the case, then why did they hold on to their religious customs and beliefs so tenaciously? That whole generation was a mystery to him!

His ruminations were cut short by the ear-splitting bellow of the conductor: "Toronto next, fifteen minutes. Toronto, next stop, Union Station."

As the rosy fingers of dawn streamed through the window of his carriage, Murray decided: *I'll check with my mother about the kids when I get to the station. Something tells me I'd better go to the theatre first.*

Murray found a pay phone just inside Union Station and called home. His mother answered and sounded a bit out of breath. She was likely cooking up a storm as always: gefilte fish; meat-and-cabbage borscht; potato latkes; baked noodles with raisins and nuts, known as lokshen kugel; stuffed derma or gefilte kishka; and her own special beef stew. Enough food to feed an army brigade.

"Is that you, Murray?" his mother asked. "Is everything all right? How were things in Miami? Did you arrange for doctors for Barry?"

"All in good shape, Ma. Barry's fine. I've made arrangements with some doctors down there to keep an eye on him. Lil's happy to stay on, and Esther's making a speedy recovery. I'm on my way to the theatre now. I'll be home about six for supper with the kids."

"Very good. Pa and the boys are being well looked after by me, of course. By the way, Lou Appleby's called three times since you've been away ... and a man calling himself Oiser or Oscar or something also phoned."

"Thanks, Ma." Murray hung up and hailed a cab just as a light drizzle began. *Ollie calling me at home? Lou, too? Something must be up — naturally!*

"Where to, mister?" the driver shouted.

"The Casino, please, at Bay and Queen."

The taxi driver chuckled. "Oh, everyone knows that place — Toronto's strip joint! You're a bit early, aren't you? You from out of town or something?"

Murray sat in embarrassed silence and didn't respond.

"Yep, a strip joint, all right," the driver continued. "Me and my buddies go there every Thursday night. We're all 4Fs. What are you? Some kind of ... what do you call it ... conscientious objector?"

Murray remained quiet, but the taxi driver didn't seem to notice.

"The Casino, eh? Boy, what a show. Those strippers take their clothes off right down to almost nothing. Gorgeous dames. And there's a chorus line of cuties and great comics. You get your money's worth there, I tell you. You can stay for a second show and the earlier shows have movies. Yep, you really get your money's worth. You ought to see some of the fares I get to and from that place. Big shots — City Hall types, you know. Some people think girls work out of that place. You know how people talk. But I have to tell you, I never pick up hookers there."

Murray's exasperation intensified. "I know all about the Casino! I'm the manager of the place!"

"Christ!" the taxi driver snorted.

Dave Sherman had just opened the theatre doors when Murray

arrived. He seemed grey and haggard and had his first cigar of the day stuck in his mouth. "Murray, Lou and Ollie have been looking for you all week."

"Well, they knew I was away and that you were covering for me, didn't they? I told them that before I left."

"I know, I know. But they still asked me a couple of times! Talking to those guys is like speaking to a pair of empty drums. In one ear and out the other. The shows have gone okay, and the box office's been good. So you don't have any worries there. I've got to tell you, though. I've been a little troubled myself since you've been away …"

"How so?"

"There's been a bit of trouble with one of the Carter brothers. And that might be why Ollie and Lou have been trying to get hold of you."

"The who?"

"You know, those two tough brothers who have been hanging around here for the past couple of months."

"Never noticed them."

"Yeah, well, those two have quite a reputation on the street, I found out. Our caretaker told me they served time for armed robbery. You must have seen them around., Murray. Sharp, good-looking fellows, but greasy, with a real tough, don't-mess-with-me look about them. The older one has tattoos on his arms and always has his sleeves rolled up to show off his muscles."

"Well, what about them?"

"One of them took a shine to Helen in our chorus, and she's been late a couple of times. So Lester Montgomery's been very upset … and maybe more importantly, Lou's upset. I don't know whether it's because of Helen being late for a couple of shows or …" Sherman paused. "You know … Lou and Helen?"

"I must admit I've heard rumours."

"I don't have to tell you about Ollie. He threatened to beat the living crap out of Carter and grabbed him by the neck at the stage door — and one hell of a ruckus broke out. Fortunately, nobody called the cops, and we've got to be thankful for that. We were able to separate the two of them. You could actually hear them fighting out there in the alley from backstage in the theatre. But messing with the Carter brothers has gotta be bad news."

"Dave, if one of our chorus girls wants to get involved with a mug, we can't very well interfere. And if Lester's unsatisfied with Helen, or for that matter anybody else in the chorus, it's up to him to make the decision to fire or not to fire. He can discipline those girls any way he thinks is appropriate. I'll get hold of Ollie and Lou today." Murray glanced at his watch. "It's still a bit early — only ten o'clock. Lou's not in till one. Don't worry. I'll get to the bottom of this. In the meantime, let's go over last week's receipts and check the bookings. You haven't had any trouble with any of the performers clearing customs at the border, have you, Dave?"

"Nope." Sherman continued chewing on his now-unlit cigar while Murray glanced at the previous week's receipts. "Looks very good, Dave. I'm certain Arthur Cohen and the Allens will be tickled pink."

"I'm sure they will, Murray. You know, I see Gersten Allen around here quite a bit, and between you and me, he sometimes looks a little pissed."

Murray lifted a heavy book off the top shelf above his desk and placed it before him. "I'm sorry, but I can't look after everybody's life, for God's sake. Let's see who's coming up at the theatre."

Sherman seemed a little surprised. "What's the trouble, Murray?"

"I just want to double-check who's booked, that's all. You know I have to go to Buffalo to screen these people now, and I like to be prepared. If I know everybody on the bill, I might not have to go traipsing off every week."

Sherman nodded, then said quickly, "Before you leave, Murray, maybe you could give some thought to an idea I've come up with." He paused, perhaps gathering courage. "What would you think about using female ushers? You know — usherettes? I thought that might be kind of unusual, and they might be easier for me to handle, too."

Murray studied him quizzically. "What do you mean by that?"

Sherman laughed nervously. "I don't have to tell you how often we have to change ushers. They're always in trouble, and Lou's always interfering, getting them to run messages for him, place bets, buy bottles of Scotch after hours. I don't know … Somehow I think girls might be more reliable and a hell of a lot more attractive for our customers. Maybe give the place a bit of class."

"That's actually not a bad idea, Dave," Murray said slowly. "But I think I'd be a little worried about girls going up and down the aisles, especially during the first show when the audience is almost all male, and a bunch of rambunctious ones at that. We could be asking for trouble. Besides, we get a bunch of servicemen in here. I don't know. I don't really want to take chances."

"Fine, have it your way. I've got things to do." Obviously annoyed, Sherman slammed the door as he left the office.

Having enough on his mind, Murray returned to sifting through the booking roster. They had Charmaine and Joe DeRita and a couple of good singing acts. So far so good. Milt Shuster in Chicago was bringing in some new strippers — Mae Brown, a "spicy new Brevitease." What did that mean? There was a black-and-white revue — the Cotton Pickers featuring "Aunt Jemima, two hundred and fifty pounds of swing," plus a few regular strippers. And there was Bob Ferguson and Mary Murray coming back over the summer. As well, there was Rose LaRose, Gaye Knight, and a couple of other strippers he'd never heard of.

Satisfied and relieved, Murray continued to scan the roster. He had to give Milt credit. The man had certainly lined up a varied collection of burlesque performers. He even had someone billed as "Superwoman, the Modern Amazon — Lois de Fee." And he'd booked Ann Corio and Sally Rand, headliners who brought in fantastic business and were easy to work with, as well. Ann, especially, was one lovely lady!

The irritating buzzer at the side of his desk abruptly interrupted Murray's musings. Lou, no doubt. What could he want? Murray supposed Lou would want to know how his mother and sister were. God, how he hated going up to his brother-in-law's office, which reeked so heavily of booze and stale cigar smoke. It always made him feel like an intruder in his own theatre.

Murray bundled together some material from his desk — last week's receipts, the booking roster, and a few eight-by-ten glossies of future performers. Lou knew as well as he did that as far as the acts were concerned, they had to take what was sent them. They really had very little choice. But it was a kind of a formality Lou liked to go through with him, particularly when he was with his cronies. At least Frank Mitchell and some of the other people, like Joe the Goof, the bookie, and for sure, Ollie, knew who they were dealing with. When the buzzer sounded again, Murray hustled to the upstairs office.

Lou was seated at his desk with the entertainment section of the *New York Sunday Times* spread before him, a half-filled glass of Seagram's whiskey holding part of the newspaper in place. Helen, the curvaceous chorus girl, was standing beside Lou, wearing shoes with spike heels that looked like metal spears. Her hair was in a neat bun, her pretty little face all but obscured by enormous mascara-laden eyelashes.

"You see this?" Lou pointed at the newspaper in front of him. "*Earl Carroll Vanities*. That's what I'm going to be like one of these days! I'm going to be another Earl Carroll, and I'm going to run my own show! Look at this. 'Through these portals pass the most beautiful girls in the world.' How's that for a great slogan! And you're looking at one of the beauties right here. The Casino's just a stepping stone for bigger and better things for me, and of course, Helen!"

Murray was caught off guard. "Lou, I thought you'd want to know that your mother's recuperating very nicely and that Lil's okay. She's still with Barry in Florida." "And what's this I hear about this fellow Carter and Ollie? Dave Sherman told me there was a big row between them."

"Naw, it was nothing. You know Ollie likes to act tough. Nothing really happened. Carter just made a pass at Helen and Ollie happened to be close by and grabbed him by the neck. Just ask Helen."

A high-pitched, squeaky voice piped in. "Yeah, that's right, Mr. Little. It was nothing, I can assure you. It was only a pass and I ignored it. Ollie knows I'm a good friend of Lou's, so he got upset. But it was nothing."

Murray remained dissatisfied. "Look, Lou, whatever you do in your private life is your own business, and frankly, I'm not interested. But if what you do reflects on the theatre or causes us trouble through bad publicity, or if one of our performers is involved, I'm very interested."

Lou took another swig of whiskey, while Helen opened her compact to apply another layer of lipstick before adding her thoughts. "You know, Mr. Little, Ollie must be a real good friend of Lou's. He put his arm around me after that Carter creep left and told me never to worry. Ollie even said that Al Capone once asked him to be his personal bodyguard. I know I'm in very safe hands. So don't worry."

Grinning, Lou crowed, "Didn't I tell you, Murray?"

Murray cleared his throat. "I've had a quick look at the receipts that came in while I was away, Lou, and the upcoming bookings, too, and everything looks nice and rosy. So I'm happy."

Lou's pleasure couldn't be contained. "See, Helen, the Casino's big potatoes and I'm going to make it even bigger." He paused, then added, "Ain't it funny? If my father were still living, we'd all still be small potatoes in that cheapy little burlesque house. I told you about his murder, didn't I, Helen?"

Murray could see the tears in Lou's eyes — a signal for him to leave.

41

BUSINESS AS USUAL

By the early spring of 1941, Esther had made an uncomplicated recovery from her broken hip and moved into the oceanside apartment with Lil and Barry.

"My accident and my stay in hospital were just other ways of God testing me," Esther bragged to her daughter. "In hospital, I prayed every day, and now God has given me new strength and has cured my grandson, too."

"Well, Ma, you did receive the best of medical care, and the doctor back in Toronto did tell us that with a warm climate and rest Barry would get better."

"There are good doctors everywhere, Lil, but without God's help I wouldn't be here today. He rewards good and punishes evil."

"Ma, you've moved in with us, and we're very happy everything seems to be turning out all right, but I don't want to get into any kind of religious discussion. I'll do my best to keep kosher in the house, but I don't want any more lectures."

Esther sighed. "I'm sure God will understand our situation."

Lil restrained herself from yet another theological interchange with her mother. "Now that Barry's going to the local public school, Ma, he seems to be enjoying himself. They've got good schools down here. I've met his teacher a number of times, and she's told me Barry's a good little student."

"I'm happy to hear that, but in the fall he'll be going back to Toronto and attend religious school, won't he?"

"Of course, he will. You know, Ma, living in Miami would be very nice. The climate's so wonderful and the people are friendly. But, of course, back home we've got the theatre and now a hotel, so it would be very difficult to make such a big move and live in Miami permanently."

"It certainly would," Esther agreed. "Besides, that would mean leaving my whole family behind."

Lil was silent, but in her mind, she shouted, *As devoted as I am to you, Mother, I certainly wasn't thinking of including you in any such move, even if we could!*

◆ ◆ ◆

In the early summer, Esther returned by train to her Grace Street home. Having received assurance from Murray that Gerry and Alan were being well cared for by Anna and Samuel, Lil decided to stay in Miami over the summer. She wrote to Murray:

Dear Murray,

The doctors down here tell me Barry has made a full recovery. They can't hear a murmur, so he's considered to be one hundred percent. Both he and I have made several friends in the neighbourhood. One of my friends is Edna Schmidt, who has an apartment upstairs from us. She's a lovely lady, and we spend much time together. Her husband's a bartender and works at night. Her sweet little blond-haired, blue-eyed daughter, Arlene, follows Barry around wherever he goes. School ended just a week ago, and the teachers report that they found Barry a very good student. To Barry, the school's different, as you can imagine. He even had to salute the American flag every morning and pledge allegiance to it. Barry loves the beach and the ocean and now goes swimming every day. We're both very happy down here, but we do miss Toronto, even with its awful climate. I hope you're well and that you and Lou are taking good care of the theatre and hotel. Regards to your parents and love to Gerry and Alan.

Love, Lil

P.S. I'll make arrangements to come home by train in late August so that Barry can get settled before school starts.

Murray promptly replied to Lil's letter:

Dear Lil,

Happy to hear all is well, especially that Barry's back to feeling one hundred percent.

I guess it's all right for him and you to stay in Miami over the summer, but I'd prefer both of you back here. I really think my parents are finding it a little difficult to look after the boys and themselves, as well. My father's now working as a night watchman at Swift and taking care of two rambunctious boys half the day. I'd really like to send all three boys to summer camp, maybe some-where in Muskoka. Or perhaps we can rent a cottage on Lake Simcoe?

Business at the theatre is just great. We've got lots of servicemen, as you can imagine, and they generally behave themselves. We've had no further formal complaints from the church people. The Statler Hotel's still holding its own. The Liberal government still hasn't changed the liquor laws so we can start serving cocktails, but we're hopeful. I'm still trying to get used to working with Arthur Cohen and the Allens. At times, they're so darn demanding.

Lou continues to drink too much, I'm afraid, but he seems to be physically all right. He's really becoming my biggest problem. I don't want him to interfere with the operation of the theatre, and I'm upset with the kinds of people he attracts to his upstairs office. I'm always afraid he'll commit the theatre to something foolish, like cutting some crazy financial deal or whatever.

Our spring's been hot and sticky so far, and I think our air conditioning in the theatre's helping to bring in better box office. I'm holding up, but I'd like to have you home a little sooner, if that's possible, even though I know you're having a good time in Miami.

Love, Murray

P.S. Gerry and Alan send their love.

Lil and Barry returned home in late August, and it was soon business as usual at Grace Street. At the Casino Theatre, it was also business as usual: four shows a day and another on Sunday at midnight. The Chinese Freemasons continued to lease the theatre for their Sunday afternoon ceremonial and theatrical presentations just as they'd done in Avner's time at the Roxy. In the early Sunday evenings, the theatre was again rented to open-minded, charitable organizations for amateur song-and-dance affairs, or upon occasion, political fundraising rallies.

The regular Casino bill had at least two strippers and occasionally three, one of whom was singled out as the featured attraction of the week. Stage productions were at one, four, seven, and ten-thirty, and the customers were guaranteed their fill of satirical comic corn and tease. Strippers came in all varieties. The hot ones strutted around the stage in simulated orgies of passionate frenzy, occasionally using the curtain as a prop to demonstrate feigned urgings. Others, more composed and reserved, gave off an air of sophistication, coyly removing their clothing slowly, even rolling down each stocking for an endless period of time, turning the strip into a real tease. Then there was the innocent-girl-next-door type with a seductive walk. If the girls incorporated a bump and grind in their dance routines, and most did, Murray insisted their movements be minimal, even though the occasional performer might forget what city she was in. Many of the strippers acted as "talking women" or "straight women" in comic routines. Since most people in the audience knew every line in the various burlesque comedy bits, it was up to the timing and delivery of the comics to extract maximum responses.

At least two large production numbers were staged and choreographed by Lester Montgomery each week, which required new sets to be built and new costumes to be fitted for the chorus line. The girls, officially called the Casinoettes, became accustomed to being referred to by theatre staff as the "poor man's Rockettes" in contrast to the chorus line in Radio City at New York's Rockefeller Center. A good four hours of rehearsal preceded these shows, and each production number had its special theme, as varied as a dance sequence in front of a Dutch windmill or a simulated underwater ballet.

Between stage shows, the Casino ran B movies; the Allen family certainly had access to first-run films but chose to place them only in their upscale theatres. Still, one could see a Saint or Falcon detective flick with George Sanders, or a feature starring Richard Arlen, followed by what were called short subjects — *Movietone News*, a Bugs Bunny cartoon, or one or two serial comedies showcasing other luminaries, often The Three Stooges. Frequently, as a time-filling prelude to the first show of the day, the fare included extended short movies, perhaps one with Blondie and Dagwood. All this cinematic activity and a live, in-the-flesh stage show, including the occasional bona fide first-rate vaudeville act, could be had for seventy-five cents. And one could sit through a second show or more if desired. The evening price was a dollar.

At the back of the theatre and in the upstairs mezzanine, refreshments could be purchased — Vernor's Ginger Ale, Orange Crush, Coca-Cola, as well as a steaming hot dog slathered in mustard and relish. It was Murray's idea to open a hot dog snack bar. Arthur Cohen and the Allens initially opposed the introduction of such lowbrow delicacies in a theatre auditorium.

Frequently, Arthur Cohen brought up objections to the food. "Murray, don't you think that's going a bit too far? I mean, hot dogs and condiments in a theatre? The place will stink! And don't you think it'll cheapen the place?"

"We'll encourage the patrons to eat their hot dogs near the stand at the back of the theatre," Murray told Cohen. "And upstairs there's room in the mezzanine. I don't see it as much of a problem, Mr. Cohen, and most of all, selling hot dogs in a theatre is innovative. I'm sure our customers will take to it and we'll a turn a nice profit." *You've been to the theatre maybe twice since we became partners*, thought Murray. *Do you have any idea of the physical layout or even how our customers really behave?*

Unable to deny the logic of a profit-making innovation, Cohen finally said, "Have it your way this time, Murray. Just show me the receipts."

42

SCHOOL DAYS AGAIN

Barry was happy to be back at Grace Street and to take up again with his brothers, Gerry and Alan, as well as all his old friends. His mother was less than enthusiastic about her return. However happy she might be to be reunited with her sons and Toronto circle of friends, she was anything but thrilled about moving back into the Grace Street home with her in-laws. Almost every conversation now between Murray and Lil ended with a similar theme. "I've told you a thousand times, Murray. With your mother living in the house, I feel like a tenant. It's tough enough dealing with my mother and her strange ways, but your mother's running the entire household. My father, may he rest in peace, left this home to my mother and me!"

Having heard this argument so many times before, Murray's only rejoinder remained. "Lil, I told you it's only temporary. I can't leave my parents out on the street."

Just before school started in September and shortly after her return with Barry, Lil gave Murray an ultimatum. "If they don't leave, I will. About the only thing left for me to do is to buy the children's clothing.

So if your parents remain here, there's no point in my staying. I might as well live in Florida where I'll be happy, then come back to Toronto from time to time to visit with the children."

"Don't be ridiculous, Lil!" Murray exploded. "I can't evict my own parents! You know my father's doing the best he can with his night watchman's job. And my mother's just trying to be helpful. They'll move out as soon as they can afford to. Try to be a little more sympathetic, Lil. You know the situation down at the Casino. I've got a million things to look after. I need you here to support me, and so do the boys. But the last thing I need is to upset my parents. Please be patient. Please try to understand!"

Gerry, Barry, and Alan greeted the school year with ambivalence. No longer able to idle their afternoons away playing baseball or stickball on the street, they knew the new school year also meant the end of the great excitement of going to the Canadian National Exhibition. Gone were the midway with its fun rides, games, hot dogs, and candy floss; the Automotive Building choked with futuristic automobiles; the Better Living Centre and its fancy new gadgets for the home; the free bandshell concerts; the spectacular theatrical productions, with fireworks, at the grandstand; the massive fairgrounds where, even with thousands of people milling about, somebody from the neighbourhood was likely to be encountered. School put an end to all that. And besides, it meant resuming the dreaded additional commitment of Hebrew school after regular school hours.

Barry's grade three teacher was Miss Jane Peterson, a tiny woman who wore sensible shoes and tied her greying hair into a tight bun. Her ski-slope-shaped nose separated two penetrating grey eyes and supported a small pair of bifocals that seemed at any moment ready to slide down the slope. She had pencil-thin lips and a soft but authoritative voice that Barry and the other children listened to carefully as she directed them to their respective desks.

This Clinton Street first-floor classroom looked so different from Miami Public School No. 32. On the wall beside the teacher's desk, in place of the Stars and Stripes Barry had gotten used to, was a Union Jack and a picture of King George VI. Miss Peterson introduced herself and asked the children to stand and sing "God Save the King."

When it seemed that Barry had forgotten the words to the national anthem, Miss Peterson glared at him. After the singing, the children quietly sat down at their desks to await their next instruction.

"Children, my name is Miss Peterson," she announced. "Instead of starting with a lesson, let's have each of you tell the class your name and a little bit about yourself. To a pigtailed girl seated two seats ahead of Barry, she asked, "And what does your father do?"

A squeaky voice answered, "My father has a grocery store on Harbord Street. I go there every day after school and help my mother behind the counter."

"That's nice." Next, Miss Peterson asked another girl, "And what does your father do?"

"My daddy's a carpenter and has his own truck. He builds houses and helped build the one we live in."

"How interesting!" Miss Peterson said with enthusiasm. She then directed her attention at Barry. "And what about you, young man? What can you tell us about yourself or what your daddy does?"

"My father owns a theatre downtown, and I often go there to watch the shows," Barry answered confidently.

Miss Peterson smiled. "Oh, and what theatre is that?"

"He owns the Casino Theatre," Barry said proudly.

A sudden *"Ooooh"* rippled through the classroom.

Miss Peterson, who had been leaning forward, suddenly bolted upright, her face lobster-red. "Did you say the Casino Theatre?"

Now it was Barry's turn to blush. "Yes, Miss Peterson, the Casino on Queen Street."

Another wave of *"Ooooh"* made a round in the classroom.

Miss Peterson seemed lost for words. "You're not trying to be smart, are you, Barry?"

Barry felt like evaporating. "No, Miss Peterson, I'm not trying to be funny. My father and uncle own the Casino Theatre."

"And your father lets you see the shows?"

"I've been going there for years."

"Well, Barry, that's all very interesting," said the still-blushing Miss Peterson.

Barry sensed that all eyes were focused on him. Suddenly, the room filled with giggling.

"Now, children, settle down, settle down," Miss Peterson ordered as she marched to the blackboard at the front of the room. "I think we can save any more questions for another day and start our arithmetic lesson."

Barry was disappointed and upset by the teacher and the class response. Had he said something wrong or funny? Hadn't he answered the teacher's question? And what was so funny about his father owning a theatre? It was a lot more interesting than owning a grocery store or working in a factory. Besides, none of these kids, even Miss Peterson herself, had ever seen what went on in the theatre. Did they think it was a filthy place? Well, he didn't, and his mother and father didn't. And wasn't that all that mattered? Barry put up his hand. "Miss Peterson, can I please be excused from the class?" *They're just jealous, that's all*, he decided.

The children continued to titter and murmur among themselves, causing Miss Peterson to scowl. "Children, settle down immediately or I'll call in Principal Austin. Barry, you can be excused if you have to go the washroom." She turned to the class authoritatively. "Come to order immediately! Barry, you're excused, but I expect you back here shortly."

Since Barry's seat was close to the front of the classroom, he was able to reach the door quickly. Before he left, he locked eyes with Miss Peterson and detected a faint smile on her face. *Maybe my dad's owning the Casino isn't so bad, after all*, he thought. *Maybe she really does thinks I'm a pretty lucky guy.*

Barry returned to the classroom after loitering in the hall for a few minutes. By now, the class had settled into a regular routine as Miss Peterson went through the multiplication tables.

At recess, a couple of the boys in the classroom approached Barry as he watched a volleyball match. Bruce Woods, a tough kid, grabbed him by the arm. "The Casino, eh? Maybe you can get me and my buddies in free."

Barry knew it was best to avoid any kind of promise to guys like Woods. He knew they were jealous. They all were, maybe even some of the girls, too. Barry thought through his best response. "Okay, Bruce, but I'll have to speak to my father first." Perhaps that would put Woods off, at least for a while. Besides, Barry knew that children under sixteen weren't permitted into their theatre unless accompanied by an adult. *I'll let Bruce find that out for himself.*

That evening, Barry related the events at school to his grandmother, Anna, who tried to reassure him. "You don't have to be ashamed of anything, Barry. Your father and grandfather are hardworking, decent people. No matter what kind of stage show or picture your father might present, there will always be someone who will find an objection. I want you to remember this, Barry. There will always be people who want to tell you what you should or shouldn't like and what you should or shouldn't think. You're lucky because you come from a tradition and family that thinks for itself."

Gerry and Alan, also seated at the table, were unusually quiet. The tone of their grandmother's voice seemed more serious than usual. Barry glanced up from the pile of potato latkes on his plate, looked over at his grandmother standing beside the kitchen stove, and said, "Don't worry, Grandma Anna. I won't ever forget what you told me. I promise."

At this point, as though mesmerized by their grandmother's sermon, Barry and his brothers finished their meal in silence and uncharacteristically walked out of the kitchen slowly. They were happy to leave the room and get out to meet their friends on the street.

43

WHILING AWAY THE WORLD WAR

On December 7, 1941, the Japanese bombed the American fleet at Pearl Harbor on the Hawaiian island of Oahu. Within twenty-four hours, U.S. President Franklin D. Roosevelt declared war on the Empire of Japan and informed the American citizenry that they were to prepare for a long conflict that "we are going to win." And as the war in Europe and North Africa continued, it seemed as though the Axis powers of Germany, Japan, and Italy would never be defeated.

At Grace Street, Anna and Samuel talked incessantly about the events of the war but strangely still never made any allusions to their people left behind in Europe. Esther showed absolutely no interest whatsoever in world events, and Murray was far too busy to become genuinely immersed in any prolonged political discussion at home. More often than not, Lou was too inebriated to grasp the implications of a world war. He'd been found ineligible for military service because of a hearing loss, Murray because of poor vision. Being the mother of boys, Lil's big fear was that the war would be prolonged and that one or all of her three sons might someday wind up as combatants.

By now, Uncle Harry's two abandoned sons had matured into early manhood. The elder one, Maxie, was rejected for active duty because of poor eyesight and spent much of his time at the local racetracks as a tout, more specifically to surreptitiously watch the trials of the various racehorses to gain information for betting purposes. Somehow Maxie was squeezing out a living. Always good-humoured, he thought nothing of taking Barry or his brothers to baseball, hockey, or football games. How he managed to obtain an adequate supply of tickets was always a great mystery to the boys.

Maxie's brother, Morris — most people called him Moishe — had become a star athlete and marathon swimmer. Shortly after Canada entered the war, he'd joined the 48th Highlanders and quickly rose in the ranks to become a commando instructor. Moishe was Barry's idol, a paradigm of physical prowess and courage. So the two forsaken boys, in a sense, became surrogate fathers for Barry and his brothers, Murray being around the house so seldom.

Morris and Maxie never mentioned their father, at least not in the company of the Little brothers. Once, while watching a minor league ball game with Maxie, seated as usual in the third-base bleachers, Barry turned to Maxie and bluntly asked, "Where's your father? I've never met him and you never talk about him."

Maxie put his arm around Barry's shoulder affectionately. "Look, Barry, as far as I'm concerned, my father's dead, and if he isn't, I don't ever want to see him, anyway. He's a no-good bastard who left my mother to scrub floors. So let's just watch the ball game. You finish your hot dog and forget about him."

Having heard Harry's name mentioned once or twice in whispered tones between Grandma Esther and Maxie's mother, Barry could recall only half-heard fragments of the conversation. But he'd noticed how the very mention of her brother-in-law twisted his grandmother's beautifully sculpted face into a portrait of scowling contempt.

Going to the games with Maxie was great fun, but Barry continued to enjoy the live theatrical productions at his father's theatre more.

It was Esther's idea that the three grandsons should spend their summer holidays at a camp where Jewish customs, rituals, and values were maintained. Accordingly, in the summer of 1943, the three boys were shipped off to Camp Yungveldt, just outside Pickering, Ontario. The boys hated the experience, particularly Barry, who wrote back to his mother:

Dear Mom,

Hardly anyone here speaks English. It's all Hebrew or Yiddish, and I don't understand very much of it. We spend half our time listening to stories told in Yiddish and the other half praying. I think I've been in one baseball game since I arrived two weeks ago. Please ask Dad to take me home as soon as possible.

Love, Barry

P.S. The food is terrible.

Murray caved and brought the boys home early. With a few weeks still left in the summer, Gerry and Alan were sent to Boy Scout and Cub camp respectively. Barry pleaded to stay in the city, so Murray found him a token job in the Casino paint shop. Curiously, the shop was located on the third floor of the old Roxy Theatre.

In fact, the paint shop was more than simply a place where sign painting was done. The weekly stage sets were constructed there, too, along with all the advertising signage, and more exciting for Barry, a full orchestra and dress rehearsal for the chorus line numbers were also held there. All work was under the watchful eye of Percy Grisewood, a formally trained illustrator from England, who shortly before the war broke out, had found sanctuary in Canada but no professional illustration work to support him. A job in a burlesque house was for him a last resort.

Percy was a master of organization, so sets were built and painted with amazing alacrity and ingenuity. Having essentially a gofer role in the shop, Barry watched and listened carefully to everything Percy did and said. His boss seemed to enjoy the company of Barry, now twelve years old, and had no hesitation engaging in conversations that ranged from politics to religion and philosophy.

The irony of Avner's grandson working in the building where the man had been murdered didn't escape Percy, either. Not that he made much of this coincidence, but one day he did say to Barry, "You know, you should write a story about irony. Here you are working in the very building where your grandfather was murdered. This kind of irony leads me to believe that someday, Barry, you're going to find out who killed him. Yes, I believe that fate is telling us something by your being here."

Percy demonstrated a constellation of interesting ideas on a whole range of subjects to Barry, who discovered early in his association with the artist to give coherent, meaningful responses to anything he was asked. To Barry, Percy seemed like the ideal of an English schoolmaster personified.

During the school year, the boys were given a small weekly allowance and on Saturday afternoons were allowed to go to the local cinemas. Barry occasionally accompanied his brothers, but he much preferred to go to his father's theatre and watch live entertainment. By the time he was twelve, he'd grown familiar with all the standard burlesque bits — Flugel Street, The Balloon Salesman, The Courtroom Scene, Pincus Pay the Two Dollars, The Schoolroom Scene, the broad spectrum of the naughty and bawdy sketches, strips, and surprise blackouts. However, the real bonus for him was listening to the music of Cole Porter, Jerome Kern, George Gershwin, and the like, albeit played by a raucous six-piece pit orchestra. Murray cringed whenever people around the theatre said, "You know, Murray, your son Barry's around here so often I'll bet he's going to end up in show business."

"Over my dead body!" Murray always replied.

44

BOXING SCAM

The year 1944 was a seminal year in the life of the Casino Theatre and in the lives of its owners as the theatre enjoyed record profits. Like moths around a flame, the theatre was now attracting not only a huge customer following but also a seemingly endless entourage of Damon Runyonesque characters. Nearly everybody in the city knew the Casino, and everyone had his or her own take on it. Still vilified as a shameful palace of sin by most people, it was championed by others as a theatre that offered pleasurable entertainment. Frank Mitchell, one of Lou's long-time lawyer cronies from City Hall, liked to say, "It's healthy for a city to have a place like the Casino. This Orange city is much too conservative."

Lou continued to hold court with his pals in his upstairs office at the Casino. And, of course, he was the de facto president of this private club as well as its chief bartender. Murray, regarded by Lou as a perpetual square and too much a voice of sobriety, if not an out-and-out prude, wasn't welcome at this "club." Ollie Baskin remained Lou's favourite confidant, perhaps his only one. Besides, they were still partners in the New Statler Hotel.

Late one bitterly cold January afternoon in 1944, Ollie rang through to Lou's private line. "Hey, Lou, I've got something great for you. A few easy bucks for both of us. I'll be right over. I'm just across the road at the hotel."

Before Ollie could sit down in the office after he arrived, Lou asked, "What's the big deal?"

"A boat race!"

"A what?"

"You know, a fight fix, a dive! Where the hell have you been, for Christ's sake? Look, you and I know boxing. It's easy to set up a dive. We pay the boxer up front and we lay our bets with a guaranteed winner. It's simple!"

Lou smiled. "Yeah, sure, everybody knows about that kind of caper, but you've got to find the right boxer. And if anything goes wrong, like the fighter doesn't take the dive, you can lose a hell of a lot and wind up serving time, too, if you're caught."

"Listen, don't you trust me? I've got this kid, Teddy Swain, in my hip pocket. He's a bantam boxer, and he'll listen to anything I say. Teddy's looking for some easy money, and he knows if he doesn't follow through with a dive, he can wind up getting hurt himself. Really hurt, you know what I mean?"

"Where the hell did you find him?"

"Are you ready for this? He works for you part-time in that sign shop with that cigar-chewing Englishman of yours. I even took the liberty of asking him to join us in your office at three o'clock. Yeah, he's going to be fighting Jimmy Rizzo at Massey Hall on February 28. He likes the deal. I told him something like three hundred bucks for him, and you and I, of course, can bet heavily."

"What if the kid squeals? Have you thought of that? And what makes you so sure he won't?"

Ollie's face ballooned with anger. "What the hell's wrong with you? I told you I've got this kid in my hip pocket. He wants some soft money, and I told my buddy, Maxie Kadin, to have a word with him. He's going to give the kid a little reminder just before the fight. You know, just in case. I promised Kadin a piece of the action. Stop worrying, for God's sake. I'm looking after all the details and I'm cutting you in because you're my pal and my partner. Or have you forgotten?"

Lou reached into his pocket and pulled out a wad of $50 bills. "Here, take $150 for the kid. By the way, I've got Joe the Goof coming by later this afternoon. How much are you in for?" Then, before Ollie could answer, Lou blurted out, "I'll be placing a thousand with Joe on Rizzo to win."

"Sounds good to me, Lou baby."

Lou poured himself a shot of Johnnie Walker and relaxed in his big office chair. Then he suddenly bolted to his feet. "Hey, what if somebody gets to Rizzo and pays him to take a dive?"

Ollie laughed. "Smart guy. I've already looked after that. The kid's going to take a blow to the head in the first round and take his dive then. Kadin's going to be in his corner. There's no way Rizzo will plan on an early dive, as well."

Thinking for a moment, Lou finished his drink, eased into his office chair again, and glanced through the viewing window at the stage. "Hey, Ollie, what do you think of our featured lady of the week, Lucille Rand?"

"Any relation to Sally?"

"Nope. She doesn't have the big name, but she's every bit as good in every other way, if you know what I mean."

Ollie peeked through the viewing window. Lucille wore nothing but pasties and a G-string. He chuckled. "I see what you mean. And by the way, Lou, I see that your advertising says 'Lou Appleby Presents.' You've got it in the newspapers and on the front billboard, too. What are you trying to do — become some kind of celebrity? And what does Murray think of all that?"

Lou was annoyed. "I'm already a celebrity in this town or hadn't you noticed? And if it weren't for my old man, Murray wouldn't even be a part of this operation. It's my theatre, so why shouldn't my name go on the productions?" Lou took a second gulp of Scotch. "If Murray wasn't married to my sister, I'd have fired him long ago!"

"Well, he's a straight shooter as far as I can see."

"Yeah, straight. Very straight. Too damn straight!"

On the evening of February 28, Teddy Swain, ex-seaman turned bantamweight boxer, entered the ring with tough Jimmy Rizzo at Massey Hall. Seventy-seven seconds after the opening bell, Swain was counted out by the referee. Lou and Ollie, seated at ringside, smiled with self-satisfaction.

A few weeks after the fight, Murray received a registered letter from a law firm in Buffalo addressed to "The New Statler Hotel, Toronto,

Ontario, Attention Murray Little, Manager." Murray often started by checking into the hotel office, and on this particular day, the mail had arrived auspiciously early. He opened the letter with haste and anxiety. Registered letters always meant trouble.

Murray scanned the letter hurriedly. The Statler Hotel chain was suing them! The letter said that Murray and his partners were capitalizing on the Statler name, implying that their hotel was part of its operation. Murray could hardly believe his eyes. The Statler people wanted $50,000 in damages ... more if they didn't immediately change the name of their hotel! Murray reflected for a moment. Hadn't he warned Lou and Ollie this might happen? He stuffed the letter into his inside jacket pocket and glanced at his watch. Lou wouldn't be in the office yet, and he didn't want to call him at home. And who knew when Ollie would show up? For the moment, the best policy was to get hold of lawyer Joe Sedgwick.

Waiting in his Casino office for Lou's arrival, Murray finally spotted him through the box office window and immediately followed him upstairs. Carrying a bunch of flowers, Lou was particularly dapper today in his Adler elevator shoes, grey pinstriped suit, and silver-grey necktie with diamond stickpin.

"Lou, I've got an important letter for us — you, me, and Ollie."

Visibly annoyed, Lou snapped, "Well, I've got an important day. There's a certain young lady I'm having dinner with — an anniversary, if you like. So what is it?"

Murray handed the letter to his brother-in-law and watched as he slowly read it, then threw it on the desk. "What the hell's this? Some kind of joke?"

"It's no joke, Lou. Didn't I predict this might happen? But that doesn't matter now. The point is, we're going to have to do something about it immediately or we'll be in very serious financial trouble. I've already called Joe Sedgwick."

"Does Ollie know about this?"

"No, I don't know how to find him. Maybe you can. And you can tell him I've already called our lawyer."

Lou reached for a bottle of Johnnie Walker. "I don't care how big those guys in Buffalo are. We're going to fight them."

"Why don't we wait until we get a legal opinion before we talk about fighting?"

"Christ, don't you ever want to fight?"

"Only if it's necessary. I like to think first!" Murray left quickly and descended the stairs from Lou's office. He had to calm himself. *This is all I need to make my life complete — a full-blown major lawsuit!*

That evening, when Murray told Lil about the letter, she listened attentively before responding. "These people certainly have a point. If you're not part of the chain, then you're misusing their name, aren't you?"

Murray felt worn out. "You know, Lil, I've had one hell of a day. Not only did I get this letter, later I had to go backstage and speak to Winnie Garrett, our featured stripper of the week."

"So what's that got to do with me? You know I don't mix in at the theatre or hotel. That's between you and Lou."

Murray persisted, somehow needing her understanding. "I told Miss Garrett she was being too suggestive in her number, so she got real upset and asked me what kind of tinpot town she was working in. She told me she was an *artiste* and an *exotic dancer* and had done her act all through the United States without any complaints. Fortunately, the discussion was very short, and when I reviewed her second show, I found she'd changed it. So the Police Commission should have no trouble with it.

"Then I had words with the comic Bobby Vail. He and the straight man were using language that could get us into trouble with the commission. I won't repeat what he said, but he didn't like my suggestions and also lit into me. He did clean it up for the second show, though. Later in the day, I got into a real argument with a reporter named Wagman from the gossip magazine *Flash*. I caught him snooping around backstage without permission, and he tried to tell me that some local gangster had threatened one of our chorus girls. I told him to leave or I'd call the police. I haven't yet met a reporter who doesn't have a red nose or dirty fingernails."

"What exactly does that mean, Murray?"

"Most of the reporters I've met drink too much and are always grovelling in some kind of personal dirt. But, wait, you haven't heard the best one yet. Just before I was going to close up for the night, one of the acts that's opening tomorrow, a brother-and-sister singing duo, complained to me that our theatre looked like a dump. They told me they were used to high-class houses like Shea's just up the way, or the Palace in New York, and couldn't believe their agent put them into a place like ours.

"I told them I'd never heard that kind of complaint before and that most of our artists, *especially* the ones who went on to become famous, *liked* working our theatre! I really got rolling and told them about Phil Silvers, who's now getting big in Hollywood. Then there's Ann Corio, one of our dancers, in that *Jungle Siren* movie. Not to mention Gypsy Rose Lee who really loved our place. She even wrote a mystery novel, *The G-String Murders*, that was made into a movie starring Barbara Stanwyck last year! Oh, I really laced into them. Then I reminded them of their contract and how, if they broke it, we could easily sue them. Boy, let me tell you, Lil, it really was some day!"

But Murray's day wasn't over — not yet. Lil, who had been seated at the side of the bed, unexpectedly leaped to her feet and began to verbally assail him. "Complaints, complaints, nothing but complaints! You're never home, and when you are, all I hear about are your problems with my brother or the theatre. My father had lots of problems, too, but I never heard him complaining to my mother. He spent time with my mother and with Lou and me. We went on Sunday picnics and drives, things like that. You never want to go anywhere. Our kids hardly know you! I hardly know you! Your father's more like the boys' father! And your mother won't even let me be their mother! I feel like a fifth wheel!"

Murray was taken aback by Lil's sudden verbal explosion. "If I could, you know I'd spend more time with you and the boys. Can't you be a little more understanding of the situation, Lil? I have to spend every waking moment running that theatre and hotel. Believe me, it's no picnic dealing with Lou and Ollie — the icing on the cake." Murray could feel himself losing whatever strength he had left.

Lil's face twisted strangely. "I can't help you in that department. Maybe you should get another job."

Murray was flabbergasted. *What a suggestion!* "You know that's absolutely impossible. You know there are no jobs out there for me. What on earth do you expect me to do?"

"To begin with, get your parents out of my house!"

"You know damn well I can't do that, Lil."

"Well, I've told you before — they go or I go."

By now, Murray was pacing the bedroom floor while Lil stood rigidly by the bedside.

"I've made inquiries," she said. "I'm going back to Miami."

"You're doing what?" Murray was incredulous.

"You heard me. The tension in this house is too much for me. I simply can't remain under the same roof with your parents."

"What about the kids?"

"They're being well looked after, aren't they? By their *second* set of parents?"

Even though he'd heard such threats before, Murray was stunned by Lil's decision to actually leave. "This … this is desertion," he stammered. "You can't leave us just like that!"

"I love the kids and I'm not leaving them. I'm only going to be away from the house for a few weeks. Maybe a couple of months at most."

"All right, have it your way. There isn't much I can do to stop you, is there? But your leaving makes it very tough for me, and for my parents. And as for the boys —"

"I'm sorry, but that's the way it is."

Murray quietly left the room and went downstairs to make himself a cup of tea. He needed something to calm his nerves after one of the most trying days of his life.

45

A LITTLE BRIBERY

Lil made good on her threats to abandon Grace Street, and in the early spring of 1944 departed Toronto by train for Miami, heading for her former oceanfront flat. Murray was angered by her actions, his parents were shocked, and the boys were surprised. Esther merely shrugged in bland acceptance. Murray drove Lil to Union Station, her large bags choked with clothing stacked in the back of the Plymouth.

"I'm really sorry you're doing this, Lil," he said to her sadly. "You're making a very big mistake leaving the kids. They'll never forgive you."

"I told you, Murray. I'm only going for a few months. I think we both need a rest, and I'll keep in touch either by phone or by mail."

"Your leaving is very embarrassing."

Lil cut in sharply. "Who cares about embarrassing! I don't care what people have to say. It's my life and nobody else's, and I'm doing what I feel is best for me ... and just maybe for the kids and you, too."

"I simply don't understand the logic. I've told you a hundred times I can't evict my own parents." Murray pulled up at Union Station just as a quiet April snow started to fall. He could see his life beginning to melt away like the snow when it hit the ground.

Lil gently kissed him on the cheek as a polite but obsequious porter took her bags, and then she was gone.

Murray drove away from the station deep in thought. Back at the theatre, he returned Joe Sedgwick's call. "Well, what do you think about this Statler business, Joe?"

"To be honest, Murray, I think the Statler people have a very good case. Adding the word *New* to *Statler* is, in my view — and I'm sure in any judge's view — simply a deceptive device to capitalize on the well-known Statler name. I don't think you have a leg to stand on."

"What should we do then?"

"I suggest you and your partners have me write a letter to the complainants with an offer. Agree to immediate discontinuation of the New Statler Hotel name and adopt a new name — Variety comes to mind — and a cash settlement of $5,000, not only as a token of goodwill but to cover any damages the Statler chain might have incurred."

"So we won't fight them?"

"I'm certain you would lose, and a court case could be very costly."

"I trust your opinion, Joe. I'll let Lou and Ollie know. I only hope they'll accept your advice. You know how combative and difficult they can be."

Much to Murray's surprise, both Lou and Ollie acquiesced and agreed to follow Sedgwick's advice. Equally amazing to Murray was the quick acceptance by the Statler chain of Joe's offer. Henceforth, the New Statler Hotel would be called the Variety Hotel.

By the time Lil returned from her Florida escapade in September 1944, the Statler issue was fully resolved. Always Lou's great defender, when Lil heard what had happened, she declared, "I told you my brother was no dope and that you'd never get away with that name. I'm sure it was Ollie's idea."

Murray couldn't be bothered to argue, preferring instead to point out, "The hotel isn't out of the woods yet. We still haven't gotten that liquor licence to serve cocktails with meals, which we were counting on when we got into the New Statler in the first place. And now with Mitchell Hepburn and his Liberals replaced by Premier George Drew and the Tories, there doesn't seem to be a chance anytime soon the liquor laws will change in this province, certainly if the Co-operative Commonwealth Federation and that Bible thumper Temperance Willie Temple continue their campaign to make Ontario as dry as possible. After all, Temple almost defeated Drew in his own seat in High Park. You know, of course, that if we had a licence for cocktails with meals, it would add considerably to our financial situation."

Lil smiled. "Murray, you're such a worrywart sometimes. Give it time. I'm sure Drew and his Conservatives will see the wisdom of letting hotels and restaurants serve cocktails. Wasn't I right about the hotel?"

"Yes, you were, Lil." Murray tried to sound warm and affectionate. "I'm happy you're showing a real interest in what Lou and I are doing."

However, as it turned out, there were bigger, more immediate problems to worry about. Ollie, Lou, and Max Kadin were charged with "conspiracy to defraud the public by means of boxing bouts." Teddy Swain, who had taken his dive in the fight in February 1944, testified in a trial in early November that after the fight he'd told his father what he'd done. It was his father who reported him to former hockey, football, and baseball star Lionel Conacher, now chairman of the Ontario Athletic Commission. Conacher suspended Swain immediately and reported the incident to the police, who then laid charges.

Murray learned about the fiasco from the radio, it being his habit to have it on while he was shaving. *My God! I can't believe it!* It was all he could do to refrain from shouting. *This could finish the hotel!* Having nicked himself more than usual, Murray ran from the house half-shaven, anxious to get downtown and pick up a newspaper.

And there it was on the second page of the *Toronto Daily Star*, November 6, 1944: "Boxer Says He Got $225 for Taking Dive."

Murray began to perspire. *My God, there are Lou's and Ollie's names right in the first paragraph, charged with conspiracy to defraud the public.* Murray read and reread the article. *This could ruin us. Forget about getting an upgraded liquor licence. We could have our wine and beer licence revoked altogether, maybe even have the hotel closed down completely. What a horrible embarrassment for us all!*

He slammed the newspaper down on the desk and continued to mutter to himself. "What a disgrace! I knew Lou would do something like this someday. I just knew it." He could only hope this Judge Parker, who was presiding over the affair, would go easy on Lou and Ollie. They could be sent to jail for months!

Suddenly, a smile crept across Murray's plump, sweating face. Maybe not having Lou around wouldn't be so bad, and that went double for Ollie, as well!

Murray's desk phone rang and shook him from his reverie. "Hello? Yes, Lil! What? Why did I have to leave the house so quickly? Some problem?" Murray hesitated as he fumbled for words. "I guess you might as well know now because you're going to find out soon enough, anyway. Lou and Ollie, and one of their sidekicks, got themselves charged with fixing a prizefight. They're going to go on trial, and it's in all the newspapers and on the radio!"

"This is terrible, Murray. What are we going to do? What if my mother finds out?"

"There's more to it than just your mother getting wind of what her son's done, believe me. Still, you don't have to be the one to tell her. She doesn't read the English press or listen to the radio. So simply don't tell her, that's all. It'll be up to the rest of the family to use their discretion. I know Becky won't tell her. And so what if someone else does? She's a tough lady. She can handle it."

The trial lasted a week, and each of the defendants was fined $5,000 and given a suspended sentence.

Murray noticed, as did the employees at the Casino, that there were fewer visitors to Lou's private upstairs office over the next several weeks. In December, Murray received a registered letter from the Liquor Control Board of Ontario. He opened the letter hastily to read terse words: "Dear Sirs: Please be informed that your beer-and-wine licence at the Variety Hotel, formerly known as the New Statler Hotel, has been revoked. Your facility does not currently meet the standards under the LCBO Act."

Without delay, Murray called Joe Sedgwick, whose secretary politely informed him, "Mr. Sedgwick's at a meeting. Would you care to leave a message?"

Murray couldn't restrain his agitation. "Tell him it's an emergency. Can you call him out of the meeting, please!"

"If you insist, Mr. Little."

Always easily excited, Murray knew he was more so than usual. When Sedgwick got on the line, he blurted, "Joe, our beer-and-wine licence at the New Statler, I mean, Variety, has been revoked. I just got a letter from the Liquor Control Board. Lou and Ollie don't even know yet, but they sure as hell will soon enough."

Sedgwick was annoyingly brief. "Well, of course, this is no great surprise in view of their recent troubles over the boxing chicanery they were involved in. That got a lot of media attention. But leave it with me. I'll make some inquiries."

Later that day, Lou met with Murray in his upstairs office. When Murray showed his brother-in-law the LCBO letter, Lou quickly scanned it, then turned to Murray in defiance. "What the hell did you expect from those bastards?"

Attempting to appease him, Murray retorted, "Not much else, I guess. In any event, I've already called Joe Sedgwick, and I'm sure he's going to appeal the decision. But for the time being, we won't be able to serve any alcohol at the Variety."

Lou glared at Murray and crumpled the letter in his right fist while reaching for his pacifying bottle of Scotch.

Exasperated, Murray sighed. How pathetic! The reason this was happening was because of the behaviour of Lou and Ollie! And they were too stupid even to understand. It didn't matter that Murray was called the manager of the hotel. They hadn't fooled anyone. The LCBO knew who really ran the Variety, so why would it want to let criminals like Lou and Ollie keep a liquor licence? His disgust mounting, Murray exited the office, leaving Lou slumped in the chair, half cursing, half sobbing.

Later that afternoon, Murray received a call from Ollie, obviously drunk and roaring with rage, his voice so loud that Murray had to hold the phone several inches from his ear.

"Those goddamn sons of bitches! Revoking our licence! Who the hell do they think they are? We're running a clean, legitimate hotel. I know what those bastards want!"

"What do you mean, Ollie?"

"Oh, I forgot who I was talking to."

Murray recognized the sarcasm.

"You gotta pay off those bastards. You know, money, green stuff. Get it?"

"Ollie, don't be ridiculous! Obviously, the licence was revoked because of your recent trouble over that fight."

"Listen and listen good. Everybody's on the take. Where the hell have you been? Just leave it with me. I've got connections and I'll use them. I'll get that goddamn licence back if it kills me." He slammed down the phone.

The conversation had been so loud that the cashier working adjacent to the office, heard it through the open door and turned to Murray. "Wow, I've never heard anything like that! I'm sorry, but I couldn't help but overhear."

Murray smiled at her weakly. "You don't have to apologize. He's one of a kind, that's for sure. But I think I can handle him."

Several days later, the phone in the office rang and again it was Ollie. "Murray, I think I can get around this licence thing. Through a friend of mine, I've got a meeting set up for you with one of the city aldermen, a man named Edward Johnson."

Murray was puzzled. "What's he got do with it, Ollie?"

"Plenty. This guy told my friend that for the right amount of money Johnson will talk to Judge Robb, the LCBO head guy, and get our licence back."

"You must be kidding, Ollie."

"I never kid!" Baskin barked.

"But what's this got to do with me directly?"

"You're our front guy, our hotel manager, aren't ya? Just call up this alderman's office and make an appointment. All he wants is $5,000."

"Five thousand?"

"Yeah, you heard me. I've never met a politician who didn't need *shmeering*."

"And you expect me to be part of that, Ollie?"

"If we don't get our beer-and-wine licence back, our hotel's history. Or haven't you looked at the books lately? We've been losing money for the past two years. So we need that licence reinstated or we're done for and we'll all lose our investment. I can't put it any more directly or nicely!"

"I guess you leave me no choice. I'll call his office."

"Geez, Murray, you sure don't sound very enthusiastic."

Murray couldn't hide his disgust. "Ollie, you must know this isn't my kind of game."

"It's everybody's game. Look, Lou and I will round up the $5,000. You make the appointment. I'll get you Johnson's private line. You feel him out and make the offer."

"But Johnson's a lawyer. He's been around a long time ..."

"You got it, baby. He knows everybody. And he's got lots of *schlep*, you know, influence. Trust me!" Saying that, Ollie hung up.

Several days later, while preparing for his meeting with Alderman Johnson, Murray carefully packed a sealed envelope containing $5,000 into his briefcase. Having received the cash from Ollie the previous day, Murray had placed the money in his safe overnight. In his briefcase, he also included the letter from the LCBO.

"If anyone calls, tell them I won't be long" Murray advised the cashier. *The sooner I get this over with the better!*

The three-block walk to the alderman's office on Richmond Street seemed like an eternity. A dizzying bombardment of ideas ran through his mind. What if this was just another of Ollie's devious schemes?

What if Murray was being set up as a fall guy and was caught trying to bribe a public official? What if this alderman wanted more money? How was it that a mere city alderman had so much influence?

Murray entered the Richmond office where a receptionist ushered him into Johnson's inner office. Seated behind an overly large oak desk was a greying middle-aged man who quickly got up and shook Murray's hand. "So you're Mr. Little, the manager of Toronto's only burlesque house, and the manager of the Variety Hotel, as well. Indeed, you must be a very busy man! Have a chair and let's get down to business."

Murray clasped his briefcase a little more tightly as he sat down and listened.

"Look, Mr. Little, I won't mince words. I'm well aware the Variety had its liquor licence revoked because your hotel partners, Appleby and Baskin, had a boxing match thrown. Naturally, the LCBO doesn't let people like that keep liquor licences. Believe me, I've got connections, but don't bother to ask me who they are because I'm not going to tell you. For a price, in this case $5,000, I'll do my best to see your hotel gets its liquor licence reinstated."

Murray sat motionless. No lie — Johnson didn't mince words! When he reached into his briefcase and handed Johnson the envelope, the man quickly opened it and counted the cash. "Yes, it's all there. Don't look so worried, Mr. Little. Just to show you I'm a fair and decent man, let me tell you what I'm going to do. As I said, I'll try to get the licence back, and I'm pretty sure I can. But if I can't, I'll return most of the money."

This was even more bizarre than he'd expected, Murray thought. He rose from the chair and said, "That's very kind of you, sir."

"Always glad to help a constituent!"

Murray walked swiftly to the Casino, and as he passed the newsstand across from City Hall outside Bowles Lunch, he noticed one of the day's headlines: "'Summer Peace Possible' — Mackenzie King." *Well, at least one war may be ending.*

No sooner had Murray relaxed in his office than Lou's buzzer shattered the silence, prompting him to hustle upstairs.

When he arrived, Lou skipped formalities and asked, "Well, how did it go?"

"The meeting was brief. I was the only one there, and Johnson promised to return most of the money if he fails to get our liquor licence back. Nothing more, nothing less, Lou."

His brother-in-law grinned. "Good! If you drank, I'd offer you one."

"Yes, well, just don't count your chickens until they're hatched."

Clearly annoyed and in a motion reminiscent of his sister, Lou twisted his face, curling his upper lip to one side.

"I'm a realist, Lou, not a dreamer, and while I'm here, I might as well get across an important point I'm going to bring to the attention of both Arthur Cohen and the Allens. I just want to run it by you again, I know I've mentioned it to you before."

"What is it?"

"Our box office receipts are down from last year. Obviously, part of that has to do with fewer servicemen being around. But I think the main reason is that our format of two or three strippers, a comic, and the occasional vaudeville act might be, if you like, a bit tired. And before you say another word, yes, I know we've got the only burlesque house in town. But, in short, I think we have to change the way we do things. At first I thought the way to go would be to introduce a variety of satirical bits like Minsky did. But I don't think that kind of gimmicky stuff will work in Toronto."

"What do you mean?"

"Well, to begin with, Minsky advertised such things as 'Anatomy and Cleopatra,' 'Panties' Inferno,' 'Dress Takes a Holiday,' 'Tease for Two,' 'Follies Brassiere.' I don't think Toronto audiences will get that sort of thing. They're just not sophisticated enough."

When Lou's face turned red, it became apparent to Murray that his brother-in-law himself had failed to understand the subtlety of the Minsky gimmickry.

"Anyway, Lou, don't you understand that burlesque is dying every-where? I've come to the conclusion that the only thing that's going to boost our box office is to bring in bigger names — actors and performers who have been seen in the movies or heard on the radio or remembered from the heyday of vaudeville."

Lou immediately grew defensive. "Hey, Murray, that's my territory, you know, the bookings."

"Well, it might be your territory, Lou, but our box office is slipping. And as a partner in the Casino, I have the right to make suggestions that might improve our returns."

"Well, I thought of the same thing myself, don't you remember? It's almost a year since we brought in Stepin Fetchit. He was some kind of movie star, wasn't he? And look at the kind of business he brought in — nothing!"

"But, Lou, he really wasn't that well known when he played the Casino. His pictures were in the late 1920s and 1930s. And frankly, his act was a bomb. What we want are people who are currently known, not has-beens."

"Well, talk it over with Gersten and the other Allens, but remember, we're still keeping the chorus line."

A few days later, Murray had his weekly meeting with Arthur Cohen, and after a few preliminary pleasantries, he broached the subject of a major change in policy to boost box office. Cohen turned to Murray, and with a sour demeanour, demanded, "What do you mean? Who do you think you are?"

"I've already spoken to Lou about it. Our regular customers seem to be staying with us, but our expenses have been going up like everything else, and we're not acquiring many new regulars. Numbers of servicemen are definitely dropping what with the war winding down ..."

Murray persisted. "I don't have to tell you that vaudeville's dead and burlesque is dying, too. We might be able to struggle along for a couple of years, but if we want to think about any future, we should be making some policy decisions now! I suggested to Lou, and yesterday in a telephone conversation to Gersten Allen, that we change to a big-name policy."

"Murray, I couldn't disagree with you more! We can't afford top movie stars — the Bing Crosbys and Bob Hopes. That's a pipe dream!"

"Well, they don't have to be exactly at that level, but it's the only thing I can come up with — a bigger-name policy."

"But didn't you once tell me that sex always sells?"

"Yes, I did, Mr. Cohen, but the kind of sex we're selling isn't working."

"What do you mean, *the kind of sex we're selling isn't working*?"

"Our kind of striptease is losing popularity."

"Murray, you know, I've discussed our situation at the Casino with the Allens. And as far as I'm concerned, there's going to be no change in policy in the foreseeable future. If we're not going to make as much money as we used to, I'm prepared to accept that. But I don't want to take any big gambles. So, for the time being, we'll stay with the B and B format."

"B and B?"

"B movies and burlesque!" Cohen was growing irritated. But then, with unexpected alacrity, his mood changed to one of paternalism. "Murray, how's the family, your three boys?"

Murray could hardly believe his ears. He'd never heard Cohen spontaneously inquire about anything other than bottom-line profits, let alone talent policy. And now interest in his family? "Thanks for asking. The boys are growing up nicely. I think the middle one wants to be a musician, but Lil and I aren't keen to have a son in the entertainment or music business. Too much uncertainty. Too many people with inflated egos."

"Now that's a little surprising to hear, Murray, your wife coming from a theatrical family, even if it was burlesque."

Cohen obviously didn't realize that his father-in-law, Avner, had been involved in live Yiddish theatre and was one of the first entrepreneurs in the movie business in Toronto! "Well, I'm not sure about it, but I don't think Barry has the talent in him. He wants to take lessons at the Royal Conservatory, but I can't see him being another José Iturbi."

Cohen frowned. "Who's that?"

Murray was astounded. *For all his pretence of being cultured, Cohen's never heard of the famous Spanish conductor and pianist.*

He quickly changed the subject. "Mr. Cohen, the building just east of us on Queen Street —"

"Yes, Murray, what about it?"

"There was a single tenant in it … a woman. I rarely saw her. She lived there for many years, but I heard she died recently. Naturally, as a Casino partner, I'm interested in knowing what's going to happen to the property. There are already too many dilapidated buildings, teahouses, gypsy joints, what have you on the south side of Queen. Well, to be blunt, I'm concerned we could have another flophouse near the theatre. That house is yours, isn't it, Mr. Cohen?" Perhaps he'd asked the wrong question, Murray thought as the look on Cohen's face changed. Feeling anxious, he made a motion as if to leave.

"Don't go yet, Murray. Pull up a chair. I want you to know something. My father, Jacob Cohen, was born in Poland and immigrated to the United States where he worked for many years as a peddler. He then came to Toronto to join his older brother and open a shoe store on Queen Street, very close to City Hall. Over time, he got involved in local politics. He became friends with a police magistrate, Colonel George Taylor Denison. My father ended up acting as an interpreter for the Yiddish-speaking community. He was a justice of the peace and a bail magistrate. It was through Denison's influence that my father was appointed a magistrate in 1918.

"That lady you mentioned was a very close friend of my father's, and he promised her that property as her home for her lifetime. I inherited the property when my father died, on condition that I keep his pledge to her. I didn't have very much to do with her over the years … and before you think another thought, Murray, she wasn't my mother. Anyway, I'm going to fix up the building and rent it out to respectable people. From the Casino's point of view, there will be no problems. Now does that answer all the questions you have?"

Not knowing quite what to say, Murray simply said, "Yes, I'll be on my way."

He hustled down the stairwell rather than wait for the slow-moving cage elevator and got to the street. *Why did Cohen tell me all of that? It sounds as if he's both proud and a little ashamed of his father. I wonder who that woman really was — his mistress?*

46

JAPAN SURRENDERS

There was great excitement in the Grace Street house on Tuesday evening, August 14, 1945. After the Americans had unleashed their "secret weapon" — bombs of unthinkable destructive power that in a few days had levelled Hiroshima and Nagasaki and left tens of thousands of people dead — the Japanese finally surrendered unconditionally. Murray's mother, Anna, who had followed the daily events of the war assiduously and was in an especially festive mood, declared, "Let's celebrate. The war's finally over!"

Samuel agreed. "We can let the boys have a little drink, too. Murray's still down at the theatre, but Lil can join us with the boys in the parlour. This is a very, very important day."

"Will we have a holiday, just like Victory over Europe Day, Grandma Anna?" asked young Alan.

"I can't answer that for sure, Alan," replied Anna, beaming. "There'll be some sort of holiday. You're probably too young to understand it all, but maybe the end of this war will be the beginning of peace forever."

Although obviously pleased with what he'd heard, Samuel cautioned Anna. "Don't be too sure. I've never been able to trust the Germans, or the Russians, for that matter."

"Stop being such a spoiler, Samuel. We should all rejoice that this terrible war is over. And I, too, don't really trust the Russians!"

Then Barry piped up. "I'm sure Dad and everybody else has heard the news by now, but I guess he has to stay at work until after the last show. We can still have a little party, can't we? Grandma Esther's upstairs. She should come down, too."

"Good idea," Samuel agreed.

Lil and the three boys gathered around the parlour table as Samuel opened a bottle of ceremonial Manischewitz wine, having put out the fluted wineglasses reserved for special events.

"I'm going to tell Grandma Esther to come down now," Barry insisted, running upstairs. When he got to her bedroom door, he paused. "It's Barry, Grandma! The war's finally over and we want you to come downstairs and celebrate." He waited expectantly with his ear glued to her door.

A soft, almost tearful voice replied, "I'll be down shortly."

When Grandma Esther finally joined the crowd, Samuel said a brief prayer to peace in Hebrew.

Lil took a small sip of wine, glanced at her mother, and began to cry. "At least my sons won't be going off to war."

Esther nodded soberly. "Only if God wishes it to be."

Gerry turned the old upright Rogers radio in the corner of the parlour up full blast and started fiddling with the dials, adding to the atmosphere of acoustical pandemonium.

Clearly irritated by her son's behaviour, Lil spoke to him sharply. "Gerry, turn that radio off immediately It's too loud!" The radio continued to blast until Lil abruptly shut it off. "Okay, boys, it's time to quiet down and go to bed. Stop your fussing or I'll have to call your father. And you know what he's like if he has to come home when you boys act up!"

The three boys quickly retreated upstairs to their third-floor bedroom, while Esther silently returned to her own room.

Murray didn't come back from the theatre until after midnight, but Lil was patiently waiting for him on the sofa in the parlour. With everyone else asleep, the house was quiet. Murray was exhausted.

"I suppose you've heard the news about Japan's surrender," Lil said.

"Of course, I have, Lil. But it seems I never hear good news without the bad, as well."

"What do you mean?"

Murray removed his jacket, hung it over the sofa arm, and flopped into an adjacent chair. "I received a call from Edward Johnson, our alderman." He held his breath for a moment as though choking on something. "It's no deal."

"No deal?"

"Judge Robb, the chairman of the LCBO, has said no to reinstating our liquor licence, and that's final. So no alcohol at the Variety. Johnson promised me we'd get most of our money back if he wasn't successful, but there was no mention of that today. I can only hope he keeps his word."

Lil's face was ashen. "That's terrible! What's going to happen, Murray?"

"The hotel and the theatre will continue to lose money slowly but surely unless we do something very different."

Lil composed herself. "You know, Murray, tonight was one of the few times I've felt I was a part of this home. We had a little celebration with your parents and my mother and the boys. But I'm still waiting for your parents to leave this house."

"Please, not now! I simply can't go over this again! I'm going to bed."

47

CHANGES AT THE CASINO

Jubilation reigned in the streets of Toronto as news of the Japanese surrender spread and Deputy Mayor David Balfour declared August 15, 1945, a civic holiday. People danced in the streets all over North America to big band tunes and The Andrews Sisters' famous hit "Don't Sit Under the Apple Tree."

At the Casino Theatre not a single show was cancelled, nor was there any special performance or announcement by any of the performers. Since V-E Day in May, there had been a noticeable decrease in uniformed servicemen, and now with the end of the Pacific War, Murray knew box office receipts would decline further. When he expressed his concerns at the weekly meeting with Arthur Cohen, the man's sarcastic response wasn't surprising.

"Don't tell me, Murray, that you want the war to continue just so a twelve-hundred-seat theatre on Queen Street can carry on?"

"Of course not, Mr. Cohen. Everybody wanted the war to be over. But now that it is, we're seeing fewer servicemen as customers, and soon we'll probably see declining prosperity across the country."

"You fancy yourself quite the economist, don't you, Murray."

"No, not at all, just a realist."

"I've heard your suggestions before, Murray. So far the figures aren't too bad. Still, I'm prepared to take a small loss, at least for now. I can write it off. The Allens have their own reasons for continuing with the Casino. The war gave us a onetime advantage, I think. We can always rethink our joint venture at the Casino." Almost condescendingly, he added, "How does that sound?"

Murray returned to the Casino after the brief meeting with Cohen, certain that tired old burlesque routines, striptease, and second-rate vaudeville acts would mark the demise of the theatre in short order. As he hurried by the box office, the cashier waved an envelope at him. *Now what?* Murray hustled into the office adjacent to the box office. "Lester Montgomery handed me this letter for you, Mr. Little. You just missed him by a few minutes. He's gone backstage."

Puzzled, Murray glanced at the envelope and opened it. Lester usually didn't send him notes if he had a problem. His choreographer and stage manager preferred to speak to Murray directly. Carefully, he read the letter.

Dear Murray,

I've enjoyed my seven years at the Casino. However, I recently got a terrific offer as assistant choreographer from Leon Leonidoff, the chief choreographer at Radio City Music Hall in New York. We met many years ago when he first arrived from Romania. I was one of his hoofers, and we became good friends. Radio City is busy preparing a big Christmas presentation, and the offer he made to me is simply too good to turn down. I hate to leave you and the girls and the staff backstage, Archie Stone and the orchestra, and all the great people I've met in burlesque at your theatre.

I know it's short notice, but as it happens, I know a fellow from New Mexico who's a great dancer, has some experience in stage production, and who's up here in Toronto seeking work. His name's Chuck Gregory and you'll find him easy to work with if you take him on.

Continued success!

— Lester

Murray hurried backstage and spotted Lester immediately. The choreographer was an angular, gangly man with a black moustache who was hardly the type anyone would think of as a dancer. Murray was still holding the letter of resignation when Lester approached him.

"Murray, you've read my note. I'm sorry I had to do it that way, but I thought you'd need formal notice. I've told some of the girls in the chorus, and they seem pretty upset about my leaving."

"Your departure does take me by surprise, but I guess we have no choice. How do we get hold of this fellow Gregory?"

"He's now living in Toronto and staying with his boyfriend, Cliff. Chuck gave me a call just a couple of days ago when he arrived."

"Did you say *boyfriend*, Lester?"

"Yes, I did. Chuck's a homosexual."

"A homosexual? Are you kidding?"

"Surely, Chuck's bedroom habits are his business. Believe me, he's a great dancer and stage director. The guy will be great and the girls in the chorus will love him."

"I've always trusted you, Lester. I'll let Lou and the front office know about your intentions. Have Mr. Gregory give me a call to talk about a contract."

"You won't regret it." Lester shook Murray's hand and then quite unexpectedly kissed him on the forehead.

Surprised, Murray took a step backward. Was Lester a homosexual, too? What should he say now? He decided to remain silent.

A few days later, when Murray met Chuck Gregory backstage after the last show of the day, he didn't know what to expect. They both arrived precisely at midnight at the dressing room door of the feature attraction of the week. Murray was nervous and wary because of what Lester had told him about Chuck's sexual orientation. He'd never encountered a homosexual before, at least not one he recognized. On the other hand, Chuck seemed quite relaxed. Casually dressed in cowboy boots, shirt collar open, black moustache neatly trimmed, he immediately picked up on Murray's apprehension. "Mr. Little, I'm Chuck Gregory."

"Uh ... pleasure to meet you, Mr. Gregory."

"We don't have to be that formal, do we? Why don't you call me Chuck? Do you mind if I call you Murray? That's the way we do things in New Mexico where I come from. I've got to get used to you Canadians. You all seem so formal. Never mind. I've worked in a couple of places in Canada, and I'm getting used to it. I do like working with Canadians in the theatre. They're so polite! I'm sure I'd enjoy working here."

Murray was pleased. "I've cleared your job with my partners, Chuck. Everybody here takes Lester's recommendations very seriously. You can pick up where he left off, salary and all. You're as good as hired."

Chuck smiled. "Great!"

"Now is there anything I can do to help? You know, introduce you to the chorus girls, the orchestra, set designer, the people at the front of the house? Perhaps accommodation in the city?"

"No thanks, Murray. Lester's been very helpful. I've already met a lot of the people, and they all seem very decent. And I've even caught a couple of the shows, so I think I know what your needs are. I don't anticipate any problems adjusting to working here. And don't worry about accommodation. I've moved into a nice apartment on Queen Street with my friend, Cliff, and we're refurbishing it. So I'm in good shape. In fact, I've already taken the liberty of calling for our first rehearsal tomorrow, subject to getting a firm job offer from you, of course!"

"You know, Chuck, your arrival corresponds with a couple of other backstage changes. You've no doubt heard that our regular house singer and MC, Bobby Goodman, is going back to Chicago. So I've hired a new man — Rex Doyle. Perhaps you've heard of him?"

"No, I haven't, but I've spoken to a number of people already about Doyle, and he's got a very good reputation. It looks to me like you have everything in order. You shouldn't have any backstage worries once I get into action with the chorus line production numbers and house staff. I've worked in burlesque in the States and know about the limitations in Canada, so you should be able to relax."

"Great, Chuck. That makes me feel good. If you have any problems with any of the staff, let me know immediately."

"Fine, Murray, and by the way, do you like chili?"

Momentarily confused by the seemingly irrelevant question, Murray hesitated for a moment. "As a matter of fact, I do. Why do you ask?"

"Now that I know I have the job for sure, I'd like to celebrate with a little party a week Sunday at my apartment. I want to invite all the backstage staff and would really like you to come, as well. I'll be serving my favourite dish — Mexican chili."

"That's very kind of you, Chuck. I'll certainly try. We have Sunday afternoon shows for the Chinese Freemasons, but I'll check with Dave Sherman to see if he can cover for me. By the way, remind me to introduce you to Dave. He's our assistant manager."

Chuck grinned. "Sounds like you work eight days a week, Murray."

"Something like that."

The Sunday following Lil's annual departure for Miami, Gerry and Alan played baseball in the local park, while Barry stayed at home with his three grandparents and father to listen to the record albums given to him on his last birthday. They included the only recordings of the great Enrico Caruso and an album of Ignacy Jan Paderewski, the famous Polish pianist, composer, and statesman.

"Dad, don't you think this music's terrific?" enthused Barry. "I'd sure like to play piano the way Paderewski does."

"You must realize these are very special people, Barry," Murray cautioned. "Musicians like these are born with very special talents and work very hard to be as good as they are."

Not about to be put off, Barry said, "I'd really like to try to play. I think I could do it! Would you let me take piano lessons, please?

Maybe I could use the piano sitting unused in the rehearsal studio. You know, the one you took from our front parlour years ago."

"You boys nearly broke that piano," Murray retorted quickly. Then half apologetically, he said, "I knew you liked music, but I had no idea you want to take piano lessons."

"I really would, Dad. I've heard the Royal Conservatory is the best place to go."

"Well, Barry, I'll talk it over with Mother … when she returns."

"Mom won't mind. She said she used to play the piano, remember? Her father gave her lessons."

"I said I'll talk it over with your mother. I promise." Then Murray changed the subject. "Maybe you'd like to come to a party with me this afternoon. I know you're enjoying the music here, but you might like to meet some of the people who'll be there. Our new choreographer, Chuck Gregory, is treating some of the Casino people to his home-made chili. How about it?"

"Sure, Dad. That sounds great."

Barry quickly got dressed in his best Sunday clothes — white shirt and tie, trousers with suspenders, and a two-toned, two-button tweed jacket.

Murray and Barry arrived at Gregory's Queen Street apartment to discover it was a second-floor walk-up in an old Edwardian house about twenty-five blocks west of the Casino Theatre. Barry had never been to this part of the city before. "Dad, why would anyone want to live on a street like this? There are hardly any houses — just a lot of grocery and hardware stores and butcher shops."

His father smiled. "I'm sure Mr. Gregory has his reasons."

As Murray and Barry climbed the stairs, they heard music, laughter, and chatter and sniffed the scent of spicy chili wafting from the apartment. Gregory's place was already filled with Casino performers and pit orchestra members.

"Dad, you seem to be the only person here who's from the office staff," Barry remarked.

Irritated by his son's inquisitiveness, Murray grabbed him by the hand and half dragged him across the room toward the kitchen door where Chuck stood with his roommate. "I want to introduce you to our host, Mr. Gregory."

Barry was startled. "Dad, he's the one with the moustache, right? That guy beside him … I've never seen a man with bleached blond hair before. I've seen men wearing blond wigs onstage, but this guy looks strange."

"Everybody's entitled to his own taste, Barry. Come, meet Mr. Gregory."

Barry's eyes darted around the room as he took another couple of steps through the partying crowd. "Dad," he whispered, trying to reach Murray's ear, "this place looks peculiar. Why are his walls all painted purple? There are white lace curtains everywhere — frilly ones! Did he do this just for the party, or is this for real?"

"Barry," Murray said softly, "let's just say Mr. Gregory and his friend are … different."

"I'll say they are!"

48

BIG-NAME ACTS GALORE

After the changes at the Casino Theatre immediately following the war, life on and off the theatre's stage didn't change much during the next two and a half years. There were still four shows a day, strippers, burlesque bits, vaudeville acts, a chorus line, an amiable MC, plus ever-decreasing box office receipts. But life on Grace Street was poised to change drastically, at least for Murray. Anna and Samuel had finally saved enough money to purchase a small home in a blue-collar district in central Toronto.

Feeling that he, too, had saved enough money, Murray was now willing to gamble on a new upmarket home in prestigious Forest Hill. As he explained it to his younger sister, Gert, "Ma and Pa will have their new place now and I'm counting on their departure to make the home setting more attractive to Lil so she'll stop running off every winter to Miami. Now she tells me she can't stand the cold winters. Imagine, all these years in the city. Thirty-nine years of age and she can't tolerate the cold. Still, I'm hoping she'll be encouraged to stay at home. Esther's going to move with us, but she's easy to handle, keeping to herself as she does. The boys are doing well at school, but I'd really like them to have a first-class education, and I think they'll get that in Forest Hill."

"Sounds fine," Gert said, "but I'm a little surprised to hear Esther would want to leave Grace Street. Everyone knows how fixed and rigid she can be."

"Becky's already moved from this neighbourhood, you know, and I think in recent years, Esther has come to see how modern and progressive her sister is. Curiously, she tends to follow Becky somewhat." Murray paused for a moment. "Don't misunderstand me. Esther's still very involved with all that religious ritual and is a hell of a stickler when it comes to observance. But at least she's not so adamant about the boys having further Judaic instruction beyond their bar mitzvahs. She's actually not as much of a problem now."

"But what happens when Lil's away?"

"Lil's promised to spend more time at home. I think it's a step in the right direction. With Ma and Pa out of the house, I honestly think she'll spend more time at home. At least I hope she will. And if she doesn't, well, I guess we'll have to hire a housekeeper to look after things while she's away. Could be three or four, maybe six, weeks each year."

"Well, I wouldn't count on it. Lil's not much of a homemaker."

"It's worth a try, isn't it, Gert? And before you say another word, I know some of the Appelbaums can be very difficult."

"Speaking of Appelbaums, what about Harry? Does anybody know where he is now? And what's happened to his two boys, Moishe and Maxie, and his poor wife?"

"I haven't heard a word about Harry's whereabouts. The Appelbaums don't mention him anymore. As for Harry's boys, Moishe is planning to go to California to seek his fortune. He hasn't been able to get any kind of decent work in Toronto since leaving the army. Maxie is still hustling the ponies. And their poor mother lives in a cheap three-storey walk-up. The boys do their best to support her, but

I honestly don't know how she keeps going. She's going to be terribly upset when she hears that Moishe is moving away. For that matter, Barry's going to be unhappy, too. He and those two abandoned boys have had a strong friendship for years. They're heroes in Barry's eyes, especially Moishe."

While get-togethers with Gert were few and far between, Murray rarely missed a weekly meeting with Arthur Cohen. One, in mid-February 1948, was very significant for both Murray and the Casino. Arriving a little late, Murray thought Cohen seemed unusually impatient.

"What was the big holdup, Murray?" Cohen asked. "You're always on time."

"Sorry, Mr. Cohen. It's snowing heavily, and in my haste to get here, I forgot my overcoat. So I had to run back to the office when I was halfway here. But when I got back to the office, there were two detectives outside the door waiting to speak to me."

Cohen's face became a wrinkled prune. "Don't tell me they're back again with this morality nonsense, Murray?"

"No, not exactly. They asked me if I knew a lawyer named John German. I told them I didn't but that I'd heard about someone by that name from Gersten Allen, that Gersten said he was a friend of a friend and was a prominent lawyer. German had written to Gersten complaining about the theatre. He said he was acting as a spokesman for one of those church groups that disapprove of our theatre. Apparently, he'd seen a number of productions he considered immoral and indecent and warned Gersten that his group intended to have our theatre closed. As far as I know, though, Gersten didn't hear anything further from him."

"What's that got to do with the presence of the policemen?"

"Well, as it turns out, this German, for all his pretensions of moral propriety and decency, was reported to the police by a neighbour. Turns out he's a Peeping Tom! He actually used a ladder to climb up to a woman's bedroom window!"

"A prominent lawyer and a friend of the Allens a Peeping Tom? I don't believe it."

"Evidently, the police laid a charge. And this morning they found him dead in his garage. He hanged himself but left no suicide note, and the police, I guess, thought I might give them further information. Have you ever heard of this man German?"

"Never! He sounds like a bloody pervert — a sick man living a double life." Cohen rose, marched around his desk, then plunked himself down again in his chair. "Don't look so upset, Murray. The world's better off without people like that."

Murray pulled up a chair and placed the receipts on the desk, thinking, *I hope I'm not in for another sermon from the old fox.*

Cohen glanced at the weekly receipts and sprang from his chair to begin pacing the room. "I don't like this, Murray. We're continuing to slip. I've given the Casino situation a lot of thought and have spoken to the Allens. I've been considering what you said about a big-name policy. It sounds logical — big names, big bucks. Financially, we're going nowhere with burlesque."

Murray leaned forward in his chair. "It was only a suggestion, but I thought it made sense."

"At this point, Murray, I think it's worth a try. As you know, I'm not much of a risk taker, but if you and the Allens want to go ahead and spend more money to make more money I'll go along with it. I've spoken to Gersten a couple of times. Nothing formal, mind you. But yesterday he called me and told me that an acquaintance of his from Montreal is in town. This man, Cooper, operates a theatrical booking agency in Montreal and handles a lot of well-known performers. Why don't you set up an appointment to meet him? Maybe he can help us. Between you and me and the gatepost, Murray, I don't care what Lou thinks. I'm game, and the Allens are willing to take a shot at it, too. And we'll let you look after Lou. It's my understanding that Gersten's bringing Cooper down to the theatre this evening. See what you make of him."

Murray rose and headed toward the door, then stopped and turned to Cohen. "You know, Mr. Cohen, I might be stepping on Lou's toes here. He prides himself as the artistic director of the theatre."

Cohen snapped like a turtle. "That's your problem. I'm not interested in talking to Lou. See what Cooper suggests and report back to me. And by the way, Murray, just remember. Money is coined liberty."

Murray nodded politely but thought, *What an odd comment to make. He reflected for a moment. But maybe he's right about the pursuit of money. Money does give you freedom from worries, and, boy, do I need that.*

Later that evening in Lou's office at the Casino, Gersten Allen introduced Lou and Murray to Roy Cooper. "Roy operates a theatrical booking agency in Montreal. He has extensive experience in the theatrical business, even burlesque. His firm, Paramount Agency, handles a spectrum of theatrical events, and for our purposes, gentlemen, Mr. Cooper can book well-known performers into our theatre, virtually anyone we want. But I'll let Roy speak for himself."

Lou and Murray shook Cooper's hand. Murray was immediately struck by the man's appearance: he looked exactly like the Hollywood actor Adolphe Menjou! A dapper and sophisticated fellow, Cooper had a kind look in his eyes and an honest face. Having seen Adolphe Menjou on the screen many times, Murray knew the actor with the waxy black moustache had a reputation as one of the world's best-dressed men.

Cooper spoke quickly and with great enthusiasm. "I caught your last show and it's pretty standard burlesque. Good, mind you, but a little dated. Maybe a lot dated. No matter. The house was half empty. Headlining your show with a well-known performer — it doesn't matter whether it's a singer or an actor as long as they're well known — is going to increase your box office. That's the story in Montreal. We're always sold out when we bring in acts like The Four Knights or the Golden Gate Quartet or Nellie Lutcher or Valaida Snow."

Lou was unusually quiet, nursing his usual Johnnie Walker, seemingly disinterested. Suddenly, he piped up. "Christ, who the hell can afford these people?"

Cooper remained unflappable. "Cut out two of your strippers and one of your vaudeville acts and you'll fill the house. I guarantee it! You'll be able to afford top-of-the-line performers and still make a profit."

Lou slumped back into his chair, sulking. "And get rid of the chorus line, too?" He was like a child who had lost his favourite toy. "I thought I was supposed to be dictating policy around here." He poured himself another shot. "But, hey, I'm outnumbered here. That's it! What choice do I have, anyway?" He was growing especially petulant.

Murray attempted to soothe Lou. "Can it hurt to give it a try, Lou, say for a couple of weeks? Let's listen to what Roy has to say."

"As it happens," Cooper continued, "I've got a cancellation for The Four Knights in the third week of February. I'm sure we can arrange a booking at the Casino. We can rebook your current people for a later date. What do you say to that?"

"I'm game," Murray enthused. "Let's give it a try."

Gersten simply nodded, while Lou muttered, "It's out of my hands."

Cooper's eyes sparkled. "Great, gentlemen, you won't regret it." He immediately reached for the telephone.

As if startled at someone grabbing his desk phone, Lou abruptly snapped out of his semi-stuporous state. "What the hell do you think you're doing?"

"I'm calling the agent for The Four Knights! Believe me, Lou, I've dealt with agents and performers long enough, from burlesque to movie stars, and I've learned you have to act fast and get a firm commitment from these people. Some of these agents are bastards, but you get a better price acting early. I like to clear up any ifs, ands, or buts and salaries quickly. That's why I have the best agency in Montreal. And I think you people here are making the right move going with big-name headliners. Toronto's just beginning to open up."

Lou seemed unconvinced by Roy's pronouncements. "Well, who the hell are these people, anyway?" He turned to Gersten and Murray. "Either of you guys ever heard of The Four Knights?"

"Well, no," Gersten admitted sheepishly.

Murray, red-faced, had to add: "I guess that holds for me, too."

"See what I mean?" Lou snarled.

"Gentlemen," Cooper interceded, "from a theatrical point of view, you all appear to be in one heck of a rut. You're completely out of touch with what's popular with a lot of people these days. This quartet's a very refined gospel group that sings beautifully. They're with Decca Records, and I'm going to bet not one of you here has even heard of Decca Records, judging from this conversation. These boys were big hits on Arthur Godfrey's radio show. Do any of you even listen to the radio?"

The office suddenly became silent as Lou, Gersten, and Murray stared at one another like three clueless kids. Murray was the first to respond, still somewhat embarrassed. "Roy, I have to admit that getting name performers at the Casino, I mean, really big stars ... well, it's new territory for us. You're right. We don't personally know the acts you've mentioned, and yes, we're in a rut!"

Gersten nodded while Lou shrugged defiantly.

Murray continued his apology. "I guess my teenage sons would know a lot more about these artists than I do."

Cooper was quick to respond. "If you think this act is just for teenagers, you're wrong, gentlemen. Trust me. Adults love them just as much as teenagers. When The Four Knights played the Monument-National Theatre in Montreal, they did terrific business! If they can do that in the French end of Montreal, believe me, they'll do great in English-speaking Toronto. You won't regret booking them."

Lou handed Cooper the telephone. Pulling a small black leather notebook out of his jacket, the Montrealer quickly dialled long distance. "Cy? It's Roy Cooper. I'm calling from Toronto and just want to confirm February 26 as an opening date for The Four Knights in Toronto at the Casino Theatre." There was a prolonged silence. "Yes, you heard me, the Casino! Never heard of it? It's like the Gaiety in Montreal. Yeah, it's a burlesque house, but they want to change their policy." Another pause followed. "No, no, it shouldn't hurt if they're on the same bill as a stripper or a burlesque comic. I'm trying to get management here to change their policy, but if we can't, surely, the boys in the group would agree to come if the date's open."

During a third protracted pause, Cooper's eyes began to twinkle. "The date's open? That's great! And you're sure they'll do it! Okay, we'll take them for one week to start. I'll send you the contract immediately!" He turned to the three men gathered around the desk, anxiously eavesdropping. "They're available, and as you've just heard, I'm sending them a contract."

◆ ◆ ◆

On Thursday, February 26, 1948, the Casino Theatre, without much fanfare, inaugurated its new big-name policy. The opening bill, a curious amalgam advertised in the entertainment section of the city's newspaper, read: "Casino Takes a Chance. The Four Knights — stars of radio and Decca Records — share their billing with a stripper, a comic, and two vaudeville acts."

Murray was backstage early on the opening date and spotted the four Black men standing quietly and occasionally whispering to one another. Nervously, he strode over and introduced himself. "I'm Murray Little, manager of the Casino. I have to tell you, gentlemen, that this is our first venture into this kind of format. As Mr. Cooper may have explained to you, we've never used big-name recording artists or radio personalities to headline our shows." Murray cleared his throat and thought for a moment as the singers nodded agreeably. "Oh, there was one," he corrected himself. "Last year we had Stepin Fetchit. But he didn't work out that well."

"We're glad to be here, Mr. Little, I can assure you," Oscar Broadway said in a sonorous voice. "You know, we've only been in Toronto a couple of days, but what we've seen here we like. And before you say another word, we don't mind working on the same bill as a stripper. Doesn't bother us one bit. We like it here in Canada, you know. There are no separate entrances for Black people, no special seating in the restaurants … things like that. We don't get treated nearly so nicely down in the States."

Before Murray could utter a response, Oscar continued as spokesperson for the group. "Stepin Fetchit? That cat's old hat now. He might have been the first Black film star white folks recognized, but he's something of an embarrassment to Black people, you know … always playing the role of some lazy, shuffling, superstitious darkie. Don't you worry about us being here in Toronto. Your theatre's going to be just fine."

The other three members of the group nodded approvingly and murmured, "Amen."

Murray was pleased. "Gentlemen, I'm really happy to hear that. Now, if there's anything you need, just let me know."

A broad smile spread across Oscar's face. "Man, we dig it!"

Murray's face must have looked puzzled.

"Ain't you heard that expression before, Mr. Little? If you *dig it*, it means you understand it and like it!"

Murray merely smiled, then shook their hands. *A new venture and now a new language*, he thought.

On the following Monday, Murray called Cooper in Montreal to say, "Roy, business with The Four Knights has been fantastic! I guess our customers have never seen popular recording stars. Or maybe these guys are just that good. Anyway, can you see if you can get them for a second week?"

"Hold the line for a minute or so, Murray. I'll try to get their agent on my other line."

Murray anxiously glanced at his watch, waiting for Cooper's response.

"Yep," Cooper finally answered. "They're clear for the upcoming week. Didn't I tell you they'd do good business?"

Murray hung up happily and quickly went backstage to meet the group before the first show of the day. "I've just been in touch with Roy Cooper, who's confirmed with your agent that you can play the theatre for another week."

Oscar Broadway clapped his hands. "Groovy, man. I'm glad Toronto digs us."

At the end of The Four Knights' two-week engagement, Murray made a special visit to Arthur Cohen's office. "I've come to show you the books, Mr. Cohen. I've got to hand it to Roy Cooper. Those Four Knights have done terrific business for us. This big-name policy might be just what our theatre needs. Did you get to see them?"

"I have to confess I didn't. I was too busy with personal affairs." He scanned the statements Murray had brought. "Well, I certainly like the bottom line. It's costing you more, but you're making more. If the shoe fits, wear it."

"Lou and the Allens aren't entirely convinced. They think the good box office is a fluke."

"I don't care how you people work it out. If they think it's such a fluke, why don't you book a few more big-name headliners and see how they do? It's sure as hell okay with me."

As usual, Murray's contact with Cohen was brief, and he quickly left the office. Customarily, he walked back to the theatre on what was a typical Toronto day in March — dull, dreary, wet, overcast, and bone-chillingly unpleasant. He'd passed the old Roxy, now the Broadway movie house, hundreds of times before, normally without much thought. But this time he stopped under its marquee as a strong gust of wind assailed him. Clutching his fedora, he leaned against the theatre building, hoping to avoid the worst of the howling wind, when the horrific events of March 3, 1935, flashed through his mind. Murray could see Avner lying bloodied in his office chair, hear the pandemonium that followed, the barking abruptness of the police, the crying and moaning at the funeral, the morbid sadness of the shiva, the ongoing frustrations at the insolvability of the murder/robbery. The images came and went as swiftly as the wind, brief but forceful. Murray continued on his way to the Casino just a few hundred feet away. *Avner always wanted to be big-time*, he mused. *What a shame he isn't around to enjoy it. But maybe he, too, would have wanted to stay in burlesque. In any case, I'll never know.*

The new Casino cashier, Margaret, motioned to Murray as he swept by the box office.

"What is it?" he asked through the small opening in the window.

"Mr. Appleby wants to see you upstairs."

Murray hurried up to the office he'd long ago euphemistically labelled "Lou's Lounge."

It was close to noon, and Lou, already into his first drink of the day, was at his maleficent best. "Hey, I see we did great business with The Four Knights. You know, don't you, it could have been an accident. I've still got my money on the girls. Even you've admitted the best business is tits and ass."

Murray frowned. "But, Lou, having a big-name headliner's a bonus. You've seen the box office receipts for the past two weeks. The Four Knights made all the difference. Without them, we'd have just about broken even."

Lou's face turned red. "I don't believe it!"

"Well, I don't think it was a chance happening. For God's sake,

Lou, burlesque and vaudeville are dead! You've got to adjust to stay in this business."

"Well, the chorus line stays no matter what!" Obviously agitated, Lou prepared another drink of what was now his favourite beverage — Seagram rye with water. "I'm as much a partner in this business as you are, if not more. You can call this Roy Cooper and book somebody else if you want, but clear it with the Allens first. And as long as I'm around, we're not getting rid of the chorus line. Is that clear?"

Murray was dismayed but acquiesced. "Fine, Lou, we'll try this experiment again. The chorus line will remain." *No doubt he doesn't want to lose Helen. And as far as Gersten and the other Allens were concerned, they like the chorus line. too, for obvious reasons … girlie time!*

Leaving Lou's office, Murray felt frustrated and mentally handcuffed. But when he called Cooper in Montreal, the booker was ebullient. "I heard from their agent that The Four Knights had a wonderful engagement in Toronto and would like to return! They're currently touring with Bill 'Bojangles' Robinson, the dancer, and they're getting some guest spots on *The Red Skelton Show*."

Murray sighed. "I'm very glad to hear The Four Knights are doing so well. However, Lou and the Allens aren't so convinced about our policy change. This is all a little unnerving for me because I really don't know who's that popular, as I've told you, and only Arthur Cohen is convincingly on my side. I've started to read *Billboard* and *Variety*, as you suggested, and that's helping a bit. I've also spoken to my sons. But I certainly can't rely on teenagers to tell me what's good for business, even though they might have heard of these performers. But, Roy, I've thought about this a lot and think we should just go ahead. Who's available?"

Cooper's animated voice bounced back. "Right now I've got Valaida Snow."

"Who?"

"Listen, Murray, you might not know her now, but take it from me, you won't regret bringing her in. Valaida's a beautiful Black singer who's been doing great box office. She was a big hit during the 1930s and has toured all over the United States, Europe, and the Far East.

She's very well known, or at least she was. Unfortunately, she was in Europe at the outbreak of the war, and not being white, she was arrested by the Germans. But she was lucky. She spent a year and a half in a Nazi concentration camp and then they released her as an exchange prisoner because of her unstable health. So she came back to the States and is now making a great comeback. A lot of people still remember her. Give her a try."

"Okay, Roy. I have to take your advice on this, so go ahead and book her." Murray glanced at his booking chart and noted that Snow would be on the same bill as Joe DeRita, the comic, and June St. Clair, a stripper.

Valaida Snow was booked into the Casino for April 29, 1948, and on the evening prior to her engagement, met with Murray in his office. "It's a pleasure to meet you, Miss Snow," he began. "What do you think of our little theatre? And have you caught our show today?" Murray felt almost apologetic.

"I love it. I've never worked a burlesque house before. I think it's kind of fun. Having a stripper on the bill with me ... well, I guess that's for the boys. I ain't got any problems with it, Mr. Little."

"Happy to hear that, Miss Snow. I'm glad you don't have a problem being on the same bill as a stripper and a comic."

"Not at all." Her smile warmed Murray. "After what I've been through and what I've seen in Europe and the Far East, and spending time in a Nazi concentration camp, are you kidding? Nothing fazes me! As long as people come to hear me sing, I'm happy."

"It must have been terrible in that concentration camp. I've never met anyone who's been through that kind of experience. We've heard stories about them here in Canada, but —"

She smiled again. "Mr. Little, that's all in the past. I'm just happy to still be alive and singing. Let's not talk about it anymore."

Murray's face turned crimson as an enormous pair of olive-brown eyes regarded him.

"Don't get upset," she said softly. "You didn't say anything bad, Mr. Little. Let's just get on with the show."

"I didn't mean to open up any old wounds, believe me, Miss Snow."

"You ain't done nothing bad, and for goodness' sake, honey, call me Valaida."

"How about I introduce you to our orchestra leader, Archie Stone, after the first show? I think our orchestra's really terrific. They're the best sight readers in the business, so you'll have no worries whatsoever. We're very professional here. I think you'll find our staff easy to get along with. And Toronto audiences are quite well behaved, I can assure you."

"Have you got a lot of Jewish people in this town, Mr. Little? I hope so. I get a big response when I sing 'Eli-Eli.' I recorded that tune just before I went overseas, and it was a really big hit for me."

Again, Murray was embarrassed. "I have to be perfectly honest with you, Valaida. I had no idea you sang songs like that. I thought you were a jazz singer."

"Man, I like to sing anything that's good!"

Several days after Valaida Snow opened, Murray enthusiastically placed a call to Roy Cooper in Montreal.

"This lady's terrific, Roy, and business is fantastic! Any chance we can get her to stay another week? I know it's very short notice, but I thought I'd ask."

"Hold the line, Murray. I'll get her agent."

Murray fiddled with his watch impatiently; the two-minute wait seemed endless.

Then Cooper's voice finally crackled over the line. "Yep, her agent says she's available. Another week at the Casino. And for the record, she told her agent she loves Toronto."

"I've got to tell you, Roy. I now know why they used to make such a fuss about Valaida. She's one heck of a performer! A Black lady who can look like a seductress singing 'Eli-Eli.' Even Lou's impressed!"

Murray hurried backstage to tell Valaida the good news. She was already into her final number in the early-evening show, and from his vantage point in the wings, Murray could see that the house was just about full. Valaida had the audience in the palm of her hand. He glanced across the stage to where the featured stripper stood watching, still wearing her kimono. *Imagine, even the stripper waits to get changed rather than miss this lady's act.*

The theatre was remarkably quiet, almost reverential, as Valaida sang the final bars to Billie Holiday's "Strange Fruit." As the final note ended, the audience burst into thundering applause as shouts of "Bravo!" resonated throughout the auditorium. He'd never heard people in the Casino yell "Bravo!" before. Valaida did two encores, then left the stage after graciously acknowledging the support of her accompanist and Archie Stone's orchestra.

Murray rushed across the stage behind the now-closed curtain to congratulate her. "That was a great performance!" he gushed with unabashed enthusiasm.

Valaida laughed. "And that was another great audience, Murray."

"I've just spoken to Roy Cooper, Valaida, and next week's available. We'd like to have you stay in Toronto for next week's show, if that's okay with you."

Valaida put her arm around Murray and whispered, "I'd love to."

Murray squirmed, not expecting the display of affection, then walked Valaida to her dressing room door. In the background, accolades continued coming from all directions. He cleared his throat. "Valaida, I have to speak to you in private."

She opened the door. "Well, let's step inside so we can talk."

"I have to ask a favour of you. A Jewish charitable organization called B'nai Brith is holding a fundraising evening, and I've been approached by the chairman to ask if you could put in an appearance. Just being there would be a big draw. The money they're raising is going to a very good cause — to help the resettlement of Holocaust survivors." Before Valaida could respond, Murray continued. "It's next Sunday evening at the Palace Pier, a beautiful dance hall on the city's lakeshore. I'd see to it that you're picked up and taken wherever you want to go after your appearance."

To his great relief, Valaida nodded and smiled approvingly, then grew tense. "Murray, I'm flattered." As she spoke, her eyes filled with tears and her mascara began to run, giving her face a strange, mask-like appearance. "I get very emotional when I think about the Holocaust and my time in a concentration camp. I was so lucky! If there's anything I can do to help those poor survivors, I'll do it. Please count me in!"

"Thank you, Valaida. I must say, you've certainly helped us at this theatre, not only by doing good business but by validating our place. You give it a sense of proper class! Being a burlesque house all these years has given us a certain reputation. And a lot of people, unfortunately, think we're in the sleaze trade. I have to tell you, at times it makes me very unhappy being known as the manager of a burlesque house."

"Oh, Murray, you shouldn't be upset." Valaida wiped away her tears and mascara. "There ain't nothing wrong with burlesque. Only squares feel that way. But I know what you're saying."

Murray left the dressing room mildly euphoric. What a sympathetic and sensitive woman! Why weren't there more like her? He hustled toward the front of the house where, much to his surprise, Lil stood waiting in the lobby. "I wasn't expecting you until next week, Lil! Is something wrong?"

"No, not really," she replied vaguely. "The weather turned bad in Miami, and I was able to get an early flight. And I miss the kids, so here I am!"

"What do you mean, you miss the kids? You were *only* away for two full months! My mother had to come over and look after the household. I really had my hands full!"

Murray's voice was so loud that one of the patrons poked his head out from his aisle seat and yelled, "For Christ's sake, shut up back there! We're trying to watch the movie!"

He grabbed Lil by the hand and escorted her to his office a few steps away. "Can you see how angry I am? These trips of yours are more than just an embarrassment to me. They've become one hell of an inconvenience!"

Lil stood back, feigning surprise. "I thought you'd be happy to see me."

"You have no business going south every winter and spring. Now that my parents have moved out, who's deserting whom, anyway?"

Lil remained stone-faced, unemotional, a carbon copy of her mother in a crisis. "I have my reasons," she snarled.

"What kind of excuse is that? Your absences are a terrible thing for me and the kids. Everyone asks about your whereabouts, and I have to give them a lame excuse that you can't tolerate the Canadian winter! Even your mother suspects something fishy."

"What does that mean? Am I on trial here? For the record, there's nothing fishy going on. I happen to like Florida, and if I must say it once again, I can't be the hausfrau like your mother. I'm not a cook or a cleaner! You do everything your own way when it comes to anything to do with the house. And I never get to share in any of the decisions you make about the kids! I'm not deserting anybody. I'm just doing the only thing I can do — letting you and your mother, even if she has moved out, run what was supposed to be my house!"

"Goddamn it! What the hell kind of family life do we have, anyway? You're never home. My parents and I try to look after the kids. I run back and forth between Arthur Cohen, the theatre, and the house … I simply can't do it all!" Lil appeared unmoved, so Murray threw himself into his office chair and lit a Sweet Caporal cigarette.

Lil quickly changed the subject. "Who's this Valaida Snow headlining the show this week, Murray? A Black stripper?"

He heaved an exasperated sigh. "Why should you care? She's a terrific singer, if you must know, and I'm hoping to convince your brother and others that people like Valaida are what we need at this theatre. In case you haven't heard, I'm trying to turn the theatre around, upgrade it, so to speak. I'm too old to become an engineer now, and the only business I know is the theatre. And even at that I'm having a lot of trouble. I'm stuck with the Casino with all its warts — and I don't like warts!"

"I thought you liked the business," was Lil's final comment before she quietly tiptoed out of the office.

Defeated, Murray slumped into his chair like a rag doll.

49

PATTI PAGE ATTACKED!

"I don't understand it, I can't believe my partners!" Murray protested to Arthur Cohen at one of their weekly meetings in the summer of 1948. "Look here!" He pointed to the week's take. "We've got all the proof we need — great receipts because of a first-class performer and still Gersten and Lou won't buy into it. Frankly, Mr. Cohen, I'm worn out."

"Well, Murray," answered Cohen somewhat sympathetically, "I'm not at all surprised. I have a sneaking suspicion that Lou and Gersten, and for that matter the other Allens, want to keep a burlesque format because they like the girls. It's as simple as that!"

"Even if we continue to lose money slowly but surely? I know I shouldn't be surprised, but don't they realize this way they'll make more money?"

"To be perfectly honest with you, Murray, I think Lou and the Allens regard the Casino as their private playpen. Maybe Lou cares a little more about money than the rest of them, but really, it's a social club for him. You know how much Lou likes to associate there with his City Hall cronies. Putting it bluntly, Murray, you and I understand that a lot of Lou's friends wouldn't be hanging around if it weren't for the free booze and girls. Need I say more?"

"I don't disagree with anything you've said, Mr. Cohen, but the theatre for me is my livelihood. As of this summer, I'm no longer involved with Ollie Baskin at the Variety Hotel. And thank goodness for that, though it's ironic after all of Ollie's machinations to get a cocktail licence for the hotel, then losing our liquor licence altogether because of the boxing scam. He's happy now no doubt, since he just got the licence back. Even happier with hard liquor being allowed in Ontario finally as of last year."

Cohen looked Murray squarely in the eye. "Well, then, you should be smiling now that you're free of Baskin."

Murray frowned. "But I've still got an expensive wife to support who spends a fortune on vacations and clothes. Not to mention three boys to put through school and university! Sure, I like many of the performers at the Casino, but not for the same reason Lou and his gang do. They're my livelihood. For me the Casino's damn hard work!"

"I can understand your situation, Murray, really I can! Your plight's not all of your own making."

"At least I was able to get a commitment from Lou and Gersten for Valaida Snow. They know she did good business, so she's coming back in September for two weeks. But you know, Mr. Cohen, so much of the time I feel like the proverbial salmon swimming upstream … and drowning."

"Just stick with it, Murray. Remember, I've got a third of the partnership, and I'm on your side on this one. I know I've got a reputation for being a penny-pincher. I know full well what people say about me. But when it comes to you, Murray, I have to admit I've developed a bit of a soft spot. And I'm willing to go along with you and whatever you want to do for the theatre. From what I can tell, I don't think Lou or Gersten are following what's going on in the world, certainly not as carefully as you are. As far as I'm concerned, you're the one reliable man in charge, and I'm going to continue to support you with your big-name policy. I'm pretty certain that in the fullness of time Gersten at least will figure it out. This new policy is definitely a money-maker. Persevere."

In September, Valaida did terrific business at the Casino again. However, her two weeks were followed, at Lou's insistence, by a succession of strippers and comics — and a subsequent decline in box office receipts.

In February 1949, Murray called Roy Cooper. "I've had a bit of a breakthrough with Lou and the Allens, Roy. At least for the time being. But I'm not sure why. Still, they've given me the go-ahead to get the best-name acts our budget will allow."

"Delighted to hear that, Murray. Just hold the phone while I look at my book and see what I can do right away."

Murray laughed. "You sure don't waste any time, do you, Roy."

"You know my style, Murray. Let's see … there's an opening for a group called the Golden Gate Quartet in March. Would you like them? They're a great singing group."

Having read a bit about the quartet in *Billboard* and *Variety*, Murray said, "I'll certainly go on your say-so."

"Great! The quartet's been around for quite a few years, Murray. They've made some personnel changes, but they're still good box office. They've got an RCA Victor contract, and lots of people have heard them over the air. They're available in the second week of March."

Murray thumbed through his big book. "Roy, we've got a stripper in the second week. Lou's gone ahead and booked her! And I don't think we can get out of the contract. Believe me, I thought we had an understanding — no more strippers! God, I can't figure that guy out."

"Who is it, Murray?"

"Her name's Rhonda True."

"Murray, I'm sure the boys won't mind having a stripper on the bill, and I don't think Rhonda will give you trouble. I know her from the Gaiety."

"It's the audience I'm concerned about!"

"Murray, don't be so nervous. I'll go ahead and get the quartet for you — and you leave the stripper alone, if I can put it that way! And, Murray, while I've got you on the phone, I see there's an opening for Oscar Peterson in the first week of April."

"Who's that?"

"Just ask Barry, your piano-playing son. Peterson's quite the sensation around Montreal — a fabulous jazz pianist just starting out on his career. He'll do very well for you, and I can get him fairly cheap."

And the deal was done.

As Cooper had predicted, the Golden Gate Quartet did first-class business, and several weeks later, a little-known but successful Oscar Peterson appeared at the Casino. Not long after that, Cooper called Murray to say he was becoming a little confused. "I've been getting calls from Lou lately to book people. He's insisting he has the final say. Just who's in charge there?"

"I have to apologize, Roy, but as soon as I think I have policy straightened away, it's broken. This is something I have to live with. Look, let's let Lou do some of the booking for now. But will you do me a favour and always check with me, as well? I have to give him some credit, or life here will be unbearable. He insists that the patrons come to see the girls and that having a name performer is just the icing on the cake. And who knows, he could be right! Somehow a lot of people who wouldn't be caught dead in a burlesque house seem to find it acceptable to come to our theatre now. For want of a better term, we'll call it a *blended policy*. You can appreciate that I'm dancing between the raindrops, Roy."

"Understood, Murray. You've got quite a juggling act there in Toronto. Here's a list of people I've tentatively booked for the Casino. Grab a pencil. There's Maxine Sullivan, a very popular singer. She's quite famous. You may remember a big hit of hers a few years ago — 'Loch Lomond.' And I've got Ethel Waters over the summer who, for sure, you've heard about. She's done a recent single with Fletcher Henderson, the orchestra leader. And then I've rebooked The Four Knights for you. After that, I've got another great performer, Rose Murphy, a first-class singer and pianist. They've nicknamed her the 'Chee-Chee Girl.' She'll do great business for you. Then we've got the Page Cavanaugh Trio. Ask your son about them if you don't recognize that name!"

"It all sounds very impressive, Roy."

"Shall I continue?"

"Sure, go ahead."

"Okay, I've got tentative dates for Josh White, a terrific folksinger, The Four Knights for a third time, followed by the fabulous Nelly Lutcher. Then there's a big band singer, Helen Forrest, who's now doing good business on her own. Next, a possible booking for a group called Red Ingle and His Natural Seven. I've also got The Charioteers, and in late October a first-class hit parade artist named Patti Page." Cooper paused. "Shall I go on?"

"Well, you might as well give me the full list."

"I've got a unique jazz singer called Sarah Vaughan and a very special singer/piano player named Dorothy Donegan, which takes you through to the end of 1949. Then, in early January next year, I've got a commitment from Larry Adler, the harmonica player. You've surely heard of him already."

"Of course, I have, though the others are still just names to me. But I'm learning!"

In late October 1949, the beautiful Patti Page appeared at the Casino. On the morning of her last day at the theatre, Murray received a phone call at home. He stepped out of the bathroom with his face covered in shaving lather to pick up the phone. "Who is this? And what's so important that I have to be called at 7:30 in the morning?"

"It's Detective Jim McNeally of the Toronto Police," an officious voice at the other end responded.

Murray almost dropped the phone. *Not again. Not another complaint!*

"Mr. Little, we'd like to see you down at the theatre right now. It appears your star performer, Patti Page, was attacked in her hotel room last night."

Murray was flabbergasted. "She was what?"

"Miss Page was attacked last night, and there's an investigation under way. We want to speak to you about this matter."

"Was she hurt?"

"No … at least not physically. Get down here as quickly as you can. We'd like to ask you a few questions."

"Right away, sir." Murray was irritated. *The way that officer talks you'd think I was the attacker or somehow responsible for the woman's assault!* He finished shaving, nicking himself several times in his haste, then dressed as fast as he could.

Esther got a glimpse of him as he darted down the hallway. "My God, Murray, your face is covered in bandages. Are you all right?"

Murray shouted back on the run, "Don't worry. I just cut myself shaving, Esther. I have to get down to the theatre right away, But I'm perfectly okay." He ran to his shiny new Cadillac parked in the garage at the side of the house.

Esther cried after him from her upstairs window, "The way you look you're going to frighten everyone."

Murray jumped into the car, ignoring Esther's shouts, and glanced at his face in the rearview mirror while speeding toward the theatre. Bits of toilet paper were plastered over the cuts on his face, his hair was uncombed, and his favourite silver-brown cravat was untied and crumpled in his shirt. No time to worry about that now.

Two enormous detectives, both wearing fedoras, greeted Murray at the theatre's front door, one in a grey suit, the other in blue. The one in the blue suit spoke first. "I'm Detective Jim McNeally and this is Detective Rick Smith. Are you Mr. Little?" The detective stared at Murray's face. "What the hell happened to you?"

Murray realized he'd failed to remove the toilet paper. He hoped he sounded casual. "I just nicked myself shaving in my rush to get down here. I'm okay."

"Can we have a word with you in your office, Mr. Little?" asked McNeally.

Murray nodded, opened the front door, and led the detectives to his office. Being nervous, he fumbled with his keys before finally opening the office door.

McNeally tried to be reassuring. "Hey, Mr. Little! Don't get upset. We're only here to ask you a few questions."

Murray glanced at him cautiously. "I guess it's just the idea of being questioned by the police, Detective."

Inside Murray's office, McNeally started his questioning. "Have you seen anybody around this area in the past several days who looked suspicious?" Before Murray could utter a syllable, the detective hit him with a cascade of questions. "Have you ever heard of a guy called William Daniel? Do you know if anybody's been harassing Miss Page? Do you know of any relationship between Miss Page and a Mr. Daniel? Has any of your staff been aware of anybody being harassed or followed?"

Beads of perspiration trickled down Murray's face. Trembling, he lit a Sweet Caporal. "Detective, the answer to all of your questions is no. I haven't seen any suspicious people around our theatre, and none of the staff have reported anything unusual to me. And I don't know anything about the private lives of our performers. There have been no reports from my staff about any kind of harassment."

The detectives seemed disappointed, even irritated, with Murray's response. "You sure aren't much help," McNeally growled.

Murray took a quick puff on his cigarette, and in an exasperated tone, half pleaded with the officers. "For goodness' sake, I'm only telling you what I know and I'm answering your questions honestly. Isn't that good enough?" He paused as the detectives became almost morbidly silent. Murray mustered some courage. "Would you please fill me in as to what exactly happened?"

"This Patti Page who's playing your theatre this week," Detective Smith ventured, "was found tied up with adhesive tape last night in her room at the King Eddy Hotel. According to Miss Page, she was in her room when the telephone rang. The guy at the other end said he had a box of flowers for her, a couple of minutes later there was a knock at her door, and Miss Page let this man into the room. The box he was carrying was empty.

"This male," Smith continued, "now identified as William Daniel, threatened her and ordered her to sit in a chair, then tied her wrists with adhesive tape. She screamed, and the guy took off. Two bellhops joined in the chase. One of our constables happened to be nearby and pursued this man to Front and Market Streets, where he was apprehended. He's now in jail. We were wondering if you might know anything about this guy, if maybe any of your other lovely ladies might have had similar experiences or know anything about this character."

"I'm sorry, gentlemen. I don't see how I can be of any more assistance. I've already told you I don't know very much about Miss Page, and none of our performers has come to me about suspicious people or harassment."

"Miss Page told us that she's leaving Toronto this evening to meet her commitments in the States," McNeally said. "Her departure from the city today gives us a problem. We're not quite sure how long we can hold this guy, and we might be forced to ask for a lengthy remand until Miss Page's schedule allows her to return to Toronto to testify. We're hoping we can nail this guy on some other charge to keep him where he belongs — behind bars. So, if you hear anything at all, let us know, Little."

"Certainly, gentlemen. Let me escort you out."

"Naw, you don't have to do that," McNeally said. "Me and my partner would like to stick around and see if we can pick up any information. There's always a chance somebody around here might know something about this creep."

Smith piped up, "Yeah, you never know what you can pick up in a place like this. Besides, we'd like to have a look at your show."

Murray countered, "As you may know, gentlemen, the free list has been suspended for this engagement. But I'd be pleased to make an exception in your case. You're certainly welcome to stay around as long as you wish."

Patti Page left Toronto after her engagement that evening, vowing never to return to the city. Her assailant was later found guilty of aggravated assault and served three months in Don Jail.

50

NIXON, MCCARTHY, AND BLACKLISTS

The Patti Page incident received little publicity beyond a day's headline and fortunately didn't reflect badly on the Casino Theatre itself. If anything, it made local people even more aware there were well-known American and European performers in town. The year 1949 continued with a succession of distinguished stars in the music business, ending with Christmas shows featuring The Delta Rhythm Boys, another popular singing quartet.

In early January 1950, the famous harmonica player, Larry Adler, appeared on the same bill as burlesque comic Herbie Barris and his beautiful stripper companion, Sherri Shannon. Lou remarked to Murray one day, "We're finally getting somebody onstage I've heard of — Larry Adler."

By now, Lou had developed a daily ritual: dropping in to visit his mother on his way to the theatre. Esther dutifully prepared a late breakfast for her only son, the meal usually consisting of a small glass of orange juice, a boiled egg, a piece of dry toast, and clear tea. She never mentioned alcohol as a beverage option, let alone served it. One of those mornings, Lou presented himself nattily dressed, right down to a white carnation and highly polished elevator shoes.

Lil happened to be in the kitchen as her brother sat down for his meal. "You look particularly sharp today. What's the occasion?"

"I'm meeting Larry Adler for dinner between the evening shows. This guy's big stuff, and I've never met anybody in his league before. You remember him, Lil, don't you? Besides being a top-notch harmonic player, you must have seen him in the movies *Three Daring Daughters* and *Music for Millions*. And he did a whole lot of Broadway musicals like *Clowns in Clover* and *Flying Colors*. The guy's world-famous!" Lou swallowed his orange juice noisily. "I gotta tell you, Lil, I have to hand it to my brother-in-law this time. He and Roy Cooper have put the theatre into the big time."

"Murray doesn't discuss much business with me, but he did tell me he was very satisfied with the new policy. But you know him. He always worries. He has to worry that a good thing won't last."

Lou quickly changed the subject. "When are you going away again, Lil?"

"Not for another six weeks or so."

"Who will look after the kids?"

"The boys are old enough to begin looking after themselves. Besides, I've got a maid lined up. She's going to be living with us and will do the cooking and cleaning from now on."

"A maid?"

"She's a lovely lady I met in Jamaica, comes highly recommended by people I know down there, and is anxious to work in Canada. She's got two young sons to support. They'll stay with their grandmother in Jamaica while she's here and will send money home. There's a lot of poverty in Jamaica …"

"Very, very fancy!"

"Never mind being so sarcastic, Lou!"

Finishing his meal quickly, Lou dutifully kissed his mother and darted out of the house.

Lil turned to Esther. "That brother of mine. I can't figure him out. He's become so cynical and sarcastic. Lou doesn't think I know it, but he and Murray don't see eye to eye on anything. And I'm sure there are a lot more quarrels between him and Murray than Murray lets me know about."

Esther rose from the table and put a hand on her daughter's shoulder. "And he drinks too much … just like your father did."

Larry Adler's week at the Casino turned out to be a great success. At the end of his Casino engagement, he was scheduled to perform at a popular supper club just outside Toronto — the Brant Inn in Burlington. Under the aegis of its owner, Murray Anderson, the Brant Inn had built a first-class reputation as a place for good food, good dancing, and good live entertainment.

On the evening of Adler's last performance, Murray went backstage, and to his surprise, saw Adler standing in the wings staring at the lovely Sherri Shannon while she performed her tantalizing striptease. The harmonica player had a big smile on his face and nearly missed the cue for his entrance as he stood hypnotized at the sight of the stripper running by him almost naked. He turned to Murray behind him in the wings, just as the master of ceremonies introduced him, and whispered, "That's some act to follow."

After his performance and several encores, Adler engaged Murray in conversation. "I really like it in Canada. I don't think anyone would believe me if I told them I was on the same bill as a stripper. This is an unforgettable engagement."

"Glad to hear it, Larry," a surprised Murray replied.

Adler smiled. "What I wanted to speak to you about was getting over to the Brant Inn. I suppose I could rent a limousine, but I thought you might have a better idea, knowing that a lot of your performers have gone there in the past."

"I can drive you!" Murray offered. "I have to meet the owner, Murray Anderson, first thing tomorrow, anyway."

The following morning, Murray drove to the Royal York Hotel to pick up Adler. Barry, whose school was closed that day, had insisted he come along to meet the famous musician. It was a sparkling, cloudless winter day but bitterly cold. Everyone on the street was moving quickly. Exhaled breath like large puffs of smoke in the frosty air gave the busy streets a surreal quality. Adler was waiting at the curbside, shivering. Murray wound down his window and yelled, "Larry, put your bags on the back seat and get in the front. The doors are unlocked."

Adler shoved two bags in next to Barry and jumped into the front seat.

Murray introduced them, then added, "My second son's a big fan of yours. I hope you don't mind him coming along."

"No, not at all," Adler said. "I'm glad when young people like the music I play. Today's hit parade is geared for kids, and most of it's junk and beyond me! I find it demeaning. I have to tell you people, though, that as much as I like Toronto, I'm up here under duress. No reflection on your theatre, of course, Murray."

Murray wrinkled his brow. "Under duress?"

"Have you heard about the House Un-American Activities Committee or HUAC?" There was pregnant pause. "It's a witch hunt originally set up by the U.S. House of Representatives in 1938 to investigate so-called 'disloyal' and 'subversive' activities by American citizens, public employees, and organizations, created under the guise of 'patriotism.' It's always been controlled by psychopaths."

Murray raised an eyebrow. "Psychopaths?"

"Psychopaths, moral imbeciles, people who have no consciences or regard for what they're doing."

Murray's curiosity was heightened. "My God, how do people like that get to run a government committee? Who are these guys, anyway?"

"One of them is Congressman Richard Nixon. You probably haven't heard of him up here in Canada. He's now running for a U.S. Senate seat and has close ties with Senator Joe McCarthy, another psychopathic 'Red' baiter. The two of them and their cronies single out people who are or were members of the American Communist Party as part of their crazy witch hunt. A few years ago, HUAC set its sights on the movie and entertainment industry. Most of that trouble began when Bill Wilkerson, the publisher and founder of *The Hollywood Reporter* magazine, published lists of supposed communist sympathizers in 1946. A year later, some former FBI agents started an anti-communist newsletter called *Counterattack*, which named names of people it deemed traitorous. HUAC used all these lists to call out people in the entertainment business as members of the Communist Party or what it called fellow travellers. As it turns out, my name was on one of those lists, but so were hundreds of others who were no more communist than I am. You could actually be on a list just for having attended a union meeting or giving a $5 donation to help the Russian cause during the war. Remember, the Russians were our allies back then."

Murray was now even more intrigued, almost flabbergasted. "What you're saying is that you've been named and it's affected your career? Am I correct, Larry?"

"It's not only been a disaster for me, Murray. It's been a disaster for the entire entertainment industry. I don't know how they get away with it. The FBI scrounges through the *Daily Worker* newspaper and takes down any names it finds and creates its own lists. You know, that paper's a rag. It just happens to be published by the American Communist Party. Can you believe it? If your name appears in this newspaper for any reason whatsoever, you're blacklisted.

"HUAC and the entertainment establishment in the United States have made life miserable for a lot of people, especially in our business. These lists are filled with hundreds of actors, screenwriters, cinematographers, music scorers, producers, and directors. And employers in the U.S. are afraid to hire them … people like myself. Theatre chains and the Hearst newspapers in particular have gone all out supporting Nixon, McCarthy, and guys like them in this witch hunt. I'm not paranoid, but they've made it personally terrible for me. I'm thinking of moving to Europe to get away from them. I've been so upset by all this stupidity that I've refused to appear before HUAC, even though I've been subpoenaed. Mark my words, Murray, you're going to see a lot more performers coming to Toronto and other places in Canada simply because they can't get work in the U.S."

"I can hardly believe what you're saying, Larry."

"Believe it, Murray. This misguided group of people pretending to be American patriots are ruining lives. My only wish is that Nixon and his committee, McCarthy, and so many others — this entire process — will be found out to be a great fraud perpetrated on the American people."

Barry was all ears as the automobile sped toward Burlington and the voluble Adler continued his story. "As I told you, for some reason, HUAC has a particular animosity toward the motion picture industry. It's labelled as un-American people like Bertolt Brecht, the famous German playwright. He gave evidence, then left the United States for Switzerland and eventually East Germany. Screenwriter Ring Lardner, Jr., refused to testify and answer any questions in front of this committee, so he's part of what's called the Hollywood Ten blacklist." Adler turned around to Barry. "Did you see *The Jolson Story* with Larry Parks? Well, Larry was the only actor in the original group of nineteen people to be named by this crazy committee. He was foolish enough to admit he'd joined the Communist Party back in 1941 but left it four years later. Parks is slated to appear before HUAC at some point soon. God knows what will happen to him."

"What an awful story," interjected Murray.

"Just imagine, these so-called patriots have harassed Lee J. Cobb, the actor, and Budd Schulberg, the screenwriter and novelist. I guess the only good thing that's come out of this for me is that I'm on lists with some very famous writers, intellectuals, and performers. I'm in the doghouse with Leonard Bernstein, Orson Welles, John Garfield, Arthur Miller, Dorothy Parker, Lillian Hellman, Pete Seeger, Josh White — a long, sickening list, but a great one."

"Did you say Josh White?"

"Yes, he's on one of the lists."

"Josh played our theatre back in August. He told me he was very anxious to come up to Toronto. What you've told me gives me a better understanding why."

"I'm sure he came up here because he's having trouble getting work in the States."

"Larry, that's a very sad story. Lots of people were, and are, sympathetic with the Russians, including my own father," said Murray sympathetically.

Barry piped up from the back seat. "So these guys, Nixon and McCarthy, believe the entertainment business is filled with communists and that these people represent a danger to the United States?"

Adler turned to respond. "Young man, you've got that exactly right. You're very lucky to be living in Canada."

"Well, it's not always a bed of roses up here, either, Larry," Murray said. "We don't have witch hunts, I guess, but we have problems with our politicians, too. They can ruin lives just as easily as they do in the United States, I can assure you. I know from personal experience."

Murray pulled the car into the driveway of the elegant Brant Inn. "Well, here we are, Larry. Seems as though the trip took only a few minutes and you kept my son and me absorbed with your account of the troubles in the States these days."

Adler smiled sadly. "You and your son were very patient, Murray. I guess I had to get it off my chest, but I still believe you people are living in a lucky country, and I'm happy to come back here any time you wish."

Murray got out of the car, and in valet fashion, opened the door for Adler. "Many thanks for the compliments. I'm sure you're going to be a big hit at the Brant Inn, just as you were at the Casino."

Barry poked his head out the window. "Thank you, Mr. Adler. This has been one of the most interesting afternoons I've ever had. Please come back."

"I'd like that very much. I only hope the people here appreciate your theatre. It's really very unique, you know, what with a stripper and a comic, vaudeville acts, and a name headliner. What a tolerant country!"

Murray blushed. "At least some people appreciate us." He turned to his son. "Barry, help Mr. Adler get his baggage out of the car. It's starting to snow, and you know how I hate to drive when it's snowing."

Barry smiled at Adler. "My father's vision isn't too good, especially in the bright sunshine and when it snows."

The musician looked at Barry, paused, then quipped, "I don't know. I think your father has great vision — the kind that really counts!"

Murray and his son returned to Toronto in a snowfall that grew heavier and more persistent. But before leaving, Barry had glanced at the side-view mirror and was just able to detect a faint smile on the face of the diminutive figure standing on the steps of the Brant Inn, baggage at his side.

Once home, Barry couldn't wait to tell his brothers about his trip to Burlington and the harmonica virtuoso's problems with the U.S. government.

Gerry's curiosity was piqued. "Does that mean Grandpa Little would be in trouble now because he liked the communists?"

"Maybe ... if we lived in the U.S."

Alan added his final comment to the discussion in Gerry's bedroom. "Boy, am I glad I don't live in America. Aren't you guys?"

Barry was less enthusiastic. "I don't know. Gerry and I think Buffalo's terrific, especially compared to Toronto. What a pokey city we live in! Besides, all the best movies and radio programs come from the States."

"Hey, you guys, let's stop all this talking," Alan interjected. "*Lux Radio Theater* is on in five minutes. Isn't that one of your favourite programs, Barry?"

"Sort of, but I like Bob Hope, Fred Allen, and *Truth or Consequences* more."

"Well, it's my favourite program, and I want to go downstairs to listen to it. You guys can do what you want." With that declaration, Alan quickly left the room.

Suddenly lowering his voice, Gerry asked Barry, "Have you got a date for the school prom?"

Sensing Gerry had something secretive to say, Barry whispered back, "No, that's not until the middle of March. Why?"

"Well, get one because it's going to be very special."

"What do you mean?"

"Believe it or not, I was able to get Page Cavanaugh's trio to appear at our high school prom!"

"You're kidding?"

"I'm not lying. Dad told me they'd be playing the Brant Inn right after the Casino. And since they're going to be around, anyway, they said they'd find it a real kick to play at a high school dance. They're only going to charge the minimum. I think they call it scale. Anyway, it's all been set up. Roy Cooper knows about it, the trio's agent has agreed, and the Prom Committee is absolutely flabbergasted!"

Barry could hardly believe his ears. "This is fantastic! Boy, Gerry, when you want to be sneaky, you're unbelievable. You could be a great spy or detective. What other tricks have you got up your sleeve?"

Gerry was nonchalant. "Nothing … for the time being."

Alan, who still hadn't gone downstairs to listen to the radio and was eavesdropping in the doorway, added cynically, "I hope they show up. Because if they don't, it's going to look bad for the three of us at school." He looked thoughtful for a moment before saying, "Well, maybe not for me. I'm not going to the prom."

51

PROM NIGHT, ELLA FITZGERALD, AND MEL TORMÉ

In late March 1950, the Forest Hill High School Spring Prom was a great success, the Page Cavanaugh Trio having appeared as promised. The day following the prom, Barry was still rubbing his eyes in disbelief, telling his brothers, "Can you believe it? We actually heard them sing 'The Three Bears' and 'Walkin' My Baby Back Home.' It was terrific! My date just stood in front of the trio, staring dumbfounded, her jaw dropping to her knees. What a coup!"

With the steady stream of well-known headliners from the movies and radio now appearing at the Casino Theatre, Barry made it a habit during the school year to catch the shows on Saturday afternoons from backstage. Stagehands Carl and Bernie were always happy to see him and placed him behind the wings in the most advantageous viewing and listening position. In the week following the Page Cavanaugh Trio, he stood in the wings mesmerized by the mellifluous voice of Ella Fitzgerald. She was simply amazing! And as for that pianist accompanying her, what he wouldn't give to play like Hank Jones! Maybe someday! Talk about lucky — he was the luckiest guy alive! He could only hope his father would continue to bring in acts like that.

That Saturday after the first matinee was over, Barry left his special behind-the-curtain box to head out of the theatre and down the side alley. He'd just exited the stage door when he saw his father coming in the opposite direction, almost running and scowling. "Dad, what's the trouble?"

"I haven't got time now, Barry. It has to do with one of the chorus girls. I'll speak to you later."

Barry continued to walk slowly along the alleyway toward the street where a small lineup of patrons was already gathering. His father was always in such a hurry! They hardly ever got a chance to talk because so often he was angry. But when things were quiet and they were alone, he could really talk to him, and his father had great things to say ... he was such a knowledgeable guy. Too bad he didn't know very much about jazz or care about it. Still, he did like Brahms and Beethoven, so maybe he was kind of musical ... in his own way.

Finding a seat at the rear of the auditorium, Barry sat through the featured movie of the week, something appropriately named *Without Honor*. He was glad they weren't using a stripper this week. How embarrassing it would be to have someone like Ella Fitzgerald on the same bill as a burlesque stripper. Maybe having these big names would soon mean no more strippers. He didn't want to hear anyone call his father's place of business a sleaze palace ever again!

Seated at the back of the auditorium, he could easily hear his father's office door open and close. When Barry heard the door open and then his dad's voice, he quickly darted from his seat and into the office. "Dad, what was all the fuss about? You looked very upset when I saw you earlier."

"The usual. Just a little tiff between Uncle Lou's friend, Helen, and Jacqueline, the chorus line captain. Seems Helen was late for rehearsal a couple of times, then told Jacqueline she didn't have to worry because she was very close to the theatre owner. So, naturally, an argument followed. Then Jacqueline called me to say she was leaving if Helen was going to continue to behave as though she was the owner of the theatre and running things. Anyway, it's all settled now."

Murray smiled. "Well, what did you think of Ella Fitzgerald?"

"Terrific! There's nothing like seeing and hearing these people live — a heck of a lot better than the radio or records. Are you going to continue to bring in people like her, Dad?"

"We fully intend to. But I have to tell you quite honestly, most of the people we've booked are still just names to me. We're relying on Roy Cooper for the most part." Murray reached for a large leather-bound book prominently displayed on his desk, sharing space with a mound of memos and a host of eight-by-ten glossies of past-and-present performers and acts scheduled to appear. "Here, have a look at who's booked and tell me if you know anything about these people."

"Sure, Dad." Barry scanned the large book with enthusiasm. The acts his father had coming read like a musical "who's who"! Mel Tormé was coming next week, then Vic Damone, and later in July, the great pianist and comedian Victor Borge! Barry could hardly contain himself. "Wow, this is amazing!" The Borsht Belt comic Henny Youngman and The Three Stooges — he could hardly believe it! "Imagine, all these famous people coming to Toronto and to our theatre!"

Murray seemed pleased and added half in jest, "I'm glad you approve, but I'm even happier that the customers do." Murray glanced at his watch, his dad's signal that he wanted Barry to leave.

The following Saturday, Barry was back at the theatre. But rather than watching from the wings, he decided to sit in the audience where screeches and oohs and aahs from the bobby soxers drew laughs from Mel Tormé as he concluded his matinee performance. Barry was over the moon. This guy was unbelievable! He not only played the drums spectacularly but was also a good piano player. And his voice was simply terrific — great timing and phrasing, so smooth. No wonder they called him The Velvet Fog! *I'll bet this is the first time these people have ever seen a real live movie star in person!* There was no stripper this week. Could that be why so many kids had been allowed to come?

When Barry arrived in his father's office, Murray asked, "Well, what did you think of Mel Tormé?"

"He's terrific! Boy, Dad, the theatre's really big-time now, isn't it?"

"We're getting there. But we've got a long way to go. We've still got that old local reputation that's a mile long."

"Why don't you just change the name of the theatre?"

"I've thought of that, but Lou and the Allens are against it. Too costly is the reason they give, but I don't buy that excuse. At least I've been able to drop the strippers from the program. And if we've lost a customer because of that, I think we've picked up another one or two." Murray paused. "At least I hope so."

There was a knock at the door of the office, and Mel Tormé walked in, taking both Murray and Barry by surprise.

"Oh, Mel, I'd like to introduce you to a loyal fan — my son, Barry."

Tormé was tanned and relaxed and wore casual loafers and a colourful open-necked sport shirt — every bit the Hollywood movie star. Tormé stared at Barry for a few seconds, then turned to Murray. "How can an ugly guy like you have such a good-looking son?"

Barry and Murray were stunned and momentarily rendered speechless by Tormé's comment.

Not at all sure about what to make of this insult to his father, Barry decided to remain silent. Murray quickly changed the subject. "Is there anything I can do for you, Mel?"

"Just wanted to double-check screening times with you, that's all." Murray handed him the schedule, and Tormé left the office just as quickly as he'd entered.

"What was that all about, Dad? What's this about screening dates?"

"Mel likes to spend a lot of time between his shows watching movies in which he makes an appearance. So we've arranged for him to see them in the private screening room at the Allens' office." Murray seemed apologetic, if not embarrassed. "You know, Barry, we have to keep our performers satisfied, and I've learned that some of them have very strange requests. But I wouldn't read too much into it. You don't have to be a famous movie star to have unusual demands."

Barry was momentarily lost for words yet again, Then said, "I guess you're right, Dad."

52

RENDEZVOUS WITH UNCLE HARRY

Living in her new Forest Hill neighbourhood left Esther more than ever isolated from her immediate family. Even her daughter, son-in-law, and grandsons rarely had time for her. She seemed amputated demographically from the main body of the Jewish community she'd come to know since arriving so reluctantly in Canada a half century earlier. No longer near her sisters and brothers and their families, she was annoyed that not even her synagogue, or the few shops she'd frequented in the past, lay within easy walking distance. Over the years, she'd acquired virtually no English-language skills and had remained unwilling or incapable of taking public transportation.

In every respect, Esther was a prisoner, not only of her physical circumstances but also of her own mind. Lou, who lived close by, visited regularly, though, possibly because it was convenient to do so and out of an acquired sense of filial obligation. Others in the immediate and extended family circle didn't. Even sister Becky was now no longer within walking distance, though she, too, had moved up the hill.

Esther had refused a separate phone line for her own bedroom, considering it an unnecessary indulgence and hence was solely dependent on the use of the single family phone, which was often engaged by Lil, when at home, or by one of the three boys.

One day, Lil was confronted by Barry in the hallway. "What does Grandma do in there all day? She only comes out for one meal a day and then goes back into her bedroom. It's always silent. She can't be praying all day long, can she?"

Lil attempted an answer. "I think she does a lot of deep thinking, and all of her praying is in whispers — sort of silent."

"Gerry and Alan think she puts herself into a trance. We all find it very strange. Was she always like that, even when you were a little girl?"

"Of course not! She changed when you were very small, when your grandfather died. A lot of things changed when we lost my father …"

"He must have been something very special, and Grandma must have loved him a lot."

Lil blotted tears from her cheek. "He was a very special person to many people. He was kind and generous, and though very quiet, he loved to meet people. He enjoyed the theatre business, had great taste in clothes, and liked fine things."

"Gee, Mother, that doesn't sound very much like Grandma Esther."

There was an embarrassing but brief silence. "Well, Barry, they were a little unusual as a couple, I have to admit, but they made the most of it."

"Do you think they'll ever find out who killed Grandpa Avner?"

Lil seemed stunned by Barry's question. Rarely, if ever in front of the children, was Avner's death discussed. Lil occasionally made references to his positive attributes, but never to his murder, or for that matter, the devastating effect it had on her, her brother, or her mother. "Everybody in the family still believes it was his business partner and that he got away with it. Does that answer your question?"

"Not really, Mother. Someday I'd like to look into Grandpa's death. The police never proved anything, did they?"

"They did what they could, I guess, and found nothing. You think you can do any better?" Lil was now clearly irritated. "Why don't we just change the subject? I've said all I want to about my father." There was another pause in the conversation. "I understand you're going to work as an usher at the theatre this summer, Barry. It'll be a great opportunity for you to see a lot of excellent performers."

Barry winced. "Being an usher is about the most boring job I can think of. Besides, I already go down to the theatre on Saturdays to catch the good acts. But you're away from home so much that you don't know that!"

"That's no way to talk to your mother!" Lil barked.

"You're away for months at a time — that's no way for a mother to treat her family!"

The heated conversation brought Esther out of her bedroom and into the hallway. "Stop the arguments and fighting immediately. It's unholy for a son to show disrespect for his mother. You must honour your father and your mother so that your days may be long in the land the Lord, your God, has given you."

"Grandma, I wasn't being disrespectful. I was simply stating a fact and I don't need a sermon. I think everybody knows how the family feels about my mother running off every winter." Barry glowered at Esther. "Maybe it's my mother who should be doing the honouring!"

The hall telephone rang abruptly, terminating the verbal fisticuffs much like the bell at a prizefight signified the end of a round. Lil quickly grabbed the phone. "Little residence. Whom do you wish to speak to?" Lil's face knotted. "Please speak louder. I can't hear you." Lil handed the receiver to Barry. "Here, I can't make out what this person wants. I'm sure my hearing's getting worse by the day."

Barry took the receiver. "Whom do you wish to speak to?" he asked, then jolted backward almost as if he'd been electrocuted. Clasping the mouthpiece with one hand, he turned to his mother and grandmother. "He says he's Uncle Harry — Harry Appelbaum — and wants to speak to his niece, Lil. At least that's what I think he's saying. He has a funny accent."

Lil snatched the receiver out of Barry's hand, while his grand-mother grimaced as if she'd just swallowed lemon juice. "Uncle Harry, is that you?" Lil shouted into the phone. Then, after a pause, she added, "I can hardly make you out."

A soft, barely audible voice in halting English tinged with a Spanish accent said, "Yes, Lil, it's … it's me, your Uncle Harry. I'm calling from Buffalo and just wanted to say hello to my favourite niece."

"I can't believe it. Is it really you, Uncle Harry?"

"Yes … yes, it is, Lil."

"Where have you been, Uncle Harry? Whatever happened to you? I've been worried sick about you. I haven't heard from you ever since you sent me that telegram years ago saying you were coming here for Passover."

"I'm … I'm fine, Lil. I'd like to answer all your questions, but it's complicated, so it's best I see you in person. But I don't think I can get into Canada until I get the right papers … because of what happened. You know, leaving the way I did. Can you come to Buffalo and meet me? I'm staying at the Statler Hotel. I'm here on business."

Lil could hardly contain her excitement. "Of course, I'll go to Buffalo to see you. As soon as I hang up, I'll call Lou and tell him about you. I'll try to get him to come with me. Just tell me when."

"I'm only going to be here for three more days. Then I have a big business meeting in Detroit. Maybe you can come tomorrow … Saturday. I'm in room 580."

"I'll be there, Uncle Harry. Expect me and Lou about one o'clock. You can count on me."

"*Adios*, Lil," came the response, and the line clicked dead.

Lil turned around and realized that her mother must have overheard the conversation. "I guess you heard. That was Uncle Harry. He's alive and well and wants to meet me in Buffalo."

Esther began to walk toward her bedroom door.

Lil yelled after her, "Mother, aren't you interested? That was Uncle Harry! Can you believe it?"

Esther stopped, glanced over her shoulder, and snapped contemptuously, "You mean the devil hasn't taken him, after all?" Then she entered her bedroom sanctuary and shut the door.

Lil quickly called her brother on his private line at the theatre. "You won't believe this, Lou, but I just had a call from Uncle Harry. You heard me, Uncle Harry, our father's younger brother. He's alive and lives in Mexico. He's in Buffalo right now, and I'm going to meet him tomorrow at one o'clock. Wouldn't you like to meet him, as well? I could pick you up at your house at nine o'clock. Is that okay?"

"Are you on the level? How do you know the guy who called you isn't an imposter?"

"Of course, I'm sure it's Uncle Harry! I'll pick you up at nine."

There was a protracted pause. "I'll be ready, but I only hope this isn't some gimmick. This guy's has been away for years … presumed dead! And if it is Uncle Harry, let's hope he doesn't just want money."

The following day, promptly at one o'clock, Lil knocked on the door of room 580. Lou stood at her side, fiddling with his suit, adjusting his tie, and clearing his throat. Suddenly, the door swung wide, and there stood Harry Appelbaum, confronting his niece and nephew after an absence of twenty years. Lou gasped, turned pale, and nearly fainted.

Equally startled, Lil cried, "Oh, my God, you look just like Father!"

The little man standing in front of her exclaimed in uncertain English, "I'm … I'm not your father! I'm your Uncle Harry. Help me get Lou to the bed. He … he looks like he's going to fall down."

As soon as they positioned Lou on the bed, he muttered, "I don't believe it … I don't believe it."

Lil grabbed a pitcher of ice water from the bedside table and splashed her brother's face. Loosening his collar, she said, "Lou, it's not Father. It's Uncle Harry."

Lou shook his head. "I don't believe it. He looks exactly like him. Nobody could look that close."

It took several minutes before the shock and excitement of the moment cleared. In the meantime, Lou moved to a chair, eyes transfixed on Harry's every move.

"Please, Uncle Harry," Lil implored, "tell us what happened to you. Until yesterday no one in Toronto except me and my husband, Murray, knew you were alive and living in Mexico. Why didn't you visit Toronto for that Passover after telling me you would? Almost fifteen years have gone by since then!"

Harry stood by the window, the afternoon sunlight catching him at an angle so that he appeared to be in a theatrical spotlight. He was hardly a matinee idol standing at five foot four with a moon face, balding head, turned-in left eye, and a thick pair of glasses slipping halfway down his nose. Lil had a hard time convincing herself he wasn't her father incarnate. Only the accent was different — a peculiar amalgam of English and Spanish with a trace of Polish thrown in.

"Things happened," he finally replied to Lil. "I … I meant to come for Passover back then. But I'm here now. And I want to tell you how … how happy I am to see you both. So much has happened to me since I left Toronto, and I'm sure much has happened to both of you. No?"

Lou remained astonished, still rubbing his eyes in disbelief, while Lil began to pepper Harry with questions much like a lawyer in a cross-examination. "Uncle, I think I know why you left Aunty Chanala, but

I'd like to hear it from you. I'd also like to know why you didn't keep in touch with her and little Moishe and Maxie."

Harry continued to stand by the window, spine arched backward, head held forward and thumbs stuck in his vest pockets, assuming a posture so much like his late brother's — almost Napoleonic. "I can explain everything. I contacted you yesterday because this was the first time I was so close to Toronto."

Lou mustered enough strength to ask, "What kind of excuse is that, Harry!"

"Well, maybe … maybe not an excuse, but that's the way it is. I was just close, so I thought it was time."

Lil held back sobs. "But why did you leave in the first place, Uncle?"

"To … to tell the truth, Lil, it was like living with the devil. Chanala was a dybbuk. Never a moment's peace. Always screaming at me. Never enough money, never paying attention to the boys. It was a nightmare. I couldn't help myself. I … I had to leave."

"But, Uncle, whatever you felt about Aunty, how could you leave her and the boys without support? They were just little babies. Aunty had to scrub floors to make ends meet and raise those two little boys on her own."

"I … I can't explain. I just wanted to forget everything. I thought I'd get over the boys. Life with Chanala was so terrible, Lil, that I had to leave." Harry seemed to be pleading. He walked over to the nearby dresser and poured himself a small Scotch. "Here, Lou, and maybe you, too, Lil — let me pour you a drink."

"Harry, what the hell have you been doing all these years?" Lou exploded after gulping down his drink.

"I told you. I wanted to get away as far as I could from Chanala, so I just kept travelling … on a bus. Somehow I was able to get across the American border without too much trouble, so I kept going south and wound up in Mexico. I kept going and going right into Mexico until I could go almost no farther. It was almost too easy getting into Mexico. I had just enough bus fare. I finally wound up in Guadalajara. I didn't speak any Spanish then, only some Yiddish and Polish and a little bit of English. There was a restaurant right across from the bus stop, so I walked in there and asked for a job. Luckily, they needed a dishwasher, and I found a place around the corner where I could stay in a little room.

"I … I saved my pesos and worked for six months in that restaurant. They treated me very nice, even though I was just the dishwasher. It was hard work, but I didn't mind. At least I was away from all that trouble in Toronto. Then one day a man came into the restaurant selling tickets for the Mexican lottery." Harry paused, reached over to the dresser, and took another swig of Scotch. You won't believe this, Lil, but I bought a ticket for two pesos, and miracle of miracles, I won the Mexican lottery."

"You what?" Lou interjected.

"I won the Mexican lottery. Would you believe it! I'm not a religious man, but I think maybe some god somewhere likes me. Anyway, I won a million pesos, which is like $100,000. Can you believe that, Lil? No education … nothing … working as a dishwasher."

"Uncle, this is like a fairy tale," Lil said. "You're not lying, are you? I wish I could believe it."

"It's true, Lil, it's true. I took the money and invested it in a business, which has been very successful. I sell machinery. I travel all through the United States and Mexico. My company's based in Laredo."

Lil was stupefied. "Uncle, tell me, why with your wonderful good luck didn't you send money back to your family? You must have known how much your boys were suffering."

"I thought about them a lot. But I knew if I sent money, their mother would easily trace me. I only trusted you, Lil. Believe me, I tried to be very generous with Chanala when I was with her, but it was never enough for her. I knew she'd never stop wanting more if she found out about my winning the lottery. Besides, I had to fend for myself when I was a young boy in Poland, and later, when I came to Canada. I thought the boys should be able to do the same."

Lil stared at him, still confused. "Uncle, you must know that no one in the family will ever forgive you for what you did, though I can understand why you left Aunty."

Harry reached into his vest pocket, pulled out a small gold case, and snapped it open. "Here's my card, Lil, with my address and phone number. You keep it, but don't give it to anybody else. You can call me anytime you want. And that goes for you, too, Lou. But I want nothing to do with the others in the family."

Lil bit her lip nervously. "Uncle Harry, I don't know whether you know what's happened to the other members of the family since you left."

"You're the first and only people I've contacted since I left. To be honest, I haven't even tried to read a Toronto newspaper. My reading English is bad. In one of your letters, you did tell me Avner was killed, but what's happened to Esther?"

"I don't know who took my father's death harder — me or my mother. She's alive, but she's stopped living. She's become a hermit and spends all her time praying. Mother continues to live with me and Murray and my three grown-up boys."

Harry nodded. "Esther was always crazy-religious, even when I knew her when she was a little girl in Poland. Your father was like me about religion. We could take it or leave it. Esther and Avner should never have married, but their fathers insisted. The brothers made a deal."

Lil pressed forward. "Uncle Harry, what have you been doing all these years?"

"I told you. I won a lottery and I'm in business. There's nothing more to say."

"Of course, there is, Uncle Harry. A lot's happened to all of us."

Harry started to fidget. "Well, there's not much else to say, Lil, only that it's all been good since I left Toronto. Maybe next time when we meet I can tell you a little more."

"Next time? How many more years will that be?"

"No … no … it won't be like that. I'm hoping to come to Toronto this summer."

Lil tried to restrain herself but continued the now-forced conversation. "Well, Chanala's still in Toronto, but Moishe went to California and Maxie's gone to Florida. Your two brothers, Moishe and Lazar, still live in Toronto. Joseph is in Detroit. We're in touch with them all from time to time. But your oldest brother, Beryl, who stayed back in Poland … we have no idea. We think he was taken by the Nazis and died in a concentration camp. Two of his children escaped."

Harry turned to Lou. "What do you do now, Lou? You were just a little boy learning to play the violin when I last saw you."

"Murray and I run a theatre. We have other partners, and it's a big business. We're the most popular theatre in Toronto. We have famous singers and movie stars. You know — live shows."

Harry stood back sagaciously. "Just like your father. He liked the live shows, and to tell you the truth, especially the dancing girls."

Lil and Lou blushed simultaneously.

53

EDWIN ALONZO BOYD, BANK ROBBER

Murray hustled across the street to join Roy Cooper, who had come to Toronto to review upcoming bookings in person with Murray, Lou, and the Allens. He had arranged to meet Murray for lunch on Elizabeth Street at the Jade House Restaurant. Although smoky and noisy, the eatery had a reputation for the best food in Chinatown. Besides, it was only about a hundred yards from the Casino Theatre.

Cooper greeted Murray in his usual ebullient manner. "I've already ordered. Hope you don't mind. I'm in a bit of a rush and need to get back to Montreal by this evening."

After gulping some green tea, Murray asked, "So who have we got lined up, Roy?"

"A great one, Murray. I've got firm commitments for Victor Borge in early July, as well as for a sensational kid who's just starting out and has cut some records with RCA. His name's Eddie Fisher. In early August, I've got a firm commitment for Kitty Kallen. And I think I've got Kay Starr for late August."

"You know, Roy, I have to be honest. I haven't heard of any of these people except Borge."

Roy gazed at Murray sympathetically. "Never mind, Murray. I can assure you, they'll all do good business for you. Borge's happy to come to Toronto, and I've got him at a good price. Eddie Fisher's a protégé of Eddie Cantor, and the Casino will be his first big theatre performance. He's been singing in the Borscht Belt, and everybody thinks that with his terrific voice and good looks he's going to be a big winner. RCA will probably send you some records to give you an idea how he sounds."

Murray shook his head and smiled. "You know me, Roy. I'm no judge. So I'll take your word for it."

"I think, too, with the people I mentioned, we should get them to make commitments for return engagements. That's how certain I am about them. We'll also get them at a better price that way, especially Fisher. I've heard him sing. He's going to be really big." Roy stared at his bowl of chicken chow mein. "You know, Murray, the food here's as good as Ruby Foo's in Montreal!"

"The performers all seem to like it. A lot of them come here between shows."

"Are you sure they like coming here just because of the food?"

"What do you mean?"

"I keep seeing a lot of people walking in and out of that backroom …" Cooper pointed his chopsticks in the direction of a tiny door at the rear of the crowded restaurant. "There's one hell of a lot of people going in and out of there — and they're not all waiters carrying dishes."

"I don't think it's any secret, Roy. The backroom here and at a couple of other places on Elizabeth Street are used for gambling. I understand it's a great Chinese custom."

"You're kidding! Don't the police do anything about it? I mean, is it legal in Toronto?"

"Every so often the police conduct a raid just to make sure they don't have too many complaints, I guess. But who knows? Maybe they realize they can't stop the gambling, or for that matter the sex trade."

"Just like Quebec! Well, at least you don't have to worry about your theatre. You're selling good family entertainment these days. But you shouldn't have had to worry back in the burlesque days, either. Haven't you always been a staunch defender of burlesque?"

"You're right, Roy, and I still am! But I must admit, I don't miss the harassment from do-gooders, churchmen, and police when I was in the burlesque business."

"Maybe it's just as well burlesque is dead, anyway. And vaudeville, too. It's a whole new era in the entertainment business."

"You know," Murray said candidly, "I knew nothing about the theatre business until my father-in-law was killed and I was thrust into it. I suppose you know that. But gradually I learned how to handle performers. Let's just say that I learned the hard way — in the school of hard knocks. But as pleased as I am with our new policy, and as convinced as I am we're making the right financial moves, I'm still a bit nervous about the whole thing — me and the theatre business — even after all these years.

"I have to admit I'm a little intimidated by some of these well-known stars," Murray continued. "I haven't had too much trouble so far, but I still worry when I run into people with a lot of temperament — not that we didn't have prima donnas in burlesque. But the performers now are so well known ... well, the last thing I need are hassles with celebrities. We've seen what the newspapers can do. And I'm always worried these people will take one look at our theatre and treat it as a joke."

Cooper frowned. "A joke? What do you mean?"

"You know ... the theatre isn't terribly elegant. It has a small stage area and no foyer to speak of at the front of the house. We've only got a small six-piece orchestra — nothing big and fancy. And I suppose the thing that worries me most is that these performers are from a world I know absolutely nothing about. So I have nothing in common with them and very little to talk to them about, other than salary and show schedules. Sometimes it really bothers me."

Cooper leaned over the small table and gazed sternly into Murray's face. "Look, the word I hear is that the performers think you're terrific and they have no problems with you or your staff or your theatre. Not one of them has complained about the orchestra. And remember, Murray, they're performers. As long as they're being paid to perform, they'll play anywhere, especially now with the situation in the States where work isn't so easy to get."

Before Murray could say another word, Cooper continued in his paternalistic tone. "Remember, performers are like everyone else — treat them well and you'll get results. I know some of them like to put on airs, but just ignore that and treat them the way you do anyone else. If they have childish whims, treat them like children. Just always be straight and on the level with them.

"Sometimes their agents can get under your skin, too, but don't worry about it. It's their job to hustle and promote their performers. They can be real bastards at times. After all, they're making fifteen to twenty percent commission, but I wouldn't get too upset by some of the comments they make. Just don't take what they say personally."

Murray sat back in the hard wooden chair, nervously glanced at his watch, and lit a Sweet Caporal. "Roy, I have to thank you for your reassuring comments. We haven't known each other all that long, but you talk to me like a real friend. And I appreciate that. I haven't told anybody, even Lil, but to build my confidence and speaking skills I've been sneaking out for a couple of hours each week to attend public-speaking classes run by a guy named Leonard Riley. Maybe that sounds silly, but I'm finding the classes helpful."

"I don't find it silly at all. I think it's a great idea. But you don't have to worry, Murray. You're doing a great job already."

"You know, Roy, I've always regretted I didn't go to university. But looking back, I had no choice. An early marriage, three kids, the Great Depression, the world war … I wish I knew a lot more about a lot of things."

"Don't we all, Murray."

"I'm hoping that learning to speak better in public will give me more self-confidence, that's all. At least it's a beginning. I'd give anything to get out of this theatrical business. And it's not simply because of my partners. either. This industry is all so airy-fairy and uncertain. Many of the people are nice and interesting and different, but I find too many are unstable. They actually make me nervous."

Murray paused as he put down his cup of green tea and lit another cigarette. "Sorry for spewing forth like that, Roy. Maybe I should just be grateful I have a good-paying, regular job in business, but I sure as hell am going to see to it that my three boys go to university and become professionals. Although I am a little worried about my middle son, Barry — the one at the Royal Conservatory. I'm trying to convince him he should go into a solid profession like medicine, dentistry, or law."

"Murray, kids are just like water. You've got to let them find their own level. And if one of them likes show business, so be it. You can only give them advice, not force them. Like you, I, too, find some of these people tough. But I still enjoy the business and I do what you should do, Murray — roll with the punches."

"Thanks for the advice, Roy. I'll try, but I wish it was as simple as all that." Murray motioned to the waiter for the check, placed a $10 bill on the table, and then he and Roy descended the steep, wooden steps of the restaurant to the street below.

Murray pointed to the Casino box office, which they could readily see. "Look at that lineup for the seven o'clock show. The Three Stooges are sure packing them in! I like their movies, but I find their act a bit silly. People seem to like it, though, so who am I to judge?"

After saying goodbye to Cooper and watching the Montrealer get into a cab and hurry off to another appointment, Murray headed to the Casino where to his surprise he found someone waiting outside his office for him — a tall gentleman with a grey fedora who introduced himself as Sergeant of Detectives Edmund Tong. "You must be Mr. Little, the manager of this theatre." Before Murray could utter a word, Tong continued. "I have to tell you that I've been a frequent patron here. However, I'm here today on official business to ask you a couple of questions."

Murray was chagrined at the prospect of yet another police interrogation. Now what? Who was in trouble this time? "Come into my office, Sergeant Tong."

When the lanky officer followed Murray into his office den, he offered him a cigarette. "Thanks, Mr. Little." Tong stared at Murray. "You can take that worried look off your face. I'm just here to ask you a few questions about some guys we're looking for. We received a tip that one of them was seen hanging around your theatre several days ago."

Seems like the police are always spotting suspects in our theatre, Murray thought.

"The tip came from a Walter Crosby, whom I believe is an employee of yours. Is that correct?"

"Yes, that's correct, Sergeant. Crosby's worked for us as a janitor and caretaker for the past two years. Surely, he's not in trouble with the police."

"Well, no, not now, but he does have a record and did serve time at the Mimico Brickyard a couple of years ago for robbery. He called us the other day to say he spotted a man we've been looking for the past several months. We have reason to believe Crosby's telling us the truth … this time."

Murray feigned surprise. "I didn't know Wally had a criminal record. He's always been honest and straightforward with us. The man's a very good worker with a great sense of humour and all the staff like him."

"Well, that might very well be the case, and I'm glad to hear it, Mr. Little. This tip from Crosby could be useful. He told us a couple of days ago that he spotted Edwin Alonzo Boyd in the alleyway beside your theatre. This Boyd first surfaced back in September last year when he robbed a bank. He wore a disguise, plastering his face with makeup and stuffing his cheeks with cotton. Then a few days later — this was in all the papers — he robbed the same bank and the same teller. This time without a disguise! We have reason to believe he's hooked up with a few of his cronies and has been responsible for further armed robberies in the city."

"Sergeant, I see hundreds of patrons every day. What does this fellow look like?"

"Slight to medium build, five foot seven, with a moustache. Good-looking fellow … has a matinee idol look about him." Tong reached into his briefcase and fumbled through a sheaf of photos. "Here's a mug shot. Have a look. We thought you might have seen him or have some further information about him. One of your girls might be seeing him."

Murray glanced at the photo. "I'm sorry, Sergeant. I haven't noticed this man anywhere around here. But I'll certainly call if I do. You must understand, of course, that I can't keep track of the private lives of our staff. And for the record, as far as I know, our chorus girls are all decent, hard-working women. I can't imagine any one of them associating with a bank robber … but perhaps I'm naive."

The detective seemed disappointed. "Well, I appreciate your frankness, Mr. Little. But if you do hear or see anything, please give me a call. This guy's a dangerous piece of work."

"Most certainly, Sergeant."

Tong turned to Murray as he was leaving the office. "Great shows, Mr. Little. Keep up the good work. I'll be seeing you."

A polite officer for a change, Murray mused.

No sooner had Sergeant Tong left the office than Murray began to look downstairs for his janitor. He spotted him stacking boxes by the furnace. "Wally, have you got a minute?"

"For you, Mr. Little, I've got all the time in the world! But remember, time's money — the only kind of money that can't be counterfeited."

Murray was bemused by Crosby's "aphorism." What a character, always clowning. Lil thought the janitor could be a movie star with his John Barrymore profile. "Wally, I need a serious moment with you. A Sergeant Tong was just in my office upstairs asking about a man named Boyd who's a suspect in some recent robberies. I understand you've seen him around the theatre recently."

"Boyd? Not that I can recall, Mr. Little. He chums around with a couple of guys I served time with, and he and his buddies occasionally catch our shows. One of them hangs around with one of the chorus girls." Crosby stopped to catch his breath. "You know I'm clean nowadays. I don't have anything to do with those guys. My sister, the one who's a model, hung around with one of them for a time. I even forget his name now."

"The rumour around here, Wally, is that you seem to have first-hand knowledge about what a lot of these underworld types are doing."

Crosby smiled mysteriously. "Honestly, Mr. Little, I have very little to do with these guys anymore. They only mean trouble. But I've got to tell you, if I did know something, I'd be a little leery about playing canary."

Murray was puzzled. "What do you mean? Didn't you contact Sergeant Tong?"

"Well, no, not exactly … I guess I did, just once. Tong was in the theatre one day, and I sort of blurted it out. Told him I saw Boyd near the stage door the other day. Call it a moment of weakness. I don't know. It just happened. Cops make me nervous."

"But why did you lie to me just now? Does that mean we can't trust you at the Casino?"

"Nah, nah, I love it at the theatre, Mr. Little. I'd never let you down. I enjoy it too much. I've always been on the level with you. It's just that I don't like ratting on people … but I did see Boyd in the alleyway and that's what I told Tong. I'm sorry I lied to you before."

"All I care about is that you be honest and above board and do your job." After a long pause, Murray added, "And not break the law."

Crosby did a fancy pirouette, garbage can in hand. "Who me? Break the law? Never again!"

As Murray began to climb the steps to the foyer, Crosby shouted, "Those Three Stooges are great!"

Well, each to his own taste, Murray reflected as he ascended the stairs and headed to the auditorium door. Suddenly, there was a crashing noise. In his Chaplinesque escapade, Crosby had dropped the garbage can on the concrete basement floor, creating a resounding noise that echoed throughout the theatre.

The omnipresent Charlie Mackie heard the loud crash, too, and was quickly on the scene. Several years previously, Mackie had taken up weightlifting, and now with his slicked-down black hair, tight-fitting pinstriped suit, patent leather black shoes, starched white shirt, and diamond stickpin he looked like a cross between Charles Atlas and Diamond Jim Brady.

Murray followed Mackie to the basement. "Don't worry, Charlie. Nothing serious. That big noise was Wally dropping a can of garbage."

"Oh, good. I was a little worried. So were some of the customers. A few of them got up and left the auditorium."

Murray half chuckled to himself. Maybe they thought it was the start of a gunfight, he thought.

"See, I ain't hurt and I didn't stop the show, either." Crosby had a half-embarrassed yet smug look about him.

"Try to forget about the dancing, would you, Wally," Murray

admonished meekly, as if to suggest that he really didn't mind the clowning. *It makes life down here a little more tolerable.*

Murray then invited Mackie to join him for some tea, and the two headed upstairs. Marg, the cashier, was leaning back in her high box office chair as the two entered Murray's office. "There's a message for you, Mr. Little. An Ida Rose says she needs to meet with you."

"Darn it! I nearly forgot. She's the lady replacing Chuck Gregory while he's away for the next six weeks."

Mackie leaned closer to Murray and whispered into his ear, "Wait till you see her. You won't believe your eyes."

Murray was puzzled. "What do you mean? Chuck told me she was a very good choreographer and director. She worked at Buffalo's Palace for years."

"Let's just say she has an unusual presentation, Murray. You'll see …"

54

HOMICIDE THEORIES

Barry was late getting to the paint shop atop the old Roxy Theatre, now called the Broadway, which was being leased by the Casino. As he climbed the three flights of stairs on the double, he knew his boss, Percy Grisewood, wouldn't be happy. "Sorry I'm late, Percy," he said a little breathlessly when he spotted his boss.

"I don't care if you are the owner's son. You're fifteen minutes late!"

Barry was embarrassed. "It won't happen again, Percy. I was watching a show and didn't notice the time."

Percy smiled somewhat paternalistically. "See that it doesn't happen again. I want you to meet Eon, my new assistant. Eon, this is Barry, one of Mr. Little's sons. He gofers for me on occasion when he's not at school."

A tall, muscular man in paint-stained overalls shook Barry's hand. "Nice to meet ya, kid."

"Eon and I are about to build a set for Ida Rose, the new director. She's got some real kooky ideas and wants me to create a Dutch mill as well as an underwater scene by tomorrow, so let's get a move on, fellas! We'll work until three o'clock in the morning if that's what it takes. Barry, you can start mixing that purple and red tempera paint over in the corner. Eon, you'll give me hand with the large beaver board over there at the side of the room."

The two men worked swiftly, cutting out the outline of a Dutch windmill while Barry mixed paints.

"So your grandfather was murdered in this building, was he?" Percy asked.

Barry was surprised by his boss's remark, though he was aware that the man had ideas and comments on virtually everything. Percy was a confirmed, card-carrying atheist, and his observations on life and his aphorisms were well known to the Casino's staff, even to some of the performers.

"Yes, I'm pretty sure I know why your grandfather was killed. People are murdered for one of two things — love or money or both! I kind of figure your grandfather was killed because of money. And I think his partner, Fred Piton, did it!"

Barry was astonished by boss's comments. "How do you know all that, Percy?" He stood up quickly, nearly knocking over a large paint container.

"Oh, I read it in a newspaper."

"You read it in a newspaper? His death was years before you came to Canada."

"Well, I became very curious when I heard the rumours going around the theatre, so I went to the library at College and St. George and looked up the case in the old newspapers. Your dad mentioned something about it to me, too — not much, though, just about the partner your grandfather had until shortly before his death."

"My dad did?" As far as Barry knew, his father never spoke about his grandfather's murder to anyone! So why to Percy?

"Yes, he told me Piton left town suddenly and has never been heard from since. He was likely the killer, I'd say."

Barry returned to mixing the large plastic containers of paints. *Gee, this looks just like I'm mixing blood,* he mused. "I'm really curious, Percy. You seem pretty sure."

"Yep, it's always a case of love or money, and in your grandfather's case, I figure it was money."

Eon, now cutting the outlines of the windmill with a buzzsaw, seemed bemused as Barry and Percy exchanged views on Avner's death.

"You know, Percy, you seem to have ideas on a whole lot of subjects," Barry said. "And you seem very sure of yourself."

"Anything wrong with that, Barry?"

"No, in fact, I find them kind of interesting. I'm learning about more than painting in the Casino sign shop."

"When you get to my age, you'll have all kinds of ideas. I think I've seen a lot of the world. You've got time yet, kid. Incidentally, was your grandfather a religious guy?"

"I don't really think so, though my grandmother sure is."

"Really? Well, she's damn foolish. I don't believe any of that religious nonsense. In fact, you could call me an atheist. Evidently, these religious screwballs haven't heard about evolution. We all started out as a bit of slime."

The three continued with their work well into the evening with few breaks. Percy finally glanced at the large grandfather-like clock and declared, "I see it's almost nine-thirty! We've got to make some room here for the final rehearsal for tomorrow's opening show."

Eon and Barry helped Percy clear one end of the large paint shop, which doubled as a rehearsal studio. Suddenly, there was the sound of girlish chatter outside the studio door. The chorus line entered, followed by the members of the orchestra led by Archie Stone. The last to show up was the substitute producer/choreographer Ida Rose. Barry could hardly believe his eyes. She was short and squat with an enormous bust, had bright carrot-orange hair, a freckled face smeared with big blotches of rouge, and brown cow-like eyes partially masked by outrageously long false eyelashes. Ida wore tiny yellow speckled dancing shorts and spiked shoes. Behind her trailed a small white dog, Skippy, which she constantly admonished for its incessant sniffing and yelping. Trailing the lady and the dog was a tall, quiet, angular man with a bulbous nose and drooping eyelids who Barry later found out was named Henry Faulkner, Ida's faithful companion.

While Eon, Percy, and Barry continued to work on the sets in a different part of the studio, the rehearsal began, and above the shrillness of the six-piece orchestra, they could hear the barking voice of Ida Rose: "Goils, goils — make a coicle." She seemed to be larger than life in Barry's mind. *I think she'd draw more laughs onstage than the comics.*

Once the rehearsal was over, the girls, musicians, Ida, Henry, and Skippy quickly left. Eon and Percy had smiles on their faces, But Barry was a bit confused. "You know something, Percy. I've never seen anybody quite like that. Have you?"

Percy chomped on his cigar. "Nope. Just another member of the human species."

Barry decided to change the subject. "What did you think of the music, Percy?"

"Oh, theatre music's all right, but a lot of it is kind of cheap and simple."

"Cheap and simple? Why, it requires near genius to come up with these catchy melodies and rhyming lyrics."

Percy continued to work away and turned his head in the direction of Barry, who had walked over to the rehearsal piano. "Sorry, kid, I think popular music is simple stuff."

"Well, if you think it's simple, then why don't you write something like that? Can you write music like Jerome Kern, Cole Porter, or George Gershwin?"

Percy put down his brush and stood upright. "Well, maybe not, but it sure as hell sounds simple to me."

"Well, it isn't easy to do. Just try it," Barry said challengingly.

Percy decided to terminate the discussion. "Let's get on and finish the set … if you don't mind."

55

KIBBITZING WITH BORGE, BEBOPPING WITH DE LYON

In the summer of 1950, Barry was working as a part-time usher in addition to working in the sign shop in the latter half of the evening. It was the night before Victor Borge's opening at the Casino, and Barry was taking tickets at the door. There was a large crowd of patrons that evening. Suddenly, he was confronted by an early-fortyish, impeccably dressed man with a stunning woman on his arm. Barry asked the gentleman for their tickets.

The man glanced down at Barry and smiled benignly. "Oh, I'm so sorry," he said in a slightly foreign accent, which Barry couldn't quite place. "I didn't know performers were required to pay their own admission. I'll go back to the box office and buy my ticket. And, of course, I'll buy one for my secretary, as well!"

Barry immediately realized he was speaking to the famous Danish entertainer Victor Borge and was appalled at his mistake. Before he could respond, the couple wheeled around and retreated to the box office. "I'll probably lose my job!" Barry muttered to himself. "Father or no father."

As soon as his shift finished, Barry rushed to his father's office to make amends. Murray was nowhere to be seen, but in the open doorway leading to the box office stood the elegant Dane talking to the cashier. Just then, the box office phone rang. Borge leaned through the doorway and picked the receiver out of the cashier's hand. Someone was obviously inquiring about who was performing that day. Borge answered, "I am." A wide smile crossed his face, and it was all that the cashier and Barry could do to restrain themselves from laughing. "No, no, madam, I told you. It's me who's playing tomorrow. No, this isn't a fool talking." There was a pause. "What do I do? I play the piano." Then there was another pause. "No, no, I'm not some crazy person. It is me,

Victor Borge. I'm the headliner tomorrow and I play the piano, and if you wish to buy at ticket, come down to 87 Queen Street in Hamilton, Ontario." Borge paused. "I mean, Toronto, of course!" Still grinning, Borge leaned toward Barry, covered the receiver's mouthpiece, and winked. "It is Toronto, isn't it?" Evidently, the inquirer seemed satisfied, so Borge hung up the phone and broke into raucous laughter. He turned to Barry. "I understand this used to be a burlesque house. I hope they haven't cancelled the strippers because of me!"

It was as if Barry's earlier faux pas had never occurred. "I don't believe there are any strippers on this week's bill, sir."

In early August 1950, after the relatively unknown singer Eddie Fisher played to great acclaim at the Casino, another entertainer not familiar to Toronto audiences appeared at the theatre. A self-taught musician, Leo De Lyon was something of a musical phenomenon. Barry was on his way to the paint shop in his usher's uniform and just happened to bump into De Lyon standing in front of Ye Olde Fish and Chip Store immediately adjacent to the stage door alley entrance. For some reason, the musician and comedian approached him and asked almost apologetically, "You work here?"

"Yes, sir," replied Barry, realizing immediately this time that he was speaking to the headliner of the week.

"Say, kid, what do you know about this theatre? I've never worked in a place that has a chorus line. What gives?"

Barry was embarrassed. "Well, sir, this used to be a burlesque house, then it became legit ... sort of."

"What do you mean ... sort of?"

"Well," Barry said hesitantly, "my father happens to be one of the owners, and a couple of the other owners insisted on keeping the chorus line from the burlesque days — something about keeping everybody happy."

De Lyon smiled benignly. "I think that's great." He paused, and for no apparent reason, asked, "Hey, kid, do you like music?"

Barry nodded.

"How would you like to hear somebody who can whistle in three parts?"

"You must be joking. Most people can't whistle one part let alone three!"

"Okay, listen to this!" He whistled "You Are My Sunshine" in perfect three-part harmony.

"That's unbelievable! That's really great!"

De Lyon was obviously pleased. "So you like music, huh?"

"I sure do, especially jazz ... you know, bebop!"

"Well, now, that's a nice surprise. So few people in Toronto seem to know much about bebop. Why don't you come backstage when you get a break and maybe I can give you a pointer or two?"

Some hours later, Barry asked Percy if he could be excused for a few extra minutes on his break. "I'm going to meet Leo De Lyon between shows, Percy."

"Okay, but be back as soon as you can. We've got a deadline to meet."

Barry quickly scurried down the steep stairwell to the street and made his way toward the stage door alley entrance. To his chagrin, he saw his father standing there, anxiously puffing on a cigarette. He knew full well that when his father smoked a cigarette there was trouble. "What's the matter, Dad?"

"Oh, the usual. Lou's upstairs drinking with his cronies. You know, the same old crowd — his buddies from City Hall. They had the peep window open and were making such a ruckus that several customers complained! I have to go up and confront Lou and his pals. And, by the way, where are you off to? Shouldn't you be with Percy?"

"I'm taking a break. Leo De Lyon's going to show me a few things on the piano!"

56

DRIVING MISS KITTY

Lil often met Murray after the last show, and the two of them would go off to Bassel's Restaurant. One evening, the conversation took a nasty turn as they waited in line in the restaurant's crowded foyer.

"You know, Lil, every time I come to this place I'm reminded of your cousin, Sam, trying to make himself a partner! What a crook! Just like an Appelbaum!"

"What do you mean?" Lil's shrill response could be heard above the background noise of chatting customers, clattering plates, and a constantly ringing cash register.

"You know what I'm talking about!" Murray shouted in response, oblivious to the crowd. "We should've had that cousin of yours thrown in jail! We never pressed charges! Cohen and the Allens would gladly have had him charged and convicted, but Lou interfered!"

"I wish you'd say something nice about my family for a change! Everyone deserves a second chance. Sam's made a big effort to stay out of mischief since then. Look at the nice movie theatre business he's now got in the east end. Leave him alone! You're always picking on him! For your information, when Lou was a youngster he was a kind, decent, hard-working kid. He would have turned out just fine, but my father's death changed all that. He was just too young to take over the business … any business. But he had to do it. He thought drinking made him look more like a man in charge of things. And now he's addicted! He can't help himself. You know that!"

"It isn't just the drinking," Murray retorted.

At this point, Lily realized their conversation was clearly audible to the other restaurant patrons. She sensed all the eyes peering at them. "Murray, try to lower your voice! You always get so excited when you talk about my brother. Can't you control yourself?"

Murray looked around the busy restaurant, cupped his hands, and whispered into Lil's ear, "All right, I'll lower my voice."

They were finally escorted to a booth at the back of the restaurant where Murray ordered his favourite midnight snack of toasted bacon sandwich and hash brown potatoes followed by a whopping portion of Boston cream pie. Lil ordered her usual coffee and Danish.

Leaning across the table, Murray attempted to apologize for his earlier outburst but simply couldn't bring himself to say he was sorry. Lil was just happy they were no longer the centre of attention.

"You know, business is booming, Lil. And we've got some great people booked. Would you be interested in hearing who they are?"

"Of course, I would!"

"Next week we've got Kitty Kallen coming and after that The Harmonicats and The Four Knights, then Kay Starr." Murray pulled a piece of rumpled paper from his vest and smoothed it out on the booth table's Bakelite surface. "Here, look at Roy's list — The Charioteers, Nellie Lucher, The Southernaires. Mel Tormé's coming back. And then we've got Count Basie and Burl Ives, even Sugar Chile Robinson and Don Cornell."

"That's terrific, Murray."

"We're booked until the end of the year, and Roy assures me that almost all of them are musical greats." Murray strained to read the list through his thick glasses, straightening the crumpled paper once again. "Oh, look, your favourite, Eddie Fisher, is coming back with The Amazing Dunninger, a master mental wizard, I hear. That blind English pianist, George Shearing, is coming, too. Also Art Tatum. Roy told me he's the world's greatest pianist. Imagine! And then there's Dizzy Gillespie, a terrific jazz trumpet player. Do any of these names mean anything to you?"

Lil had to admit that most of them were unfamiliar to her.

On August 10, 1950, Kitty Kallen was booked into the Casino Theatre. She'd been a well-known big band vocalist in the 1940s singing with Jack Teagarden, Jimmy Dorsey, Artie Shaw, and Harry James. Her husband ran the Copacabana Club in New York City. Lou asked Murray to invite her to his Lake Simcoe cottage on the Sunday of the performing week. Barry was designated to chauffeur her.

"Look, I'm just too busy to drive her to the cottage, and besides, I don't want to spend any time up there, Barry," Murray explained. "I've made arrangements for her to be picked up at ten o'clock at the front door of the Royal York on Front Street."

That Sunday, Barry, who had recently acquired his driver's licence, pulled up in front of the hotel driving Murray's shiny new black Cadillac. He spotted a petite, doll-faced young woman standing at the curbside and shouted through the open passenger door window, "Are you Miss Kallen?"

"Yes, that's me. Are you from the Casino?"

"Yes, I'm Murray Little's son." Barry jumped out of the car and around to the curb and opened the passenger door for Kitty in perfect chauffeur style.

"How old are you, young man?" she asked, easing into the passenger seat.

"I'm old enough to have my driver's licence. I'm sixteen."

"Obviously, your father puts great trust in you."

"He does in some things and knows I'm a good driver."

"Quite honestly, young man, I thought Murray would be driving me … and I didn't catch your name."

"My name's Barry. And my father's tied up today."

"I'm sorry to hear that."

Barry closed the passenger door and hastily returned to his seat. Soon he was driving north up Yonge Street and out of the city. A long silence ensued. Then it was broken.

"So you work at the Casino and your father and uncle are owners?"

"Yes, Miss Kallen. And my kid brother's been in some stage productions."

"Don't tell me your mother's a performer, too?"

"No, but her father was in show business back before the mid-1930s."

"A real family affair, eh? Sounds interesting. Someday someone should write a story about your family and the theatre."

"Ending up in the theatre business has been a bit of an accident, at least for my father, and it hasn't been always so great. You see, my grandfather was murdered in 1935, and my father and uncle had to take over his theatre business."

"How terrible. Do you know who did it?"

"No, the killer was never found. A lot of lives were changed because of the murder."

"I'm so sorry to hear about all of this." An embarrassing moment of silence ensued. Sensing she had touched a raw nerve, Kitty quickly changed the topic of conversation. "Well, young man, there are lots of nice people in the theatre business. I'm sure you've met many of them. You've heard of the Sinatras, haven't you? Well, Frank and Nancy are very good friends of mine. My husband and I recently visited them. They have a gorgeous home, and Frank has a swimming pool in the shape of a grand piano. There are lots of wonderful people in show business."

If Miss Kallen only knew the problems within our family, she wouldn't find show business so loving! Barry mused.

It was a scarlet afternoon by the lake. Lou had invited his neighbours for a picnic, and the afternoon passed very quickly. The drive home from the lake was quiet and uneventful, and by the time Barry returned home, it was close to midnight.

Murray was still up. "How did things go, Barry?"

"Miss Kallen seemed to enjoy herself, and the afternoon went quite well. However, toward the end of the afternoon, Uncle Lou had one beer too many and began to talk about his late father, repeating what a wonderful, kind guy Grandfather was, how naive he was, how he loved the theatre business, how stupid he was to be a partner with a drunken Irishman. It was very embarrassing to hear, especially with all those people around and Miss Kallen, too. And then he went on to brag about how well known the Casino was becoming, how it was his idea to have famous people such as Miss Kallen come up to Canada, and how he was going to turn the Casino into the most famous theatre in North America."

"I wouldn't be too worried about what Lou has to say, Barry. You know how he gets when he's had a little bit too much to drink. I'm pretty certain he knows deep down what the truth is — his bad fortune to lose his father and his good fortune to inherit some money and a theatre."

And his good fortune to have a tolerant brother-in-law, Barry thought.

57

LUNCH WITH GYPSY ROSE LEE

On Thursday, August 31, 1950, the Casino advertised "The Renowned Recording Artist, Kay Starr — Featured Voice of Capitol Records."

There were five other acts on the bill, including a comic duo, a trio who performed zany harmonica antics, a European "novel" act, a dancer labelled as "Shades of the Roaring Twenties," and another dancer described as "A Fantasy in Fans." The screen featured a classic B movie entitled *Secret Agent of Japan* starring Preston Foster and Lynn Bari.

Murray was outraged. "What's "A Fantasy in Fans" doing on the bill!" he bellowed into the phone at Lou. "That's a stripper!" "For goodness' sake, what are you trying to do? Put off our customers and offend our headliner?"

A somewhat slurred voice at the other end of the line answered, "Don't you ever forget, Murray, that I have the final say when it comes to billing! I've gone along with your big-name policy ideas, and yeah, they've worked, but I wanna spice up the program. You know, a little biz-zaz, something for everybody."

"Listen, Lou, please don't cause me any more embarrassment. Miss Starr will likely be very upset. Roy Cooper couldn't have known about this!"

"Of course, he does," Lou countered.

"You cleared it with him first?"

"Damn right I did!"

"I don't believe you, Lou! Can't you get it straight? You're going to drive away the better performers and the customers with strippers!" Murray slammed down the receiver in disgust. *I don't know how many times I have to tell him we must be consistent and keep strippers off our bills. Isn't it enough for him and his cronies that we've kept the chorus line?*

On the day of Kay Starr's opening, Murray hurried backstage to introduce himself to her. "Miss Starr, I'm Murray Little, the manager here. I hear you've had a quick rehearsal with the orchestra already, but perhaps you haven't had time to check over the bill, coming in late as you did. I must be honest with you. An exotic dancer's been included this week. I had no knowledge of this until recently, and it was too late for me to do anything about it. I do hope you're not offended."

Kay Starr, an exotic-looking woman, the daughter of a North American Indigenous father and an Irish mother, gazed at Murray with astonishment. "Absolutely not, Mr. Little. I play a lot of clubs in the U.S. and nothing surprises me. Besides, people are coming to the show to see me, not a stripper!"

"You mean, it doesn't upset you?"

"Not at all!"

I'll never understand performers. Murray was about to leave when he remembered he'd had a call from the owner of CKEY Radio on University Avenue. "Miss Starr, Jack Kent Cooke called me and asked me to convey a message. He'll have a car waiting for you after your first show today."

Kay smiled. "Thank you. He's quite a fan of mine, you know."

Best not to ask any questions! Murray thought, a little flustered. "Have a good stay at the Casino, Miss Starr." As he hurried to leave, he reached into one of his pockets and handed her a scrap of paper. "Here, these are my phone numbers — both here and at home. If you have any problems whatsoever, don't hesitate to call me."

By the early 1950s, the Casino had become respectable, a place where one could be seen in attendance without social embarrassment. Performances at the theatre were now regularly reviewed in the major Toronto newspapers — Helen McNamara and Stan Helleur in the *Telegram*, Hugh Thomson and Jack Karr in the *Toronto Daily Star*, and Rolley Miles in the *Globe and Mail*.

In early 1951, though, Gypsy Rose Lee was booked to play the Casino.

"Isn't Gypsy a stripper?" Lil asked one morning.

"She certainly used to be one," Murray told her, "but at present she's an international celebrity, a stage personality, and Roy Cooper has assured me there's no offensive nudity in her act. It's nothing like her old burlesque striptease."

So, in May, Gypsy Rose Lee, "The One and Only," the queen of glamour and star of stage, screen, and radio, and the author of mystery *The G-String Murders*, played the Casino with her "Royal American Beauties" in an all-star vaudeville show direct from New York's Capitol Theatre. Gypsy had been a feature on the Minsky circuit as a prototypical stripteaser but had never played the Casino in the burlesque days of the 1930s and 1940s. Her 1951 engagement was a special event, at least for the Casino.

Jack Karr, in his May 4, 1951, column in the *Toronto Daily Star*, wrote:

> The girl who used to strip for a living before she got culture and wrote a book is at work at the Casino Theatre stage this week ribbing the "art" that used to pay for her rent and groceries. In her salad days, Miss Lee found it quite profitable to peel down to her rhinestones, but of late she's found it more rewarding just to jam her tongue in her cheek and kid the whole process. She does this with a hearty and gutsy good humour. For the first show yesterday she crammed the joint, a situation that sent manager Murray Little darting around, rubbing his hands and wishing no doubt for a few extra hundred seats to accommodate the sold-right-out crowd. And the mob packed in the stands waited for Miss Lee to get naughty. Miss Lee for her part seemed to be hovering on the brink of being naughty much more often than she was actually taking the plunge. Gypsy saves her famous strip for the finale and when she goes into it, it turns out to be a gag act. The idea roughly was to appear in a modest and voluminous gown and by releasing a series of zippers and fasteners — to which only Miss Lee knows the combination — to remove the clothing from the inside out with a brassiere, garter belt and other dainties floating about the stage before the gown itself is removed for a glint of the rhinestones. While this is going on she is reciting a little song about what a stripper thinks about when she is stripping. She thinks about fine art and good books says Miss Lee. Gypsy's two contributions to the bill are separated by other acts. For her first appearance she surrounds herself with four long-stemmed stripped-down beauts at whom she cracks robustly in a mock lecture on etymology. Since the girls couldn't get much barer than they are without feeling the hot breath of the law the reverse process is used. By the time Gypsy has finished throwing materials extracted from her bustle around them they are clad in pretty dodgy fashion. Frankly, there isn't much to it and the audience members who came looking for sensationalism certainly

aren't going to get it from this gal. Miss Lee is too slick an operator to be playing up to the bald-headed row at this stage of the game.

"I hope Miss Lee isn't upset by Jack Karr's review," Lil said to Murray after reading Karr's column.

"I do, too. By the way, Miss Lee asked me to lunch after tomorrow's first show. She's a delightful person and a real lady. Would you like to come along? I'm sure she wouldn't object."

"I'd love to."

The following day, Murray and Lil joined Miss Lee in the Victoria Room of the King Edward Hotel. Murray was reluctant to mention the review, but before the waiter even arrived to take their orders, Gypsy said, "I read that review in the *Toronto Daily Star*, Mr. Little. Don't give it a second thought — I don't. I've been roasted in bigger towns than Toronto. I enjoy thinking about those kinds of reviews all the way to the bank! One of the best reviews I ever got — what a laugh — was published by the *Daily Worker*, the communist paper. They claimed that striptease was a capitalistic cancer and a product of the profit system and that it was girls who turned away from street-walking who took up stripping. Can you believe that?"

Murray and Lil were almost speechless with embarrassment, but Murray nevertheless managed to blurt, "I really admire your candour, Miss Lee."

Gypsy shot back, "Oh, what part of the anatomy is that?" She then went on to share other anecdotes about her theatrical experiences and soon had Murray and Lil completely at ease and chuckling. The lunch came to an end with everyone on a first-name basis and with an agreement to get together again before Gypsy left Toronto. As they were about to part company, the former stripper reached into her large handbag and drew out a book, which she quickly inscribed and handed to Lil. "Here's a copy of my second mystery novel, Lil." The book was entitled *Mother Finds a Body*, and the inscription read: "To Lil with love from Gypsy Rose Lee. Someday this book will be a movie like my first novel!"

Lil was thrilled. "Thank you very much, Gypsy. I'm sure it'll make terrific reading."

On the drive home, Lil declared, "You see, Murray, mixing with the performers isn't so bad, after all. You should do it more often."

"She's an exception. I spend enough time already with performers!"

In late February 1952, the phones at the Casino began ringing off the hook. The famous and fabulous Johnnie Ray was to make his first appearance at the Casino. By 6:00 a.m. on the day of Ray's first performance, there was an enormous queue on Queen Street; the line extended in both east and west directions and numbered close to a thousand people. There was a fever of anticipation in the crowd not seen previously. Ray was a teenage idol, but there was a healthy sprinkling of adults in the line, as well, and the following day a newspaper report noted there was even a man with a sleeping child in his arms standing in the crowd. Ray was often labelled "The Prince of Wails" and billed as "Mr. Emotion." He was also called the "Nabob of Sob" and the "Howling Success," all because of his famous recordings of "Cry" and "The Little White Cloud That Cried."

On the Saturday of Ray's opening week, Murray spotted Barry with a young female companion standing in line at the box office and made his way through the milling throng. "Barry, you didn't tell me you were coming to the theatre. And who's your young friend here?"

"Dad, this is Cheryl, a friend of mine from school. I promised I'd bring her to see Johnnie Ray. Cheryl, meet my dad."

Murray smiled benignly and shook Cheryl's hand. "You aren't going to get seats in the auditorium tonight, I'm afraid. We're sold out. Would you like to see Mr. Ray perform from backstage? Maybe you'd like to meet him, too?"

"That would be terrific, Mr. Little," squealed Cheryl.

"Then follow me." Murray led Barry and his young date through the crowd to the side alley, then down the alley to the stage door and into the backstage area. He motioned them to position themselves behind the large proscenium curtain. "I'll meet you here after the show," he said, then hurried off.

Barry and Cheryl, hidden by the curtain, stood no more than ten feet from Ray as he performed to the delight of the enthusiastic audience. The audience, especially the young girls, oohed and aahed with the singer's every move and utterance. Ray was accompanied by a Toronto singing group, The Four Lads. Barry quietly whispered in Cheryl's ear, "At least the boys sing in tune!"

Cheryl was simply mesmerized.

There was loud hooting and cheering and clapping at the end of Ray's performance and were calls of "More, more, more!" The curtain finally descended, the audience settled down, and the movies began.

Murray reappeared and led Barry and Cheryl to Ray's dressing room. He knocked on the door, and it quickly opened. There stood the singer in his dressing gown, still in pancake makeup and wearing a hearing aid. Murray announced, "Johnnie, this is my son and his girlfriend, Cheryl. Barry's a big fan of yours. Would you mind giving him and his friend your autograph?"

"Delighted to meet you," said Ray, reaching for two signed eight-by-ten glossies of himself on his dresser. "Sorry I can't spend much time with you. I'm in a bit of a hurry right now."

Murray, Barry, and his date thanked Ray and hastily left the room. Once the door was shut, Barry turned to his father and said, "I'm not a fan of his, Dad. You know that. He sings out of tune! And I don't ever ask for autographs!"

"But I'm sure your young friend's a fan," Murray quickly retorted.

Cheryl was oblivious to the father-and-son conversation and was in what appeared to be a trance, tightly clutching her autographed photograph.

TELEVISION VERSUS THEATRE

The boom days of the big-name policy continued. In the second week of May 1952, Larry Parks and his wife, Betty Garrett, appeared on the Casino stage. Parks was a famous film star, having played the tempestuous and popular Al Jolson in *The Jolson Story* in 1946 and again in the 1949 sequel *Jolson Sings Again*. He'd gained notoriety because he starred not only in an extraordinarily popular movie but also because he appeared before the House Un-American Activities Committee in 1951 where he openly admitted to joining the American Communist Party ten years earlier. And though he'd left the party in 1945, he was blacklisted from performing in the United States. Parks was still an internationally famous person, though, when he appeared at the theatre with his equally celebrated wife, Betty Garrett.

Murray was full of praise for Parks. He found him gentlemanly and self-effacing. "He has no pretensions whatsoever," he confided to his sons. "He's one of the easiest performers I've ever worked with. He and Betty have a great act. You have to see it."

The act avoided all mention of Al Jolson, which had, of course, become Parks's professional trademark. In spite of repeated requests from the front row to perform an impersonation, he refused to do so. The boys enjoyed the performance, which was memorable for its diversity — singing, dancing, and joke-telling. The actor liked kidding the smoochers in the balcony, if there were any, and indulging in repartee with members of the pit band.

In the early 1950s, a parade of movie stars appeared, the names and faces of the majority being immediately recognizable to the Casino's audiences. The list included Marilyn Maxwell, Gene Nelson, Jack Carson, The Andrews Sisters, Dorothy Lamour, Jane Powell, Van Johnson, Gordon MacRae, Dorothy Dandridge, Chico Marx ... the roll seemed endless.

Murray continued to have his weekly meetings with Arthur Cohen in the man's office. At one in particular, Cohen said, "Well, Murray, you must be very happy with the way business is going."

"Yes, business is very good. And it's easier, too. The headliners are a lot more painless to deal with than I anticipated. I find that almost always the bigger the star, the more trouble-free they are to handle. I only hope our good luck at the box office doesn't run out too soon, Mr. Cohen."

"What do you mean by that?"

"I see a major problem ahead for the business."

"Ahead? What's ahead?"

Murray was stern-faced. "Television!"

"Television, Murray? Are you kidding? That's no competition for the Casino. Besides, television is in its infancy and many people still can't afford a set."

"I disagree. Sales of television sets are definitely increasing rapidly as costs come down. And programs are improving. Lil and I have a TV, and though reception's awful at times, we really enjoy programs like *Your Show of Shows* and *What's My Line?* It won't be too many years before most people will be able to sit in their own living rooms and watch the very performers we now have onstage. And all they'll have to do is turn a dial! And perhaps more importantly, we're going to have problems hiring our performers in the future. They're currently doing four shows a day, sometimes five on Friday, at least two dozen performances a week. I predict they'll choose television engagements over theatre ones any day and be paid as much for one television performance as we pay them for a week, maybe more! What's more, I hear Canada will have a TV version of CBC later this year."

"I see your point, Murray, but I think you're being unduly pessimistic. What does Roy Cooper think?"

"Like I do. But it won't affect him the way it will us. Roy can book performers into any venue, including television studios, concert halls, and the like. It's the Casino and other live theatres that will suffer. And there are few if any theatres like ours left anywhere."

Cohen looked thoughtful and stared out the office window. After a few moments, he said reassuringly, "You're really pushing things, Murray. I wouldn't worry about it just yet. Keep up the good work."

Murray grabbed his weather-worn briefcase, and as he opened the office door to leave, he turned to Cohen. "I won't lose any sleep over it, Mr. Cohen, not yet." Murray couldn't help but reflect on his mother's perpetual reminder that nothing lasts forever.

"He wanted you to do what?" Murray exclaimed as he and Barry drove home after the day's last show.

"He wanted me to join his act," Barry repeated.

"You must be kidding!"

"No, I'm not! I was marking time before the one o'clock show, dressed in my uniform and noodling away on the rehearsal piano. I had no sooner started when I felt a tap on my shoulder, and when I swung around, there was Rudy Vallee asking me if I could read music. I replied I could and he then asked me how old I was. When I told him, he was surprised. He thought I was around thirteen or fourteen, not seventeen! He then said he was always looking for something different in his act and that it would be a nice gimmick to have a kid accompanying him. And he asked me if I'd like to! Before I could reply, he went on to tell me about how he got started in the theatre business, how he did everything around the theatre, including being an usher like me. He also told me he played the saxophone before he became a singer. I eventually got a word in and told him I was a student and that my usher's job was just for the summer. He persisted, though, and asked me to think about it."

Murray chuckled. "Well, I hope you made it clear you didn't want a career in show business."

There was an awkward silence as they travelled another two blocks. Exasperated, Barry finally replied, "Other than thanking him for his interest, I didn't say anything. And I'd like to know something. What have you and the rest of the family got against us boys going into show business?"

Murray was taken aback. "I care a great deal about you boys. You must understand that I know a lot more than you do about how the world works. All I'm trying to do is give you the best possible advice for your future," he added defensively, thinking about his meeting with Arthur Cohen and their discussion about television.

Not another word was spoken for the remainder of the homeward journey.

◆ ◆ ◆

In the autumn of 1952, Murray received a phone call from Gersten Allen. "Murray, we've got a great opportunity to grab hold of a money-making film that I think we could fit into the Casino."

"A film, Gersten? Are you serious? The Casino's in the live theatre business!"

"It'll only be for a week. The film's done great box office everywhere it's played."

"What do you mean? What's it about?"

Gersten cleared his throat. "It's a film about sex."

"Sex? You mean to tell me you want to run a stag movie? Gersten, are you out of your mind?"

"Calm down. It's a legitimate film. It's advertised as a movie that dares to discuss sex as never before seen or heard. Theatres aren't admitting anyone under high school age unless they're accompanied by a parent."

"We've already had enough trouble with churchmen in this city. Do we need more, Gersten?"

"Listen for a moment. It's an educational film, a story about the birds and the bees. Believe me, it's legitimate. It shows how a young woman has her life ruined by an unwanted pregnancy when a guy robbed her of her virginity and is killed in a plane crash a month after their encounter."

"Don't be ridiculous," Murray retorted. "That would tarnish the theatre's reputation!"

"Don't be ridiculous, Murray. It's a wonderful opportunity to make a good buck. Lou's in favour of it."

"Do we really need this? What will our headliners think? They may not want to play the theatre again."

"Christ, Murray, stop being such a pessimist. As soon as there's an opportunity, we want to show this film. It'll be a winner!"

Under protest, Murray finally agreed to the proposal. The film was shown a few months later when a headliner cancelled unexpectedly. There were record-breaking box office sales despite admonishments from several pulpits to boycott the film. Still, Murray viewed the whole affair with the sex film as another sign of an uncertain future for the Casino Theatre. Television? Stag films? What else loomed on the horizon?

59

TWO SISTERS VISIT

It was a late morning in March 1954 in the Little household in Forest Hill. Esther was alone in the house when there was a knock on the door. She hurried down the stairs and peered through the peephole. It was Becky.

"Quick, Esther, open the door!" Becky shouted. "It's raining. I'm getting drenched standing here."

Esther opened the door, and Becky stepped inside, simultaneously waving goodbye to her husband, Sam, who had brought her over. "Becky, it's so good to see you! I haven't seen you in such a long time. Is everything okay?"

"Of course, it is. But, Esther, you're so short of breath. What's wrong with you?"

"Well, I did just run down the stairs, but even walking makes me short of breath these days. The doctor tells me my lungs are bad." The two sisters entered the living room and sat next to each other on the long, deep leather sofa. Esther continued. "The doctor's given me some medicine and it helps … a bit. Never mind, though. I'm okay, God willing. How are you and the family?"

"We're all fine," Becky answered cheerfully.

"I'm so glad to hear that. And what about the Appelbaums? Have you any news of them?"

"I've heard Chanala isn't well. She's living in a small downtown apartment now, and her two boys are supporting her. She misses her boys terribly. Both are well settled in the United States — Moishe in California and Maxie in Florida. By the way, I hear things are going well at the theatre. Have you been taking in any shows?"

"Becky, you know I don't mix in. Murray, Lil, and Lou tell me business is good and that's all I care about. You know I never went to the theatre when Avner had the Roxy, and I'm not about to start now."

"But, Esther, the Casino's different. They no longer have strippers and they've even dropped the chorus line. They've got famous performers now! This week they've got Julius La Rosa, the world-famous singer! Sam and I are going to see him tomorrow evening!"

"Becky, I don't want to hear about it. It's for a different generation. I'm not interested. Murray's Sam and Anna don't go, either. But if you and your Sam want to go, that's fine with me. All that matters to me is that everybody's well."

Becky glanced around the living room. "I see you have a television set."

"I never watch it. The boys do — and Lil and Murray."

"You shouldn't isolate yourself so much," Becky admonished. "Television's a big thing. Just about everyone on our street has a set now."

"How do you know that?"

"I can see the antennas on the roofs. Television's so popular now that no one wants to be seen without a set. I've heard that some people who can't afford one have actually installed false antennas to avoid feeling embarrassed!"

"It's of no interest to me, Becky."

"You know me, Esther. I like to keep up to date. I watch a lot of television. There is great news on and very good entertainment. Just as good as the entertainment at the Casino! Julius La Rosa is a good example. I saw him on a live television show a few months ago. He was wonderful. I'm telling you, Esther, you really shouldn't be so out of touch with what's going on."

"Becky, I don't need any sermons from you. If you want to have those interests, fine. Mine are different."

A protracted silence ensued — the two sisters embarrassed by each other's comments. Finally, the silence was broken by Becky. "How's your Lou?" she asked softly.

Esther's face lightened a bit. "Lou's become such a mensch in recent years, Becky! He stops in to say hello every day now on his way into work. I always prepare a little breakfast for him. Esther stared at her dainty diamond-studded watch that Avner had given her so long ago. "He should be here any minute now."

"And Lil?" There was a sustained silence.

"Neither here nor there," Esther responded, rotating her wrists to the right or left for added emphasis.

"What does that mean?"

"Well, she's good to me, but I'm unhappy with the way she runs off and leaves the kids and Murray. And Murray works so hard. You can see it on his face. And another thing that's bothering me — I can tell he and Lou don't always get along together. Brothers-in-law should care for each other, especially when they're partners." Esther paused, looking wistful for a moment, then said brightly, "Come, Becky, let's have some tea in the kitchen."

STRIKE!

"I won't be home for dinner this evening, Lil." Murray was clearly agitated and had nicked himself more than usual while shaving earlier.

"Why not?" muttered a half-awake Lil as she fumbled for her dressing gown.

"I've got a late meeting with Lou and Gersten. We've got a situation at the theatre."

"A situation?"

"We need a new contract with the Toronto Musicians' Association, and we're getting nowhere with them. Walter Murdoch, their president, is one tough guy to deal with. He's threatening to close the theatre."

"Really?"

"Yes, though he doesn't see it that way. Murdoch's insisting the new contract contain a clause stating that musicians in Toronto won't be required to play for members of the American Guild of Variety Artists. Put it another way, Lil, Murdoch wants Toronto musicians to play only for all-Canadian acts."

"You must be joking?"

"Nope," said Murray as he bent to tie his shoelaces. "He thinks his proposal will get more jobs for his members. But it'll have just the opposite effect. We couldn't operate the theatre for more than two weeks with only all-Canadian acts."

"He wouldn't want that to happen, would he, Murray?"

"Nothing I say seems to convince him he's on the wrong track. And he's threatening a strike if we don't agree to his terms."

Murray straightened his tie in the mirror and hurried out of the house. He'd arranged a special early-morning meeting with Arthur Cohen and was anxious not to be late.

Cohen was waiting for him at the door of his office. "Did you make any headway with Murdoch yesterday, Murray?"

"Nope. I couldn't reason with him."

"Well, surely you've done something about it other than speak to Murdoch, Murray?"

Murray was surprised and annoyed. *Cohen has no idea how much work I've put into this!* "Yes, of course! Joe Sedgwick's been helping me. As I already mentioned, we applied to the Ontario Labour Relations Board a few weeks ago for a conciliation officer. We heard just yesterday that the application was approved. Under the law, there can be no strike until the conciliation process is completed. The problem is that Murdoch isn't buying into this, and I'm afraid he'll call an illegal strike any day now!"

"Those sons of bitches! I've hated unions all my life."

"We can curse all we want, Mr. Cohen, but we have to face reality. We have to have plans in place to deal with a strike!"

"Well, what are your plans, Murray?"

"We'll cancel all the acts and just run movies. Lou, Gersten, and I will meet tonight to sort out details so we're ready for anything."

On Thursday, September 9, 1954, the pit musicians and the live acts failed to show up and the Casino featured two movies being premiered in Canada — the French *Companions of the Night* and the British *Eight O'Clock Walk*.

Murray returned to the theatre with three of the Toronto dailies tucked under his arm. All three contained articles on the death of Canada's only remaining vaudeville house.

> The Casino, one of only five such houses on the North American continent, from here on in will be showing movies.
> We hope the theatre does well but movies, like TV, will never be a substitute for live performances.
> It may be just sentiment but every time the curtain goes up, we experience the satisfaction of seeing performers in person … whether they be recording stars, musical groups, acrobats or tap-dancing fools. Sometimes the acts were not always up to par, but we loved their tireless efforts just the same … from the buck-and-wing dancers to the salsa-squirting comics. And when the act is first-class, well, the movies and TV can take a back seat in any time period.
> Who for instance can ever forget the polished performances of people like Eartha Kitt or Pearl Bailey, especially La Bailey's languid air as she drags a chair onstage and whispers, "You people are sitting down … why shouldn't I?" And from there on working with faultless timing gears her performance to the reactions of the audience. Try and get that on your TV set!
> But though the clowns and the contortionists were missing last Thursday that final show was good theatre. You might not think putting people into a trance is entertaining, but the Great Morton is a showman all the way. His 90-minute act is so good, especially the way his volunteer assistants follow every command that we couldn't help thinking the wrong people were onstage. It should have been the bigwigs of the American Guild of Variety Artists and the musicians' union.

Upon reading this, Murray chuckled. *It's nice to know someone's on our side.*

Three days later, the phone in Murray's office rang. It was Walter Murdoch. Murray could hardly believe his ears. "You mean you've changed your mind. You're not going to insist on all-Canadian acts?" Murray reached for his cigarette pack. "That's wonderful, simply wonderful! What's that? Yes, of course, I'll meet with you and Archie Stone at five o'clock at the union office. See you then!"

On Thursday, September 16, 1954, the Casino advertised "Bigger, Better Stage Shows Are Back! Direct from a sensational run at New York's famous Copacabana, Diosa Costello and her torrid, tuneful, tantalizing Brazilian Brevities."

The report of the death of the Casino Theatre was premature.

MONEY WORRIES

Murray picked up the phone in his office.

"Congratulations, Murray! It's Arthur Cohen. Glad the strike's been settled, but I'm not pleased about what I see in today's newspapers."

Murray was taken aback. "How so, Mr. Cohen?"

"I turned to the entertainment section, and what do I see advertised for next month, 'Maria Elena in her daring dance of sacrifice – breathtaking, spectacular, mystical'? And I see you have a Canadian premier of a movie called *Rossana* — 'Latin America's torrid picture of the year'! I thought we were through with this kind of stuff, Murray. What in tarnation's going on? I thought you and Cooper were dead set against bringing back strippers!"

"Look, Mr. Cohen, you know full well that box office receipts have been slipping for months now. Even Eartha Kitt and Dorothy Dandridge failed to fill the house. We're still booking legitimate acts and have managed to get The Crew Cuts, The Four Lads, Louis Armstrong, and Cab Calloway, but we're finding it impossible to sign some others. And it isn't just television that's cutting into our business. Places like Las Vegas are paying double or triple the salaries we can offer for big names — and with less performance time! I've been under tremendous pressure from Lou and Gersten to bring back strippers and resisted them for as long as I could. But I've finally faced reality. Something had to be done. And let's face it, sex always sells, television or no television."

"Murray, I'm disappointed to hear that. This is a radical change. But you do what you must to keep the theatre alive. Just don't cause me any embarrassment!"

Within moments, the phone rang again. Murray's broker from Thomson McKinnon was on the line. "It's Norm, Murray. Your margin account's overdrawn. It's that oil stock you bought. It's taking a dive. I'll cover for you for now, but I need $50,000 from you within the next few days. Get the money to me as soon as you can."

"I'll go to the bank straight away, Norm. You'll have your money by tomorrow. I'm sure that stock will come good."

"You know my opinion about oil stock, Murray. I'm with O'Henry, the American writer. He says an oil well is a hole in the ground surrounded by suckers. I warned you about that stock. You should sell it right now!"

"Norm, it'll be okay. Relax."

"Tell anybody who calls that I'll be back in about an hour!" Murray shouted to the cashier as he hurried out of the theatre toward the bank at the corner of Queen and Bay Streets.

"Yes, Mr. Blenkenship can see you right now," the teller informed Murray after he entered the bank.

Walter Blenkenship frowned when Murray explained the situation. "Your credit's good with the bank, Murray, but I'm a little uneasy that you're using this money to buy oil stock."

"I'm very confident about this stock, Walter. If the stock goes as I think it will, my financial problems will be nicely settled."

"Murray, I have to tell you that I have no faith in the stock market. The little-guy investor is a pawn in a chess game rigged by inside players. That's why I have to insist that you put up your home as collateral if we loan you $50,000."

"My home?" a disappointed Murray replied. He slumped in his chair and released an exasperated sigh. "I guess I have no choice."

Blenkenship handed over the necessary documents for Murray to sign. *Lil's not going to like this. How will I tell her? But maybe I won't have to.* Murray left the bank in a cold sweat. *I suppose Walter's is right. The stock market's another form of robbery.*

◆ ◆ ◆

"What's going on with you?" Lil asked Murray at the breakfast table. "You look as pale as a ghost and you're shaking. You haven't touched any of your breakfast and that's certainly not like you." She stared at Murray but couldn't make meaningful eye contact with him. "Is it something I said?"

Murray remained mute.

"For goodness' sake, Murray, at least say something. Something's obviously happened, and if you can't tell me, who are you going to tell? Or is it something between you and your mother?"

After a further seemingly endless silence, Murray took a deep breath and spoke in a slow, hushed voice. "Lil, I've lost a lot of money. I thought I had a sure thing in an oil well stock. I still don't know how much I've lost, but it's considerable. I was trying to make up for a bad investment in a furniture company. I've been very naive losing all that money. This couldn't have happened at a worse time. With the way the Casino box office is going, my salary's going to be cut back even more. I really don't know how we're going to continue living in this expensive house."

"You've never shared any of this with me!" Lil spluttered angrily. "Why have you kept it from me?"

"It just never occurred to me, Lil. You know nothing about the market or business and have never expressed an interest."

"Well, how much have you lost?"

"I told you, I don't know how much, but it's probably most of our savings. We might have to sell the house." Murray nervously reached into his pocket, pulled out a Sweet Caporal cigarette, lit it, then quickly butted it in his coffee.

"Murray, you're a mess. What are we going to do? Especially if the theatre fails! Are we going to go on relief?"

"No, not as bad as that! After all, I've got my motion picture projectionist licence and can always work as a projectionist. So we'd get by. But maybe it won't come to that, anyway. Roy Cooper and the others feel the theatre would have a chance to survive if we went back to burlesque."

"Burlesque? You mean back to bump-and-grind, a chorus line, and baggy-pant comics?"

"Well, no, not the comics. Most of those performers are dead or retired, and survivors like Red Buttons are on television or working in Las Vegas. And we can't afford a chorus line. It's back to just bump-and-grind." Murray sighed. "What a comedown for the Casino."

"This is very depressing, Murray."

"I have something else to tell you. Dr. Richard says I'm depressed and wants me to go into the hospital for a week's rest and have shock treatments. ECT, they call it."

"You're depressed? So that's what's going on with you! Well, I can understand you might be a bit down about our financial situation, but surely not to the degree to have shock treatments? The situation isn't that hopeless. You just said so!"

"The financial worries don't help, Lil. But it's more to do with our family life … with you and me. You must know that. You go away for weeks on end, and when you're in town, we hardly see each other. We're living separate lives. We're worlds apart."

Flustered, Lil rose to pour herself another coffee. "When are you going into the hospital?"

"In about a week's time. It'll give me a chance to finalize some work at the theatre."

Lil steadied herself against the counter, anxious to change the topic. "Has anybody got any ideas besides going into burlesque?"

"Roy's keen to have us combine country and western music acts with burlesque. He's got some acts booked already. I'm not so sure, but I guess it's worth a try. At least there's no extra overhead. Remember that East Coast singer Wilf Carter? His lineups were almost as big as Johnnie Ray's. At the time, we thought it was a bit of a fluke. But Roy assures us this country and western stuff is big business. There's also something called rock and roll that's becoming popular. A young American kid called Elvis Presley does it. He wiggles about and makes a lot of noise apparently, but the kids go crazy for him. And Roy says he's caught on with the country and western fans, too. So we'll see. If that doesn't work, we'll be into burlesque full-time, I'm sorry to say."

"I've heard of Elvis Presley! Have you tried to get hold of him?"

"Yes, but his asking price is much too much. He has a very tough agent — some kind of colonel."

A week later, in the cold January of 1955, Murray entered Wellesley Hospital and received three electroconvulsive therapy treatments. That same week the Casino featured Little Jimmy Dickens of Grand Ole Opry fame. The day after Murray was released from the hospital he was back at the Casino directing traffic. Charlie Mackie, Wally Crosby, and the grumpy but reliable Dave Sherman were still around to help the aging Jezebel of Toronto.

When Murray returned to the Casino office, the cashier shouted, "It's Roy Cooper on the phone!"

"I'm calling from Montreal," Cooper said when Murray got on the line. "How are you feeling? I heard you were in the hospital."

"Fine, Roy, but I don't remember anything that happened to me in the past week. I guess those shock treatments made me forget my troubles."

"The theatre's going to be fine, Murray. Don't be so pessimistic. I think the Casino's going to attract a new audience with country and western and rock and roll, and yes, with strippers, too. As long as we keep overhead down, the theatre will be just fine."

The last big name to appear on the Casino stage was Louis "Satchmo" Armstrong with his sextet of internationally known jazz musicians, including Trummy Young, Barney Bigard, Arvell Shaw, and Velma Middleton. As usual, the engagement was for one week and was advertised as "fine family entertainment." The same advertisement boasted the following attraction: "Melba, the Toast of the Town in Her Exciting Bubble Dance."

62

THE END COMES

It was early morning, and for some reason Esther had left her bedroom following her morning prayers and had come downstairs. She spotted Murray in the hallway about to leave the house. "Please don't leave yet, Murray," she said breathlessly. "I must speak to you."

"Of course, Esther."

"Come and sit in the breakfast room." The morning light streamed through the breakfast nook windows, highlighting Esther's silver-grey hair. Her gold necklace with the pendant containing her cherished picture of Avner glistened.

"What's the problem, Esther?" a concerned Murray asked.

Esther could hardly catch her breath. "You see, Murray, I know it's God's will for me to leave this earth very soon. The doctors have told me there isn't much more they can do for me. I want to tell you something important before I die."

Murray was startled. *This sounds like a deathbed confession.*

"I want to thank you for being such a mensch. You've worked so hard on behalf of us all. This family couldn't have survived without you. I also want you to know how sorry I am that you've suffered over the years. I know how difficult Lou has been for you as a partner at the theatre. And my Lil hasn't been the best wife for you."

"Esther, none of this is necessary."

"There are certain things that must be said before it's too late." Esther had become increasingly excitable and short of breath as she struggled to express herself. "I want you to make a promise to me, Murray."

"Of course, Esther. Try not to get so upset."

"I want you to someday see that justice is done. See to it that Fred Piton goes to jail for what he did to my Avner. Whatever his faults, there hasn't been a day gone by when I haven't thought about Avner and prayed for him."

Murray was flustered. "Esther, there's very little I can do. For all I know, the police have closed the case." He anxiously glanced at his watch.

"I'm counting on you, Murray. Avner must not be forgotten."

Murray looked at his watch again. "Esther, I have to go now, but be assured, I'll never forget Avner."

A barely audible Esther whispered, "Thank you, Murray. Now go already."

Murray arrived at Arthur Cohen's office for his regular weekly meeting fifteen minutes later than usual. "You're late, Murray." Cohen snapped, then got straight to the point. "I think we should seriously consider selling the Casino!"

Murray was startled.

Cohen continued. "The past few years have been an absolute disaster for the theatre. If it weren't for the confectionery stand at the back, we'd be dead broke."

"You're right, Mr. Cohen. But before we do that, don't you think we should wait to see what sort of business country and western will do for us?"

"Well, how's it doing so far?"

"Roy Cooper's got some great acts lined up. Here's a list of some of the people. There's Ray Price, Jimmy Reeves, Justin Tubb, Hank Snow, Marty Robbins, Roy Acuff, and Johnny Cash."

"Murray, you know very well those names mean nothing to me."

"The same for me," said Murray, attempting to placate Cohen.

"Well, if country and western changes things soon, fine. Otherwise, we should sell the whole operation."

Murray left a copy of the week's receipts on Cohen's desk and quickly left the office. *I'm going to wind up being a motion picture projectionist, after all,* he mused as he hustled back to the Casino.

By 1960, the Casino was almost broke. Grand Ole Opry and strippers were as incompatible as oil and water. Neither was doing anything to save the Casino.

"It's time to stop the bleeding and sell up, Murray," said Cohen at one of their later weekly meetings. "And we already have an interested party! There's bound to be a developer who wants to put up a hotel complex near City Hall. Between the Casino and the other property I own, we can offer a perfect space on the south side of Queen Street. I want you to organize a meeting with all the partners as soon as possible."

Murray was relieved to hear about the prospects of a quick sale. He'd been fretting for weeks about the Casino's financial woes. "Agreed, Mr. Cohen. I'll attend to that right away."

Heading back to the Casino, Murray immediately went upstairs to Lou's office. His brother-in-law had been entertaining some of his pals from City Hall and had apparently stepped out on a brief errand with one of them. The room was choked with cigarette and cigar smoke and reeked of alcohol. Frank Mitchell, one of Lou's old City Hall cronies, was still in the room and leaned in Murray's direction. "Hey, Murray, how'd you like to go on a deer hunt?"

"You must be kidding, Frank. You know I'm not interested in that sort of thing. That's Lou's idea of fun!"

"We're not including the little guy," replied Mitchell in a conspiratorial tone.

Murray was startled. "That's your business, but keep me out of it. I'm here to discuss some business matters with Lou."

At that moment, Lou entered his office with another of his old pals, Willie Anderson, but ignored Murray. Almost childlike, he immediately showed Mitchell his Winchester rifle.

Murray was peeved. "Lou, I need a couple of minutes of your time … in private."

"You can say anything you want in front of my buddies," Lou retorted.

Buddies! They're not including him in their deer hunt. Some buddies! "Lou, I've just come from Arthur Cohen's office. He intends to sell the Casino and wants a partners' meeting to discuss it. He thinks there's a good chance of finding a buyer."

Lou seemed to sober up momentarily. "That son of a bitch! Who does he think he is? What a stupid idea!"

"Listen to reason and face facts, Lou. We've got competition from two other burlesque houses."

"You mean the Lux and the Victory? Christ, I hear the Lux is going broke. And the Victory's a sleaze palace. That's no competition! We've got the top professional strippers in the business and great country and western acts besides!"

"Maybe so, Lou, but the bottom line stinks and short of a miracle we're going to have to close the theatre at some point soon. Best to do that when it looks like there's an opportunity."

Lou poured himself a Johnnie Walker and turned to his cronies. "Listen to my brother-in-law! Mr. Doomsday!" He turned toward Murray. "There's no way I'm agreeing to sell the theatre. I think we should carry on just as we are!"

The partners subsequently met, and surprisingly, Lou got his way. The classiest striptease artist on the circuit was to be recruited to turn business around. A $2,000 contract was drawn up with Tempest Storm — twice as much as the Casino had paid any stripper since 1936. The two appearances of the beautiful redhead, who gave her measurements as 40-22-34, failed to save the ailing theatre.

In the early fall of 1960, the partners finally decided to close the Casino and sell the property. Later that evening, Murray told Lil about the plans.

"I was expecting this to happen," Lil responded sadly. "And what's going to happen to Lou and the others?"

"Don't worry about them. Your brother hasn't spent all of his inheritance, and he'll do well in his new hotel on Queen Street. As for the Allens and Arthur Cohen, they're millionaires, so don't shed any tears."

"I really hate to see the place shut down. There was always some kind of excitement around the theatre. I'm going to miss Wally, Charlie, and Percy. And Archie and the band. They were like family to us."

Murray was momentarily lost for words.

"Are you absolutely certain nothing can be done to keep the theatre going?" Lil asked.

"Well … I don't think it'll amount to much, but a couple of days ago one of Barry's friends called me and asked if the theatre could be leased. His name's Harvey Hart, and he and his partner, Antony Ferry, want to produce legitimate theatre. I warned him that the Casino was structurally not very suitable. It didn't matter for any of our productions over the years and Percy's hanging sets always created the illusion of depth, but the stage is a bit too shallow for legitimate theatre. Hart said he wasn't put off by that. I then pointed out to him that the name Casino might be bit of a curse, and he came up with a new name — the Civic Square Theatre. Hart persisted that he was genuinely interested, so I finally agreed to arrange a meeting with the partners."

"That sounds wonderful, Murray!" Lil exclaimed gleefully.

"Just remember, it won't involve us directly. It's just a matter of leasing the theatre."

Several days later, the Casino partners met with Harvey Hart and Antony Ferry, who confirmed their interest in leasing the Casino and shared their plans. "We propose to sell a subscription series," said Hart. "Our aim is to subscribe $7,500 for each play. We expect to do one play a month, each running for three weeks with no performances on Monday nights but both matinee and evening performances on Sundays. We think we can get two thousand university students subscribed, and the tickets should range from $1 to $2.50 to encourage the younger playgoer."

"Plays? Off-Broadway plays?" asked Arthur Cohen.

"No, no, Off-Broadway's is going out of our territory. We're not interested in the Broadway success format. We're out to sell an idea. And we've been encouraged by the activity in the city at the Royal Alexandra, the Crest, and the O'Keefe Centre. We want to use the theatre to the fullest extent, and we want the theatre itself to have a different orientation for each play produced. To do this, we're prepared to use dance, mime, graphics, sound, music — everything. It won't be epic or expressionistic theatre. We'll work from the core outward to involve the audience in a meaningful experience."

The Casino partners were somewhat bewildered but listened intently as Hart continued with unstoppable enthusiasm. "We want to put on plays by all the angry young men out there and the angry old men, too! We're not adverse to the classics, though we're not thinking of Ibsen, Chekhov, or Strindberg. We're also interested in Canadian writers and hope two of our five plays in the first season will be originals. We're also thinking about holding actors' workshops."

"What sort of theatre background do you two have?" Gersten Allen finally interjected.

"Well," Hart replied, "I've been a television producer for a few years now, and Antony's a journalist and critic who's worked with theatre clubs in the past. We've also got commitments from several successful producer/directors."

"It all sounds very ambitious, Mr. Hart," Cohen said. "We wish you all the luck in the world. Give us a day or two to consider your proposal."

The Casino partners were sufficiently impressed by Harvey Hart's presentation to put plans for the sale of the theatre on hold and enter into a lease agreement with the two entrepreneurs. They also agreed to the proposed name change.

The Civic Square Theatre failed miserably — at least financially, if not creatively. The first production, Eugène Ionesco's *Rhinoceros*, met with some critical success, but the two following productions simply flopped. Insufficient subscriptions were sold, and the venture collapsed after the third attempt at avant-garde theatre.

For several months afterward, the Casino was leased to Bennet Fode, who ran so-called art films. It, too, flopped miserably, and the beloved old dump was finally torn down in June 1963. The marquee outside the theatre read: "Another Smash Hit by Tepperman," alluding to a local building wrecker.

Epilogue

The murder of Avner Appleby on March 3, 1935, was a horrific event for the Appleby and Little families. Avner's death altered the life course of not only his widow but his son and son-in-law and their families. Two young men, Lou Appleby and Murray Little, were suddenly thrust into the position of owning and operating a burlesque house. Neither had theatrical or business experience.

For my father, the Casino was strictly a place of business — a source of great frustration and embarrassment much of the time. It was such a source of angst for him that he didn't retain any memorabilia. For myself, it was at times a microcosm of reality, and at other times, one of fantasy. I encountered the kind of people few would ordinarily meet — chorus girls, showmen, choreographers, graphic artists, a spectrum of musicians and musical tastes, disingenuous politicians, ex-cons, incorrigible drunkards, petty gamblers, racetrack touts, celebrity-gazers, and sycophants.

Of course, most of these people made only a cameo appearance in my life. But so did some members of the family. Uncle Harry lived out his years as a bigamist, passing away in his eighties. There was an attempt at reconciliation with his wife, Chanala, which didn't work. Of all my grandmother's sisters and brothers, I knew Becky best of all. Perky and optimistic, she lived a full life with a happy large family, always supportive of her God-fearing sister, Esther.

My father sold the Forest Hill home after the sale of the theatre and started work as a projectionist, a job he held for many years thereafter. My mother went to work as a part-time saleslady for Simpson's. My parents' stormy relationship mellowed somewhat as the years progressed, though my mother continued to take annual extended trips south by herself until well into her nineties.

◆ ◆ ◆

I was very young when my grandfather was murdered. I can't recall the word *murder* or *killing* ever being used within the household. I never heard any family discussion about the murder, the robbery, the police investigation, or other circumstances surrounding my grandfather's death. My mother rarely talked about him, and when she did, she spoke of him reverentially; my grandmother never mentioned him to me. I remember on one occasion about age five asking why Grandfather Appleby was dead. My mother was evasive. "Look up there at the full moon. Your grandfather's there looking down on you," was all that she said. I sensed there was something being kept from me … something secret.

I first learned of my grandfather's murder from a school classmate when I was about ten. "Is it true somebody shot your grandfather dead?" I was asked. Something told me it had to be true. So that was the secret! I felt frightened and ashamed and couldn't bring myself to say anything to my parents. My only confidants were my brothers, Gerry and Alan, who, like me, felt embarrassment and shame.

From that point on, I noticed that at intervals Avner's murder would be mentioned in the popular press as one of the city's famous unsolved crimes. (The 1919 disappearance of Ambrose Small, also a theatre manager, was invariably included in the short list of famous unsolved Toronto crimes.) A few years later, I saw my grandfather's name mentioned in a story about bank robberies in the city. My curiosity was heightened. Still, I didn't approach my parents, or for that matter, other adult members of the family. Although there were frequent contacts with Avner and Esther's kin in Canada, the Roxy murder issue never surfaced.

While a medical student, I made a startling discovery. One afternoon at the Banting Institute in Dr. William Boyd's pathology museum, I discovered my grandfather's brain. It was preserved in a formaldehyde jar and the label beneath it read: "Brain Trauma — Two Bullet Wounds." I was startled, horrified, and angry all at once. And then I was tormented by the choice between equally unfavourable options — telling my family of my chance discovery or keeping it a secret. I elected for the latter. The image of the brain specimen has never left me. I promised myself that one day I'd find out exactly what happened to my grandfather. However, I was shortly thereafter locked into a busy medical career and had little time to devote to personal research. The years passed by with the unresolved Roxy murder nagging at me from time to time, especially when there was a media reference to it. For example, some forty years after the killing, I chanced upon a television program featuring six of Toronto's most famous unsolved murders, and my grandfather's murder was included.

Unfortunately, I missed the credits and was unable to find out who had produced the program. (Even a subsequent search of the various newspaper and television network archives failed to uncover the program. It appears that any recording of it must have been destroyed.)

It was the 1990 meeting in my clinic room with Adolph Frankel — detailed in the prologue at the beginning of this book — that finally spurred me into concrete action. Some weeks later, I arranged to meet with Adolph for a taped interview. He informed me that he'd been a close friend of my grandfather, even gave me the street address where they'd lived together for a time. Adolph told me that he and a friend of his had overheard a fearsome quarrel in front of the Roxy Theatre. The quarrel was between my grandfather and two plainclothes police officers. Adolph swore he could still identify their faces, though he couldn't name them specifically. Priding himself in his knowledge of the people on the street, he told me he knew all the merchants on Queen Street, at least those in the general area of the Roxy and all the police officers, many on a first-name basis. He informed me that he was no more than twenty feet away from the altercation and then mimicked what my grandfather did and said — lifting his right arm and wavering his index finger in the direction of City Hall, shouting in broken English, "I'm going to fix you on Monday morning. I'm going to tell everybody what you're doing!" The following day, March 3, 1935, Avner was found murdered.

Adolph went on to state that he believed the police who were threatened by Avner on March 2, 1935, were on the take and that Avner had been murdered to prevent him from reporting this to the authorities. He felt that the police were implicated in the murder, conjecturing that this was the reason why the crime was never solved. He was aware that the investigation appeared to go only so far before it was squelched. Adolph also told me of his knowledge of the partnership and the conjoint life insurance policy with Fred Piton, their bitter disagreement some months prior to the murder, and how Piton had been cleared as a suspect early in the investigation. He then went on to tell me how he'd attempted to tell my Uncle Lou and my father about what he knew and how they had dismissed him.

That evening, I mustered enough courage to tell my father what Adolph had shared with me earlier. I simulated as best I could the posture and words that were quoted to me by Adolph. My father was visibly shaken at first, appearing embarrassed and ashamed. He finally responded, "That's about the way he would have said that. That was a typical gesture with his index finger wavering when he was angry."

As time passed, my father gradually became more comfortable talking to me about events surrounding his father-in-law's death. I also approached other members of the family. My mother refused to talk about the murder. Some family members remembered the shiva, and one of them told me that Esther had confided in her then that she'd told Avner not to go to the theatre on that fateful Sunday morning. She didn't elaborate further and apparently didn't tell anyone else. I tried unsuccessfully to follow up the report that Avner had been seen near the Ford Hotel around midnight and that he hadn't returned home until 3:00 a.m. on the day of the murder, an inference of an extramarital affair. I questioned many of the surviving relatives, but no one had knowledge of an affair, or found it credible that Avner had been involved in extramarital affairs at any point. Everyone interviewed extolled his virtues as a family man.

It wasn't until after I retired that I finally attempted to seek out official information about the murder. In the early summer of 2000, I contacted the curator at the Toronto Police Service archives. I had several lengthy, interesting talks with him. He knew about the Roxy murder and was able to speak about the lead investigator who was a good friend of his. I expressed an interest in seeing the file, and he told me that by coincidence he'd recently seen it and that he would get it for me. When I followed up with him a few short weeks later, he informed me that he was going on vacation but that he would have one of his assistants in the archives department locate the file.

On August 6, 2000, I received a letter from the Toronto Police Service that read in part:

> I'm responding to your access request under the Municipal Freedom of Information and Protection of Privacy Act concerning the death in 1935 of Avner Appelbaum/Abe Appleby our file 0001224. Please be advised that a thorough search for investigative records regarding this case was conducted on your behalf. Unfortunately, the search produced negative results. Access to the contents of the investigative file cannot be provided as such records no longer exist. However, two records concerning your grandfather were located, the first in a long listing of homicides on a yearly basis and the second in a Services 1935 report. Copies of these reports are enclosed. You have been provided with complete access to information on these two pages which is relevant to your request. However, any non-responsive information has been severed from the record copies provided to you. The Coordinator is responsible for these decisions.

The copies of the two records supplied to me read as follows, though the police misidentified my father as Avner's son:

Homicide Listing
1935 Mar. 3 Abe Appleby (shot) Unsolved.
1935 Services Report

On Sunday, March 3, about 3.05 p.m. the body of the proprietor of the theatre located in the main business section of the city was found in front of his safe in his office in the theatre with two bullet holes in his skull. Three hundred and seventy-five dollars was missing from the safe. The Murderer, who had apparently been hiding in the office since about midnight on Saturday, shot the victim twice killing him instantly and stole the money in the cash box and then escaped. The dead body was discovered by a son of the murdered man and the police immediately notified. Although a most exhaustive investigation was made and numerous clues traced, the murderer has not yet been apprehended.

I didn't appeal the decision. The curator retired shortly thereafter and I subsequently heard that he'd died. I would have liked to have spoken with him further. Avner Appleby's murder at the Roxy Theatre on March 3, 1935, remains unsolved.

But is it?

Performers at the Roxy and Casino Theatres

ACTORS

Robert (Bob) Alda, house singer, master of ceremonies, and father of
  actor Alan Alda
Pearl Bailey
Red Buttons
Jack Carson
Diosa Costello
Dorothy Dandridge
Leo De Lyon
Stepin Fetchit
Betty Garrett
Burl Ives
Van Johnson
Eartha Kitt
Dorothy Lamour
Gordon MacCrae
Marilyn Maxwell
Gene Nelson
Larry Parks
Jane Powell

COMICS AND ENTERTAINERS

The Amazing Dunninger, mentalist
Herb Barris, burlesque comic
Fred De Lyon, whistling virtuoso and comedian
Joe DeRita, eventual member of The Three Stooges

Bob Ferguson, burlesque comic
The Great Morton, hypnotist
Pinky Lee, burlesque comic
Red Marshall, burlesque comic
Chico Marx, comedian, actor, and pianist
Phil Silvers, eventual movie, stage, and television star
Bozo Snyder, burlesque comic
The Three Stooges
Bobby Vail, burlesque comic
Henny Youngman, stand-up comedian

MUSICIANS AND SINGERS

Roy Acuff, country and western singer
Larry Adler, classical, jazz, and pop harmonica player
The Andrews Sisters, close-harmony vocalists
Louis Armstrong, jazz trumpeter and singer
Count Basie, jazz orchestra leader
Barney Bigard, jazz clarinetist
Victor Borge, comic conductor and pianist
Cab Calloway, jazz singer and band leader
Wilf Carter, country and western singer
Johnny Cash, country and western singer
The Charioteers, pop and gospel group
Don Cornell, jazz and pop singer
The Cotton Pickers, early jazz band
The Crew Cuts, Canadian pop group
Vic Damone, pop singer
The Delta Rhythm Boys, pop quartet
Little Jimmy Dickens, country and western singer
Dorothy Donegan, jazz singer and pianist
Rex Doyle, house singer and master of ceremonies
Eddie Fisher, pop singer
Ella Fitzgerald, jazz singer
Helen Forrest, pop and swing vocalist
The Four Knights, doo-wop and gospel group

The Four Lads, Canadian pop quartet
Dizzy Gillespie, bebop jazz trumpeter
Golden Gate Quartet, gospel group
Bobby Goodman, house singer and master of ceremonies
The Harmonicats, pop harmonica group
Hank Jones, jazz pianist
Kitty Kallen, big band and pop singer
Julius La Rosa, pop singer
Nellie Lutcher, rhythm and blues and jazz singer
Velma Middleton, jazz vocalist
Rose Murphy, jazz singer
Page Cavanaugh Trio, jazz and pop group
Patti Page, pop and country singer
Oscar Peterson, jazz pianist
Ray Price, country and western singer
Johnnie Ray, pop vocalist
Red Ingle and His Natural Seven, country music and comic
    entertainers
Jimmy Reeves, country and western singer
Marty Robbins, country and western singer
Sugar Chili Robinson, jazz pianist and singer
Arvell Shaw, jazz double bassist
George Shearing, jazz pianist
Hank Snow, country and western singer
Valaida Snow, jazz singer
The Southernaires, pop vocal group
Kay Starr, pop and jazz singer
Maxine Sullivan, jazz singer
Art Tatum, jazz pianist
Mel Tormé, pop and jazz singer
Justin Tubb, country and western singer
Rudy Vallée, pop singer, musician, and actor
Sarah Vaughan, jazz singer
Ethel Waters, jazz singer
Josh White, folksinger
Trummy Young, jazz trombonist

STRIPPERS

Mae Brown

Charmaine

Ann Corio

Maxine DeShone

Maria Elena

Lois de Fee

Winnie Garrett

Gaye Knight

Rose LaRose

Gypsy Rose Lee

Joan Lee

Melba, Toast of the Town

Stella Mills

Mary Murray

Lucille Rand

Sally Rand

Sherri Shannon

June St. Clair

Tempest Storm

Rhonda True

Acknowledgements

I am deeply indebted to the following people for assisting me in various ways — professionals: Michael Carroll, Daniel Crack, Marjorie Green, and Rosemary Shipton; family members: Beth-Ann Little, Robert Little, Hailey Simpson, and Diana Thomson; and friends: Mary Clarke, the late Ruth Morawetz, and Carolyn Taylor-Watts. To all of them, thank you!

www.ingramcontent.com/pod-product-compliance
Lightning Source LLC
Chambersburg PA
CBHW070902120626
46546CB00001B/111